Economic Development

An Anthropological Approach

EDITED BY JEFFREY H. COHEN
AND NORBERT DANNHAEUSER

Published in cooperation with the
Society for Economic Anthropology

PRESS

A Division of
ROWMAN & LITTLEFIELD PUBLISHERS, INC.
Walnut Creek • Lanham • New York • Oxford

ALTAMIRA PRESS
A Division of Rowman & Littlefield Publishers, Inc.
1630 North Main Street, #367
Walnut Creek, CA 94596
www.altamirapress.com

Rowman & Littlefield Publishers, Inc.
4720 Boston Way
Lanham, MD 20706

12 Hid's Copse Road
Cumnor Hill, Oxford OX2 9JJ, England

An earlier version of chapter 2 appeared in *Ethnology* 39 (3): 225–242.

The photographs in chapter 2 used with permission of Fidel Ugarte, Calle Alonso
Cano #88, Colonia Alfonso XIII, Mexico D.F., fidelugarte@hotmail.com.

Chapter 10 reprinted from *Human Organization* with the permission of the Society of
Applied Anthropology.

British Library Cataloguing in Publication Information Available

Library of Congress Cataloging-in-Publication Data

Economic development : an anthropological approach / edited by Jeffrey H. Cohen
and Norbert Dannhaeuser.
    p. cm.— (Society for Economic Anthropology monographs)
    "Published in cooperation with the Society for Economic Anthropology."
    Includes bibliographical references and index.
    ISBN 0-7591-0211-2 (cloth : alk. paper)—ISBN 0-7591-0212-0 (paper : alk. paper)
    1. Economic anthropology. 2. Economic development. 3. Sustainable
development. 4. Capitalism. I. Cohen, Jeffrey H. (Jeffrey Harris)
II. Dannhaeuser, Norbert, 1943– III. Series.
  GN448 .A56 2002
  306.3—dc21   2002001961

Printed in the United States of America

♾ ™ The paper used in this publication meets the minimum requirements of
American National Standard for Information Sciences—Permanence of Paper for
Printed Library Materials, ANSI/NISO Z39.48–1992.

Economic Development

SOCIETY FOR ECONOMIC ANTHROPOLOGY (SEA) MONOGRAPHS

Deborah Winslow, University of New Hampshire
General Editor, Society for Economic Anthropology

Monographs for the Society for Economic Anthropology contain original essays that explore the connections between economics and social life. Each year's volume focuses on a different theme in economic anthropology. Earlier volumes were published with the University Press of America, Inc. (#1–15, 17), Rowman & Littlefield, Inc. (#16). The monographs are now published jointly by AltaMira Press and the Society for Economic Anthropology (http://nautarch.tamu.edu/anth/sea/).

Current Volumes:

Vol. 1   Sutti Ortiz, ed., *Economic Anthropology: Topics and Theories.*
Vol. 2   Sidney M. Greenfield and Arnold Strickon, eds., *Entrepreneurship and Social Change.*
Vol. 3   Morgan D. Maclachlan, ed., *Household Economies and Their Transformation.*
Vol. 4   Stuart Plattner, ed., *Markets and Marketing.*
Vol. 5   John W. Bennett and John R. Brown, eds., *Production and Autonomy: Anthropological Studies and Critiques of Development.*
Vol. 6   Henry J. Rutz and Benjamin S. Orlove, eds., *The Social Economy of Consumption.*
Vol. 7   Christina Gladwin and Kathleen Truman, eds., *Food and Farm: Current Debates and Policies.*
Vol. 8   M. Estellie Smith, ed., *Perspectives on the Informal Economy.*
Vol. 9   Hill Gates and Alice Littlefield, eds., *Marxist Trends in Economic Anthropology.*
Vol. 10 Sutti Ortiz and Susan Lees, eds., *Understanding Economic Process.*
Vol. 11 Elizabeth M. Brumfiel, ed., *The Economic Anthropology of the State.*
Vol. 12 James M. Acheson, ed., *Anthropology and Institutional Economics.*
Vol. 13 Richard E. Blanton, Peter N. Peregrine, Deborah Winslow, and Thomas D. Hall, eds., *Economic Analysis beyond the Local System.*
Vol. 14 Robert C. Hunt and Antonio Gilman, eds., *Property in Economic Context.*
Vol. 15 David B. Small and Nicola Tannenbaum, eds, *At the Interface: The Household and Beyond.*
Vol. 16 Angelique Haugerud, M. Priscilla Stone, and Peter D. Little, eds., *Commodities and Globalization: Anthropological Perspectives.*
Vol. 17 Martha W. Rees and Josephine Smart, eds., *Plural Globalities in Multiple Localities: New World Border.*
Vol. 18 Jean Ensminger, ed., *Theory in Economic Anthropology.*
Vol. 19 Jeffrey H. Cohen and Norbert Dannhaeuser, eds., *Economic Development: An Anthropological Approach.*

Contents

Figures and Tables

Acknowledgments

The papers collected here were originally presented at the annual meeting of the Society for Economic Anthropology (SEA) held on the Texas A&M University campus in March 1999. We would like to thank the SEA for selecting our theme for its annual meeting. We also thank the Department of Anthropology, the Center for Science and Technology Policy and Ethics, and the Anthropological Society at Texas A&M University for their conference support. In addition, we want to recognize the efforts of people who contributed their work to this volume. And we thank Deborah Winslow, the series editor, and the reviewers she selected to comment on this collection. Their efforts greatly improved our work. Thanks also to Miriam Aune, who copyedited the text and to Rosalie Robertson and Erin McKindley, our editors at AltaMira. The selections by Michael Chibnik and Cynthia Werner originally appeared in the journals *Ethnology* (Chibnik) and *Human Organization* (Werner); we thank the staff at both journals for allowing us to reprint the works here in their entirety. Finally, we dedicate this collection to the local folks throughout the world who daily struggle to make development work.

Jeffrey H. Cohen
Department of Anthropology
The Pennsylvania State University
State College, PA

Norbert Dannhaeuser
Department of Anthropology
Texas A&M University
College Station, TX

June 2001

camps. Practicing anthropologists publish in venues like *Practicing Anthropology* and *Human Organization* and author countless reports that focus on projects and innovative approaches to meeting the challenges of development (albeit often with a critical eye to the positive and negative effects development can have on local communities and populations) as well as a host of other issues in the applied social sciences. Critical anthropologists tend to throw the baby out with the bath water and condemn development, relegating successful as well as problematic projects and programs to the scrap heap of history. The critique is often done carefully, pointing out the ways in which development leads to dependency and undermines local social practice (see, for example, Black 1999; Cardoso and Faletto 1979; Escobar 1995). However, critiques of development often disregard the positive contributions anthropology makes. The critics bemoan the loss of native cultures in the name of morality, based on Western assumptions about what is good for local and native populations. Perhaps more important, such critiques often play into the collective guilt that inflicts many in the West and concerns what are seen as the devastating effects of capitalism's march toward global, economic dominance (see Verhelst 1990).

Our purpose in this volume is not to suggest that development is problem free and above the need for critique, or that all practicing anthropologists and the projects they design are successful. Rather, the contributing authors argue that it is unwise to dismiss or condemn development outright. There are numerous and important successes to be examined and learned from, just as our failures help us better to plan for future projects. The value of successfully organized development programs and the growth that comes from reviewing our failures does not mean we are released from the need to discuss critically anthropology's role in the history or the current organization of economic development. Nevertheless, in anthropology we have largely lost our ability to talk about the theory and practice of development in a meaningful and cohesive way. Furthermore, the separate realms that characterize contemporary discussions of development have caused us to lose sight of anthropology's historical interest in the overall process of development or what Harold Schneider (1975) described as "formal development theory in anthropology" (p. 273). In this volume, we bring together thirteen essays that consider economic development from historical, theoretical, and practical perspectives and point toward ways in which we can reintegrate the practice of development with the growth of formal development theory in anthropology.

CLASSIC APPROACHES TO DEVELOPMENT

Modern economic development is rooted in the programs and policies of post–World War II U.S. administrations. It can be grouped into several overlapping types.

Classical and neoclassical approaches (Bauer 1976; Hayek 1988) emphasize the efficient allocation of resources through the dynamics of supply and demand, by means of a competitive market and an assumption of a homogeneous economy and economically motivated actors (Smith 1970[1776]). Proponents use Ricardo's comparative advantage principle to argue that market specialization and trade can maximize consumption for the poor and rich (Chenery 1961).

Radicals (Amin 1976; Baran 1957; Frank 1979; Kahn 1978; Lenin 1934) stress the internal and external systems of collective exploitation and define an approach that makes economic development with rational rules only possible under socialism, especially if it were to benefit all people. In this paradigm, supply-and-demand–driven markets are detrimental to development beyond the capitalist stage and harmful to large sectors of the population within that stage.

Structuralists and institutionalists recognize that market dynamics foster efficiency and economic growth in the long run, but that social impediments often exist that demand attention and reform for the full benefits of competitive markets to have an impact across a population (Fei and Ranis 1964; Lewis 1955).[2]

Finally, the cultural/psychological approaches stress the variables of cultural orientation, value systems, and shared psychological characteristics within populations. These are factors that affect development outcomes and the likelihood of a society gaining sustained growth through market-driven processes (Boeke 1953; Foster 1973; Landes 1999; McClelland 1961; Weber 1958[1904/5]).

Missing in these approaches (with the exception of the radicals and dependistas who authored their own radical approach [see Cardoso and Faletto 1979]) are the complicating issues of income inequalities and concentrations of capital, to name but two. Nevertheless, writing in the late 1950s and 1960s, Walter Rostow operationalized the goals of postwar development and the hopes of the Marshall Plan in his *Stages of Economic Growth* (1960). Rostow argued that once countries left their static and irrational non-Western economic models, economic "take off" and self-sustained growth would occur. In other words, once kin-based, subsistence, and state-driven models of the economy were abandoned in favor of market-based systems, growth and prosperity would closely follow. So, too, would the arrival of unstoppable capitalism and market-based economies that paralleled, caught up with, and came to resemble those found in Western Europe and the United States (see Nurkse 1953).[3]

Debates concerning development remain largely anchored in attempts to understand colonial and postcolonial societies and their economies in the emerging Third World (see Boeke 1953; Hoselitz 1960; Myint 1965). Interest in development through the 1970s lay in critiquing Rostow and understanding the negative effects of trade relations between peripheries and centers within and between countries (Myrdal 1957, 1970); ways to foster development in societies burdened by surplus labor conditions (Fei and Ranis 1964); what to do about indivisibility (the minimal input needed to get an economy going on the trajectory of development (Rosenstein-Roden 1957); how to maintain a balance between industrial and agricultural expansion (see Nurkse [1953] on the big push debate); and how to create investment incentives along a production stream (backward and forward linkages) given that resources in poor countries are scarce (Hirschman 1958).

ANTHROPOLOGY AND DEVELOPMENT

For anthropology, some of the issues that motivated interest in development included the outcomes and effects of Western development on native populations (defined largely as the social and cultural costs and benefits of development projects and programs); the history of development in non-Western and lesser-developed nations (what has today become largely the concern of colonial and postcolonial historians); and alternative models for development that might be found in non-Western settings. Among the historical studies of development and its long-term effects on local/native populations are Epstein's analyses of economic change among the Tolai of Southern India (1962), Geertz's work on agricultural development (and involution) in Indonesia (1963a, 1963b), and Boserup's analysis of the relationship of technology to population growth (1966). Even Sahlins's *Stone Age Economics* served a purpose in the development debate; it argues for the Domestic Mode of Production and that accumulation can be achieved by producing more (the classical view) but can also relate to consuming less (1972).[4]

Discussions of the outcomes and the costs and benefits of development revolve around the logic (or lack thereof) of development and critiques of estimates concerning the adoption of non-native economic models by local populations. Typically, the anthropologists show that the locals are neither naive nor unwilling to adopt new technologies, production strategies, or work regimes. Rather, the locals are often eager adopters, although the long-term costs and benefits of adoptions were not always well known (Nash 1958). Anthropologists also find alternative avenues for development in their work with non-Western natives, just as sociologists often find local models of development that have little to do with large-scale governmental work programs (see Stack 1974). We also see the first strong critiques of Western development during this period (Frank 1966; Schneider 1975).

Anthropologists (and scholars in related disciplines) are also interested in establishing correlates between traditional institutional setting and modernization (Adelman and Dalton 1971) as well as examining the impact of religious and other institutional factors on development potentials/outcomes of particular communities (Belshaw 1964; Benedict 1968; Epstein 1962, 1968; Nash 1958, 1965). The cultural-psychological dimension received considerable attention in McClelland's (1961) and Hagen's work (on need-achievement) (1962), stimulating interest by anthropologists in entrepreneurship (Barth 1963; Geertz 1963b; Greenfield et al. 1979; Kunkel 1963). On a more general level, studies of peasant communities show that cultures adapted to high-risk environments contain elements that help people to adjust to local conditions, but that also make it difficult for them to escape such conditions (Foster 1965; Lewis 1966).

A third current in anthropology seeks to apply ideas concerning development (here development is broadly conceived to include social, economic, and political realms) to real-world problems and inequalities. Perhaps the most important of these projects was the Vicos "research and development" project managed by Allan Holmberg at Cornell University in the 1950s and 1960s (see Holmberg 1966, 1971). The Vicos project brought social scientists in the United States and Peru together with Peru's

Institute for Indigenous Affairs, and the local population and leadership of the Vicos hacienda community. The project was based on the assumption that social values (i.e., morality, respect, and skill) and economic worth needed to be developed together as well as through the regular consultation of locals with experts to increase the success of development programs and projects. The project used local models of association and community (particularly the *varayoc* system—seventeen individuals who lead the community in decision making) to disseminate information and encourage changes that were designed to reduce socioeconomic inequality, foster democracy, and improve health among other goals.[5]

A fourth area of interest, and one with deep historical roots in our field, is the politically sanctioned work of anthropologists to develop native and peasant populations in the effort to modernize and build nations. In the United States, particularly under the auspices of the Bureau of American Ethnology and later the Bureau of Indian Affairs, and in Mexico, anthropologists associated with indigenous affairs within the government planned and executed large-scale projects and organized long-term programs to facilitate the acculturation of native peoples (Nahmed 1997).

Anthropological approaches to development reflect our increasing understanding of the development process, but also (one suspects) fashion trends and what is currently considered politically acceptable. Project designs of rural development have experienced several such phases since development became an agenda of international concern in the early 1950s (Ruttan 1984). During the 1950s—the decade of development euphoria—the community development approach dominated the field in and outside of anthropology.

This was replaced with the technically oriented Big Push and Trickle Down emphasis of the 1960s (e.g., the Green Revolution) in which anthropological contributions played only a marginal role (Miller 1977). With amendments to the Foreign Assistance Act (the New Directions) by the U.S. Congress, the integrated and basic needs approach to development became the focus in the 1970s/80s, including a greater emphasis on the participation of the poor majority among target populations and on equitable income distribution as well as growth (Johnston and Clark 1982).

The 1980s/90s saw an ecological/environmental component incorporated in the construction of sustainable development programs (DeWalt

1979; Netting 1993; Schaffer 1995). And, most recently, concerns about globalization/localization processes have become major issues in development/applied work, at least on the theoretical level, as world trade relations have been liberalized and as the post-Soviet era has witnessed greater economic and cultural integration, fostered by new technologies, such as the Internet (Black 1999; Escobar 1995).

DEVELOPMENT IN PRACTICE

Anthropology has long been involved directly in development, as our field's roots in such institutions as the Bureau of American Ethnology attest. Nevertheless, since the Vicos project, there has been little large-scale intervention by anthropology programs or by anthropologists seeking to develop a local community in its totality. Rather, what we have seen since the 1970s are an increasing number of small-scale projects in which anthropological methods are applied to the challenges of project design and implementation. Projects range from issues in health care to education, from native populations dealing with the impacts of Western markets to refugees coping with the loss of homelands, to Western communities coping with changes in their social, economic, and political systems. What links the various applications of anthropology in development are (1) the organization of culturally appropriate projects; (2) intercultural brokering between program sponsors and program recipients that takes account of conflicting goals and miscommunication between the parties involved in projects; and (3) the analysis of a project's outcomes with an eye to the cultural and social ramifications of development and not simply to discern whether a project "worked" (see examples in any issue of *Practicing Anthropology*).

No matter the goals of a project (and no matter the support that exists for a program), it is imperative to understand the sociocultural costs and benefits of development. Black (1999) points out that the poor of any community or population see few of the benefits of development. In effect, development, even when successful, does not benefit a population equally. There are often hidden or unanticipated costs associated with any project. These include, for example, pushing up property values and reducing the ability of lower-class members of a population to keep or build homes. In addition, as an economy is commodified, relationships shift and social links can weaken as newly wealthy households compete for local status and authority with traditional leaders (Cancian 1992).

The point is not to judge the morality or immorality of these outcomes; rather it is to plan for and perhaps mitigate some of the effects, to work with a community toward ways in which lower-class and lower-status families might be enfranchised rather than disenfranchised. Anthropologists working outside the academy and within the confines of economic development, whether as policymakers, project designers, implementers, and/or facilitators, make programs that take local sociocultural variation into account more possible. These programs also make it easier to test non-Western ideas and approaches to development problems. Perhaps in a more hopeful mode, anthropologists working within the framework of development can help empower the individuals with whom we work and communities within which we work.

DEVELOPMENT IN THEORY

What is an unfortunate outcome of the separation of development in practice from its more theoretical discussion in anthropology is the failure to create a "midlevel theory [that] might bring more of the findings of the various social sciences to bear on work of planners and make implementers, or field agents, less vulnerable to blindsiding—to seeing their projects sabotaged by sponsoring agencies, local leaders, or supposed beneficiaries" (Black 1999:20). To Black's list we can add that the construction of grounded theory for development would also empower local actors and help donor agencies and nations realize the costs and benefits of their projects for recipients who have little if any voice in the organization of most large-scale programs. Furthermore, applying theories of development to real-world situations and using real-world experiences to critique and assess theory adds to the growth and coherence of those theories over time.

How can theory and the experiences in the field help specialists as they deal with their project, local populations, sponsors, or specialists? First, it is important to remember that the local recipients of development's largess typically are not waiting for handouts. Rather, people constantly devise and revise their models for survival. They calculate the costs and benefits of participation and regularly check on outcomes and their "take" (although this is a calculation that is made with sometimes imperfect knowledge). Second, local communities are not as homogeneous or as isolated as government workers, the media and early anthropologists portray.

Rather, local variations (whether social, economic, or political) have ramifications for a project's success (Cohen 1998). Third, when local populations are given the opportunity, they can and do integrate development programs into their lives; nevertheless, the poorest of the poor in most communities typically do not benefit from development (Chambers 1983). Fourth, donor nations must realize they are no more isolated from the woes of the underdeveloped community or population than the rest of the world. Rather, both developed and underdeveloped worlds (however they are defined) are linked, and outcomes in the West have ramifications for the rest, just as the events occurring in the Third World involve First World decision makers.

Theories of community, social action, and practice in anthropology and sociology are of crucial importance as specialists work to deal with project managers (particularly governmental workers) who typically have little background knowledge of the people they hope to help. More troubling, project managers and funding agencies often think of themselves as the last hope for a community or population, and that any program will improve the lives of recipients. What we now know is that local recipient populations are far from passive in their actions. Rather, local populations respond to situations as best they can, and, as Escobar (1995) suggests, we might start by listening to their criticism before we launch a new phase of development.

Anthropologists historically describe local populations as largely homogeneous and isolated (see critique in Kearney 1996). Power might not be shared equally, but, in general, the native, poor, and non-Western community lacks the strict divisions of Western mainstream (read middle-class) society. What we have learned over the last two decades is that local populations are heterogeneous and integrated into regional, national, and global systems. Using models that are built around understanding social process, cultural beliefs, and economic production, we can begin to identify and understand this complexity. Defining and describing local hierarchies (whether social or economic) and their transformations help us understand how individuals negotiate social life not always successfully, but actively and in an engaged and thoughtful manner. Thus, we can argue that recipient populations are able to implement projects and readily make sense of development goals. In fact, implementers, donors, local leaders, and local populations share many of development's goals.

However, programs and projects very often are tailored to the ideas and desires of the granting agency or nation and pay little attention to the local population. Finally, anthropologists are often brought into a project as it begins to fail, too late in the processes effectively to help either the donors or the recipients.

TOWARD A SYNTHESIS

We live at a time when it is crucial to understand the many ways development is defined and realize that economic growth should not be the only goal of development programs and projects. Furthermore, we need to understand the costs and benefits that are associated with various kinds of development. What anthropologists must do better are (1) effectively balance the discussion of development in practice (whether economic or social, grass roots, or large scale) against debates concerning development in theory; and (2) carefully deploy our methods better to serve the needs and desires for development as defined in the boardroom, the stateroom, and the community.

Robert Hackenberg (1999) describes a dilemma that "show[s] one of our members clinging to a lower rung of the academic ladder in a college department while another, who has already lost his grip, takes up a hopeful position, resume in hand, on the front steps of the World Bank" (p. 106). Hackenberg's challenge is for anthropology to regain a relevant role in the development debate. Further, he argues it is not enough simply to publish more critiques, overviews, and textbooks; he asks that we produce formal theory and construct practical models through which we can effect change and exploit opportunities for the people with whom and for whom we work and study.

In this collection, we have organized thirteen papers that meet Hackenberg's challenge and cover a variety of issues in development. Our hope is that this collection highlights the value of anthropology to theory and practice in development and points toward exciting new possibilities for development specialists. To this end, we have organized the papers into three parts addressing respectively theoretical issues, practical concerns, and future possibilities.

Part I examines development in theory and in the history of anthropology. Gilman's paper considers one of anthropology's most important actors, Clifford Geertz, and examines how he went from his central role in development anthropology (particularly in his work *Agricultural Involution*) to his more interpretative contemporary interests. Using the example of Oaxacan wood-carvers, Chibnik argues that market systems follow life cycles. He models the concept of ecological succession to define the ways in which market systems evolve over time. In the process, he reminds the development specialist how local market systems can change before we have the opportunity to organize programs for growth. Similarly, Cronk and Steadman suggest that meddling with local control, while perhaps beneficial in a gross economic sense, can have devastating effects on environments. They look at the pitfalls of local control of common pool resources (in their case including both tourists and reefs off the coast of Utilia, Honduras) to talk about the costs and benefits of local versus international development. Halperin develops a similar argument in her analysis of local political activism in Cincinnati, Ohio, and points out how the socioeconomic status of an area can directly impact its future and limits the ability of local leaders and organizers to mediate change. What is encouraging is the ability of locals to rally supporters; what is discouraging is the limited effectiveness of this organization.

Part II focuses on development in practice. Using the example of Balinese agricultural development, Jha argues that our field has played an important role in the incorporation of local knowledge into program planning. However, he also points out the limits of that knowledge as it comes up against local contests over social, political, and economic status. Woost makes a similar argument in his paper on Sri Lankan participatory development. He shows how local participation and its goal of bringing the "common folk" into the debate creates new discourses about development that are in their own way exclusionary. Clark's analysis of the lack of participatory development among Asante market women makes the alternative point; we often forget to listen to local populations and forget that they are experienced actors whose insights can help in the planning and evaluation of the costs and benefits (in social as well as economic terms) of projects for development. Kennedy, in her discussion of risk perceptions among Costa Rican and Panamanian farmers affiliated with the conservation of the La Amistad Biosphere, brings up the importance of bridging local, national, and international knowledge, markets, and social practices in the organization of development. As she shows, locals define risk in ways often quite different from specialists, and those definitions can vary in relation to national borders and international market outcomes. Finally, Johnson examines how Bangladeshi women suffer a "double" marginality, first as members of a Third World nation and second as women within that country. While her paper notes the hopeful and positive outcomes of family planning in Bangladesh, she bemoans the failures of projects aimed at economic development for that country. Johnson asks, what are the costs to families and particularly Bangladeshi women as their husbands migrate in search of wage labor that does not exist locally?

Part III examines new areas for the discussion of development in anthropology. These papers note the growing transnational and transcultural links that exist between nations. Focused on problems coming from the collapse of the Soviet Union, Werner examines the "crisis" of corruption in Kazakstan. She notes that there is little agreement over just what corruption is (sometimes it is a gift, sometimes a bribe). More important, the lack of a solid, "anti-relativistic" conceptualization of corruption makes it difficult to work with locals in efforts to achieve the economic and political goals of governmentally driven international development. The outcome, rather than helping struggling democracies, may be effectively to encourage blatant corruption. Matejowsky points to another problem resulting from the penetration of Western market ideals to Third World settings in his discussion of the growth of malls in provincial Philippine communities. He notes the loss of public places is fundamentally changing the organization of Filipino society and thus reminds us of the geographic implications of development. In the final papers of the volume, Lindh de Montoya and Montoya use anthropology's lens to analyze stock markets in Sweden and Venezuela, respectively. As stock trading grows more common and stock markets open throughout the world, they point toward new areas for investigation and ask important questions such as: How do individuals deal with market risks? and How do small investors in new stock markets deal with economic instability at home and abroad?

NOTES

1. Defining just what is meant by development is often a complex exercise in itself. For the purpose of this volume, economic growth involves increases in the

scale of an economic system—total capital production and income—without necessarily a per capita improvement or any accompanying structural transformation of the economy or society. Development entails processes by which a society improves its control over resources by increasingly competent technology and complex organization, and involves the rationalization of the production and exchange accompanied by mass consumption, mass transportation, and improved health and comfort. Implied in this definition of development are a rise in per capita income levels and the structural transformation of the economy and society. Moral issues and those relating to happiness are not considered in this definition. Modernity can be approached in a broad or narrow framework. The narrow meaning is rooted in the Enlightenment and is tied to the ideals proposed by Western thinkers (especially in America, Britain, France, and Germany) during the second half of the eighteenth and early nineteenth centuries. Elements that are usually included are: equal rights and the notion of citizenry (civil society); decrease of inherited privilege; social and physical mobility; industrialization and material wealth acquisition; bureaucratization and rational organization; mass literacy and education; complex division of labor and urbanization; nationalism; democracy; freedom of expression; and an emphasis on science as a source of inquiry and knowledge (Bendix 1967; Tipps 1973). A broader approach to modernity relates the term to the characteristic of society in recent times or the present; modern here is relative to time and similar in meaning to contemporary.

2. In the 1950s and 1960s, historians and anthropologists pointed out—similar to the Old Institutionalists (Commons 1934; Veblen 1953[1912])—that social and cultural contexts shape human goals. Means to reach them are influenced by social process and cultural context, rather than some pristine proclivity for humans to act rationally according to classical microeconomic theory. Through the more recent works of North (1981), Williamson (1985), and others, economists in the 1980s and 1990s rediscovered the institutional dimension and the New Institutional Economics (NIE) was born. Practitioners of NIE stress that certain institutions are to be regarded as integral to economic systems rather than external to the economy and therefore dismissible in economic modeling. NIE differs from substantive approaches in economic anthropology by constructing quantifiable models and testable theories. Through the effort of Acheson (1994) and others, NIE has been introduced into anthropology where so far it has flourished less than one would have expected—perhaps its stress on how formal model building can complement microeconomics makes it suspect. Of special interest to anthropologists, however, should be the effort by economists, historians and political scientists to apply NIE to issues of development (Bardhan 1989; Harriss et al. 1995; Nabli and Nugent 1989). Transaction costs, imperfect information,

and collective action (how self-interested individuals can benefit a collectivity), areas of considerable interest to NIE, are affected by the institutional settings typically found in lesser-developed countries and not in economically prosperous countries. The NIE approach can help explain the existence of various distortions in such societies, such as the use of personal means to gain trust, the importance of households and kinship in the production process, the preference for sharecropping among tenants, the widespread existence of fragmented market channels, and so on (see Dannhaeuser 1993). Given their comparative orientation and preference for empirical work in microsettings—areas in which economists are not as strong—it stands to reason that anthropological contributions to development issues from the NIE perspective could be considerable and would complement the quantitative and deductive approach of economists (Epstein 1975; Ruttan 1989:183–185).

3. It should be noted that the inequalities encountered in Rostow's model, income disparities, for example, were resolved at least theoretically, by the buoyant lift it was assumed "take-off" would provide to all sectors of an economy. Further, it is important to remember that the goals of development (i.e., market expansion and higher productivity) were seen as natural or innate qualities of most of the world's people (see Buchanan and Ellis 1955).

4. It can be argued that anthropology's very roots are in the study of development over time (e.g., Morgan's work on stages in human sociocultural evolution [1995] or White's work on technology and the rise of civilization [1959]). However, for our purposes, we will concentrate instead on contemporary issues in economic development.

5. During this period, the Vietnam War encouraged many anthropologists to adopt a politically derived critical attitude toward development/applied work, an attitude that found its confirmation in the fiascoes of Project Camelot and the Thailand Project, both of which involved counterinsurgency research (Belshaw 1976; Horowitz 1967). At the same time, much of development/applied work carried out by anthropologists also came under attack for its lack of professionalism (Cochrane 1971). Concern about both issues led to the implementation of an ethical code by the American Anthropological Association and the establishment of programs designed to tighten the training of anthropologists involved in applied work (Hoben 1982).

REFERENCES

Acheson, James M., ed.
    1994 Anthropology and Institutional Economics. Lanham, MD: University Press of America.

Adelman, Irma, and George Dalton
    1971 A Factor Analysis of Modernization in Village India. In Economic Development and Social Change: The Modernization of Village Communities. George Dalton, ed. Pp. 492–517. New York: Natural History Press.

Amin, Samir
    1976 Unequal Development: An Essay on the Social Formations of Peripheral Capitalism. New York: Monthly Review Press.

Baran, Paul A.
    1957 The Political Economy of Growth. New York: Monthly Review.

Bardhan, Pranab
    1989 The New Institutional Economics and Development Theory: A Brief Critical Assessment. World Development 17(9):1389–1395.

Barth, Fredrik, ed.
    1963 The Role of the Entrepreneur in Social Change in Northern Norway. Bergen: Universitetsforlaget.

Bauer, P. T.
    1976 Dissent and Development. London: Weidenfeld and Nicolson.

Belshaw, Cyril S.
    1964 Under the Ivi Tree: Society and Economic Growth in Rural Fiji. Berkeley: University of California Press.
    1976 The Sorcerer's Apprentice: An Anthropology of Public Policy. New York Pergamon Press.

Bendix, Reinhard
    1967 Tradition and Modernity Reconsidered. Comparative Studies in Society and History 9:292–346.

Benedict, Burton
    1968 Family Firms and Economic Development. Southwestern Journal of Anthropology 24(1):1–19.

Black, Jan Knippers
    1999 Development in Theory and Practice: Bridging the Gap. Boulder, CO: Westview Press.

Boeke, J. H.
    1953 Economics and Economic Policy of Dual Societies. New York: Institute of Pacific Relations.

Boserup, Ester
1966 The Conditions of Agricultural Growth: The Economics of Agrarian Change under Population Pressure. Chicago: Aldine.

Buchanan, Norman S., and H. S. Ellis
1955 Approaches to Economic Development. New York: The Twentieth Century Fund, Inc.

Cancian, Frank
1992 The Decline of Community in Zinacantan: Economy, Public Life and Social Stratification, 1960–1987. Stanford, CA: Stanford University Press.

Cardoso, Fernando H. and E. Faletto
1979 Dependency and Development in Latin America., M. M. Urquidi, trans. Berkeley: University of California Press.

Chambers, Robert
1983 Rural Development: Putting the Last First. Essex, England: Longman.

Chenery, Hollis
1961 Comparative Advantage and Development Policy. American Economic Review 51(1):18–51.

Cochrane, Glynn
1971 Development Anthropology. New York: Oxford University Press.

Cohen, Jeffrey H.
1998 Craft Production and the Challenge of the Global Market: An Artisans' Cooperative in Oaxaca, Mexico. Human Organization 57(1):74–82.

Commons, John R.
1934 Institutional Economics: Its Place in Political Economy. New York: Macmillan.

Dannhaeuser, Norbert
1993 The Social Limits of the Family-Operated Firm in a German Town. The Demise of a Traditional Institution in the Context of Rapid Development. Journal of Developing Societies IX:11–32.

Dewalt, Billie R.
1979 Modernization in a Mexican Ejido: A Study in Economic Adaptation. Cambridge: Cambridge University Press.

Epstein, T. Scarlett
1962 Economic Development and Social Change in South India. Manchester, England: Manchester University Press.

1968 Capitalism, Primitive and Modern: Some Aspects of Tolai Economic Growth. Ann Arbor: University of Michigan Press.
1975 The Ideal Marriage between the Economist's Macroapproach and the Social Anthropologist's Microapproach to Development Studies. Economic Development and Cultural Change 24:29–46.

Escobar, Arturo
1995 Encountering Development: The Making and Unmaking of the Third World. Princeton, NJ: Princeton University Press.

Fei, John C., and Gustav Ranis
1964 Development of the Labor Surplus Economy: Theory and Policy. Homewood, IL: R. D. Irwin.

Foster, George M.
1965 Peasant Society and the Image of Limited Good. American Anthropologist 67:293–315.
1973 Traditional Societies and Technological Change. New York: Harper and Row.

Frank, Andre Gunder
1966 The Development of Underdevelopment. Monthly Review 18:17–31.
1979 Dependent Accumulation and Underdevelopment. New York: Monthly Review Press.

Geertz, Clifford
1963a Agricultural Involution. Berkeley: University of California Press.
1963b Peddlers and Princes. Social Change and Economic Modernization in Two Indonesian Towns. Chicago: University of Chicago Press.

Greenfield, Sidney M., Arnold Strickon, and Robert T. Aubey, eds.
1979 Entrepreneurs in Cultural Context. Albuquerque: University of New Mexico Press.

Hackenberg, Robert
1999 Advancing Applied Anthropology. Human Organization 58(1):105–107.

Hagen, Everett
1962 On the Theory of Social Change: How Economic Growth Begins. New York: Feffer and Simons.

Harriss, John, Janet Hunter, and Colin M. Lewis, eds.
1995 The New Institutional Economics and Third World Development. New York: Routledge.

Hayek, Friedrich A. von, ed.
1988 The Fatal Conceit: The Errors of Socialism. Chicago: University of Chicago Press.

Hirschman, Albert
1958 The Strategy of Economic Development. New Haven, CT: Yale University Press.

Hoben, Allan
1982 Anthropologists and Development. Annual Review of Anthropology 11: 349–375.

Holmberg, Allan R.
1966 Vicos: Método y práctica de antropología aplicada. Lima: Editorial Estudios Andinos.
1971 Vicos: A Peasant Hacienda Community in Peru. *In* Economic Development and Social Change. G. Dalton, ed. Pp. 518–555. Garden City, NY: Published for the American Museum of Natural History by the Natural History Press.

Horowitz, Irving, ed.
1967 The Rise and Fall of Project Camelot: Studies in the Relationship between Social Sciences and Practical Politics. Cambridge, MA: MIT Press.

Hoselitz, Bert F.
1960 Sociological Aspects of Economic Growth. New York: Free Press.

Johnston, Bruce F., and William C. Clark
1982 Redesigning Rural Development: A Strategic Perspective. Baltimore: The Johns Hopkins University Press.

Kahn, Joel S.
1978 Marxist Anthropology and Peasant Economics: A Study of the Social Structures of Underdevelopment. *In* The New Economic Anthropology. John Clammer, ed. Pp. 110–137. New York: St. Martin's Press.

Kearny, Michael
1996 Reconceptualizing the Peasantry: Anthropology in a Global Perspective. Boulder, CO: Westview Press.

Kunkel, John H.
1963 Psychological Factors in the Analysis of Economic Development. The Journal of Social Issues XIX(1):68–87.

Landes, David S.
1999 The Wealth and Poverty of Nations: Why Some Are So Rich and Some So Poor. New York: W. W. Norton.

Lenin, V. I.
1934 Imperialism, the Highest Stage of Capitalism. Moscow: Progress Publishers.

Lewis, Oscar
1966 La Vida: A Puerto Rican Family in the Culture of Poverty. San Juan and New York: Random House.

Lewis, W. Arthur
1955 The Theory of Economic Growth. London: G. Allen and Unwin.

McClelland, David C.
1961 The Achieving Society. New York: The Free Press.

Miller, Frank C.
1977 Knowledge and Power: Anthropology, Policy Research, and the Green Revolution. American Ethnologist 4:188–198.

Morgan, Lewis Henry
1995 (1877) *Ancient Society*. Tucson: University of Arizona.

Myint, Hla
1965 The Economics of the Developing Countries. New York: Praeger.

Myrdal, Gunnar
1957 Economic Theory and Underdeveloped Regions. London: Duckworth.
1970 The Challenge of World Poverty. A World Anti-Poverty Program Outlined. New York: Pantheon Press.

Nabli, Mustapha K., and Jeffrey B. Nugent, eds.
1989 The New Institutional Economics and Development: Theory and Applications to Tunesia. Amsterdam: North-Holland.

Nahmed, Salomon
1997 Mexican Applied Anthropology: From Founder Manuel Gamio to Contemporary Movements. *In* The Global Practice of Anthropology: Study in Third World Societies. M. L. Baba and C. E. Hill, eds. Publication 58. Pp. 229–244. Williamsburg, VA: College of William and Mary.

Nash, Manning
1958 Machine Age Maya: The Industrialization of a Guatemalan Community. Chicago: University of Chicago Press.

1965 The Golden Road to Modernity: Village Life in Contemporary Burma. New York: John Wiley.

Netting, Robert McC., ed.
1993 Smallholders, Householders: Farm Families and the Ecology of Intensive, Sustainable Agriculture. Stanford, CA: Stanford University Press.

North, D. C.
1981 Structure and Change in Economic History. New York: Norton.

Nurkse, Ragnar
1953 Problems of Capital Formation in Underdeveloped Countries. Oxford: B. Blackwell.

Rosenstein-Rodan, P. N.
1957 Notes on the Theory of the "Big Push." Cambridge, MA: MIT Press.

Rostow, Walt W.
1960 The Stages of Economic Growth. Cambridge: Cambridge University Press.

Ruttan, Vernon W.
1984 Integrated Rural Development Programmes: A Historical Perspective. World Development 12(4):393–401.
1989 Institutional Innovations and Agricultural Development. World Development 17(9):1375–1387.

Sahlins, Marshall David
1972 Stone Age Economics. Chicago: Aldine-Atherton.

Schaffer, Ron
1995 Achieving Sustainable Economic Development in Communities. Journal of the Community Development Society 26(2):145–154.

Schneider, Harold K.
1975 Economic Development and Anthropology. Annual Review of Anthropology, 4. Palo Alto, CA: Annual Reviews Inc.

Smith, Adam
1970[1776] The Wealth of Nations. New York: Penguin Books.

Tipps, Dean C.
1973 Modernization Theory and the Comparative Study of Societies: A Critical Perspective. Comparative Studies in Society and History 15:199–226.

Veblen, Thorstein
(1953)[1912] The Theory of the Leisure Class: An Economic Study of Institutions. New York: Mentor Books.

Verhelst, Thierry G.
1990 No Life without Roots: Culture and Development. London: Zed Books, Ltd.

Weber, Max
1958[1904/5] The Protestant Ethic and the Spirit of Capitalism. New York: Charles Scribner's Sons.

White, Leslie A.
1959 The Evolution of Culture. New York: McGraw Hill.

Williamson, O. E.
1985 The Economic Institutions of Capitalism. New York: Free Press.

I

DEVELOPMENT AND THEORY IN ANTHROPOLOGY

Involution and Modernization: The Case of Clifford Geertz

Nils Gilman

"The tragedy is not that they suffered. . . . The tragedy is that they suffered for nothing."

—Clifford Geertz, *Agricultural Involution*

Anthropologists have played a Janus-faced role in what David Engerman has referred to as "the romance of economic development" (Engerman 1998). On the one hand, they have helped sensitize scholars and the public to the impact on indigenous peoples of colonialism and development. Especially in the more innocent early postwar years, many anthropologists saw themselves as advocates if not spokespersons on behalf of the people they studied. As Lucy Mair observed, "Most of us have come to regard the people we have lived among as our friends, and have wished to give a sympathetic interpretation of them to readers who may include impatient emissaries of material, and indignant emissaries of moral, uplift" (1957:19). On the other hand, anthropologists have contributed to the formulation of postcolonial power relations by producing knowledge about local peoples that would contribute to the more effective control of these populations by elites with privileged access to this knowledge.[1] Postwar development anthropologists in the United States were interested in determining, as Vera Rubin suggested, "the possibilities of scientific engineering of social problems" (1961:122). Thus, anthropologists often found themselves in the uncomfortable position of sympathizing with the plight of their subjects in principle, but aiding policymakers responsible for that plight in practice.

Accepting the meliorist premises of the postcolonial development ideology known as modernization theory was crucial in negotiating this cognitive dissonance. By 1968, at the apogee of modernization theory's influence, the same Lucy Mair could declare that, "Those who held that any help they might give to a colonial government must be a kind of treachery to its subjects need have no such inhibitions about independent territories" (1968:328). Although Americans pointed early on to the relationship between British anthropology and colonialism (Kroeber 1953), American anthropologists in the early postwar years rarely recognized the parallel dynamic between their work and the aims of the American government. The postcolonial rhetoric of nation-building and independence intersected with development discourse to provide anthropologists with a way to rationalize their complicity with the changes being imposed on their subjects.

During the late 1950s and early 1960s, American social scientists increasingly equated development and modernization. Formulated as an antidote to Communist development strategies, modernization theory was the first full-blown interdisciplinary theory of development to emerge in the United States after World War II. Although modernization theory has been associated primarily with sociology and political science, American anthropologists helped formulate modernization theory by providing basic research about so-called traditional societies. As purveyors of knowledge about formerly remote areas of the earth now considered of high strategic significance, postwar anthropologists found themselves regarded as a valuable national resource in the project of modernizing traditional societies while preventing peasant insurgency. This chapter examines how modernization theory informed the early work of one of the most acclaimed American anthropologists of the century, Clifford Geertz.

CLIFFORD GEERTZ: MODERNIZATION THEORIST

While best known for his introjection of hermeneutics into anthropology and cognate disciplines (Ortner 1997), much of Clifford Geertz's early work addressed problems of economic development. Perhaps the most influential postwar work on the Javanese agricultural system, Geertz's (1963a) *Agricultural Involution* was greeted with rave reviews (Benda 1965; Nash 1965; Murphy 1967) and has remained a touchstone for debates about Indonesian agricultural policy ever since. Although Geertz published *Agricultural Involution* in 1963, drafts containing the basic argument had been circulating since 1955 at the institutions in which he had been working (Geertz 1955, 1956a, 1956b).

When Geertz began his research in 1953, he was a graduate student at the Harvard Department of Social Relations, the fountainhead for modernization theory in sociology. The brainchild of Talcott Parsons, the Department of Social Relations sought to develop what Geertz later called "the sociological equivalent of the Newtonian system" (Geertz 1995:100). Geertz's involvement with Indonesia began almost by chance as he was looking for a dissertation topic. Geertz heard through the graduate student grapevine that the Center for International Studies (CENIS), a think tank across town at the Massachusetts Institute of Technology (MIT), was preparing an interdisciplinary team to go to Indonesia. The MIT Indonesia project wanted to develop a comprehensive theory of Javanese culture and society, a project that connected both in theory and spirit with the kind of work being done at the Department of Social Relations (Geertz 1995:103). Max Millikan, director of CENIS, suggested that Geertz could do the research on Javanese religion. Although by his own testimony he could scarcely locate Indonesia on a map, Geertz jumped at the opportunity to become part of the MIT research team. The dissertation he produced out of this research would be published as *The Religion of Java* (Geertz 1960).

But Geertz did more than study Javanese religious practices. When Geertz returned to Cambridge in 1955, Millikan suggested that he write a study about Javanese agriculture in connection with Indonesia's prospects for economic development. In the 1950s and 1960s, CENIS was the base of operations for an influential group of development economists including Paul Rosenstein-Rodan, Everett Hagen, Benjamin Higgins, and Walt Rostow. Like the Department of Social Relations, CENIS wanted to construct a generalized theory of social and economic development, the best-known expression of which became Rostow's (1960) *Stages of Economic Growth: A Non-Communist Manifesto*, which outlined how societies could achieve take-off into self-sustained growth. CENIS was at that time also receiving funding from the Ford Foundation to help research how best to turn Indonesia into a "modernizing country." According to Francis X. Sutton, the foundation's vice president for International Development (and also a student of Parsons), the explicit aim was to help Indonesia build a modernizing elite (Ransom 1975).

Geertz's youthful work can best be understood in light of the more general project in which he was participating. As Benjamin Higgins suggested in the preface to *Agricultural Involution*, "each of the researchers, using the methods of his own discipline, had arrived at essentially the same broad analytical framework and the same general conception of the task facing the Indonesian people" (Geertz 1963a:viii). Higgins recollected that, "Rostow was formulating his stage theory of economic development while Geertz was at MIT, and Geertz was certainly not alone in falling under the spell, at least for a while, of Rostow and his theory" (Higgins 1989:132). While Geertz did not have much direct contact with other members of CENIS, modernization theory grounded his work. According to Geertz, the modernization idiom emerged as a way to phrase the relationship between industrialized and nonindustrialized countries in a forward-looking way. "And for that," Geertz has said, "the modernization idea seemed especially well made, convenient at once to ex-masters and ex-subjects anxious to restate their inequalities in a hopeful idiom. . . . The whole pattern of global connections was reformulated in these terms—as an effort to 'close the gap' and bring the world up to speed" (1995:137).

AGRICULTURAL INVOLUTION AS MODERNIZATION THEORY

Millikan wanted Geertz to explain why Java had failed to achieve an agricultural revolution that would have set the stage for industrialization. In *Agricultural Involution*, Geertz claimed that the Javanese ecological-cultural response to land shortage was responsible for inhibiting industrialization. Because of the ecological particularities of the *sawah* (wet rice terrace), unique opportunities existed for agricultural intensification in Java. By adding additional cultivators to the sawah and continually refining the cultivation techniques to account for this additional labor, the Javanese could almost indefinitely increase the marginal productivity of the sawah. This "amazing . . . capacity of most terraces to respond to loving care" (Geertz 1963a:35) encouraged (or at least permitted) high fertility rates, the end result of which, after several hundred years, was the severe overpopulation and land shortage for which Java was renowned.

According to Geertz, the Javanese solution to land shortage was "shared poverty"—whatever little work there was, was to be divided among all those wanting work. Geertz's notion of shared poverty exemplified the Parsonian epistemology at the root of his analysis; the putative existence of a widely held value consensus, exterior and prior to the social actors themselves, was made the primary vehicle of sociological explanation. In Geertz's interpretation, the thesis of shared poverty implied a lack of class divisions, which in turn explained why Indonesia lacked an elite group to lead the development process. It imputed to the Javanese a generalized nonentrepreneurial, noninnovative cultural attitude, and made this supposed cultural trait the proximate cause for Indonesia's failure to industrialize. In short, Geertz believed that Java had failed to industrialize because its traditional values had never given way to modernizing ones.

The failure to institutionalize modern values meant that instead of achieving social evolution and industrialization, the Javanese had settled into a pattern of "involution," by which Geertz meant "the overdriving of an established form in such a way that it became rigid through an inward overelaboration of detail" (Geertz 1963a:82). In other words, blocked from advancing in the appropriate manner, the culture had settled into stagnation. If he appreciated the wild variety and detail of Javanese culture on an aesthetic level, Geertz also believed that it was a cause of the island's poverty. As Geertz put it,

> The Javanese village has come into this century with . . . a set of values which commit those who hold them to a communalistic rather than an individualistic approach to economic problems. . . . Unable either emotionally or technologically to reorganize agriculture on an extensive basis, and unable to increase output through further intensification, the *abangan* [commoner] has been forced to solve his population problem by lowering his standards concerning what he will accept as a decent level of living for one of a set of equally privileged peasants. . . . This general pattern of response to a worsening economic situation through a division of the economic pie into smaller and smaller pieces might well be called "shared poverty." [Geertz 1955:11–12]

In other words, the Javanese cultural response to poverty led inexorably to the worsening of that poverty. Rather than pursuing the individualistic ideal of lifting themselves up by their own bootstraps, the Javanese alleg-edly preferred to lower their standards and share their poverty.

Beyond this cultural explanation for Javanese poverty, Geertz had a his-torical explanation for the genesis of cultural involution: colonialism. On top of his synchronic analysis of the involuted Javanese culture—which he used both to explain why self-starting industrialization was unlikely to occur today and to account for Javanese cultural patterning—Geertz over-laid a diachronic, historical analysis of how this culture of involution had come into being as a response to colonialism. Following the analyses of his colleagues at CENIS, Geertz's analysis pinned the historical blame for the current involuted nature of Javanese culture and economy on the Dutch colonial administration.

Beginning in the 1830s, the Dutch had imposed on Indonesia a system of extraction—the culture system—mandating the delivery of plantation products to colonial authorities. The Netherlands East Indies government forbade native growers from selling cane to local sugar refineries, thereby preventing the accumulation of local capital, nipping incipient local industrialization in the bud, and encouraging population growth by increasing demand for unskilled labor (Boomgaard 1989). As Geertz observed, "The existence of colonial government was decisive because it meant that the growth potential in the traditional Javanese economy . . . was harnessed not to Java's (or Indonesian) development but to Dutch" (Geertz 1963a:141). By demanding that sugar production compete with rice growing, the Dutch administration greatly increased the subsistence pressure on the Indonesian peasantry, leading to a population explosion, which, in turn, promoted the cultural and economic intensification described by involution (Utrecht 1973:41). "What makes this develop-ment tragic rather than merely decadent," Geertz concluded, "is that around 1830 the Javanese (and, thus, the Indonesian) economy could have made the transition to modernism with more ease than it can today" (Geertz 1963a:82).

Geertz sealed the cultural-ecological argument of *Agricultural Involu-tion* with a brief comparison of the failure of Java to the success of Japan. In the nineteenth century, Geertz noted, Japan had shared Java's ecologi-cal-demographic predicament—a high population engaged in irrigated rice production. But Japan, in contrast to Java, had not involuted. During the critical period between 1830 and 1870, during which time the Javanese economy had been subordinated into the Dutch colonial system, the Japanese had successfully laid the foundation for an indigenous industrial revolution.

By 1920, Japan and Java had been set on definitively different paths, "in take-off into sustained growth on the one hand and in involution into static expansion on the other" (Geertz 1963a:137). The reason for this differential outcome was plain: "The existence of colonial government in Java is replaced in Japan by the existence of a powerful indigenous elite" who had chosen to industrialize Japan (Geertz 1963a:140). In other words, this Japanese elite had successfully industrialized the country and thereby created an effectively modernized people. As Geertz put it, "The Japanese peasant had to go to town and become a full-time, reasonably disciplined member of a manufacturing system" (Geertz 1963a :142). This comparison of Java to Japan underlined the fundamental cultural determinism of Geertz's argument; ecological conditions set certain limits on cultural responses, but ultimately it was the cultural response to the ecological problem that determined a nation's fortunes.

The concept of involution was Geertz's gloss on the central question of modernization theory: Why hasn't development happened outside of the West (including Japan as an honorary member of the West)? Involution described both the current state of Javanese culture and economy and the historical process that had led to the current economic and cultural impasse, a state Geertz represented as the final result of a long-term pathological mode of development. Consider the epigram Geertz chose for *Agricultural Involution*: "Just as the progress of a disease shows a doctor the secret life of a body," Geertz quoted from Marc Bloch, "so to the historian the progress of a great calamity yields valuable information about the nature of the society so stricken." Involution constituted a pattern of macrosocietal deviance, constructed in contrast to what Alec Gordon has called a "norm of evolution" (Gordon 1992:495). Instead of moving forward, the Javanese economy and culture had spiraled in on itself, becoming more and more intricate and complicated, but without advancing as it should have. Instead of achieving modernity, the Javanese village had become merely "post-traditional" (Geertz 1963a:90).

In implicit contrast to a normative "modernism," Geertz described the Javanese development as "late Gothic" (1963a:82). Like other modernization theorists, Geertz assumed that social evolution meant inevitable and desirable progress, and that therefore the central problem was to explain why this salutary destiny had not come to pass in Indonesia. As Gordon put it, "Economic and social evolution appears in *Agricultural Involution* not as a theory forming the essential starting point but as a background sort of secret faith" (1992:496). CENIS's theory of economic growth, and the normative theory of social and cultural evolution that went with it, was thus the subtext of *Agricultural Involution*.

To be fair to Geertz, his cultural explanation for Java's poverty did represent a revision of earlier racist explanations for Indonesian poverty, which attributed the archipelago's backwardness to the innate characteristics of "the oriental" (Boeke 1953).[2] But even the abjection of racist discourse constituted only a partial break with older analyses. In a move characteristic of postwar American social science, Geertz replaced the term "culture" with the term "race" as the critical explanatory variable, leaving intact other assumptions of older racist theories (Michaels 1992). This move was less difficult than one might suppose since, as James Clifford has pointed out, the category of culture, like the category of race, contained embedded within it a "bias toward wholeness, continuity, and growth" (1988:338). Or rather, in the case of the Javanese, a bias toward wholeness, continuity, and stagnation. As Frans Hüsken and Benjamin White have argued, *Agricultural Involution* echoed colonial "ideas of the stagnant, subsistence-minded, poverty-sharing and homogenous 'post-traditional' village society incapable of modernization and economic growth" (Hüsken and White 1989:238–239). Both the earlier racialist and Geertz's culturalist explanations for the Javanese situation buttressed the notion of the Western-trained administrator as the proper arbiter of social relations. Whereas earlier racist discourses had justified direct metropolitan political rule over the allegedly inferior colonial peoples, the postwar culturalist explanations called for a scientific, technocratic elite to implement reformist, meliorist programs of social engineering. In both the colonial and postcolonial contexts, the desires of the peasantry were systematically ignored.

THE POLICY IMPLICATIONS OF INVOLUTION

Funded by a grant from a think tank, Geertz researched and wrote *Agricultural Involution* with an eye toward policy recommendations. As we have seen, these recommendations assumed the desirability of industrialization.

They also provided a special role for social scientists in general and anthropologists in particular in the generation of those recommendations. As Geertz put it in *Peddlers and Princes*, which he published as a companion volume to *Agricultural Involution*,

> The value of systematic studies of particular communities for the understanding of the national economic development lies (1) in their more intensive probing of particular dynamics that are, nevertheless, of broader general significance; and (2) in their more circumstantial depiction of the nature of the social and cultural context within which development *inevitably* will have to take place. [Geertz 1963b:142, emphasis added]

As an applied science, postwar development anthropology's main contributions to policy were, first, to help locate and delimit the population sectors capable of promoting gradual change in the direction of non-Communist industrialization, and second, to evaluate the potential utility of existing indigenous institutions as instruments for inducing industrialization. To see how Geertz's work fit into this discourse, let us consider his essay, "The Rotating Credit Association: An Instrument for Development" (Geertz 1962).

In this paper, Geertz started from the premise that economic growth required the indigenous population to increase its propensity to save. Following development economics orthodoxy, which called for deliberate, planned, and subsidized efforts to increase the rate of savings and capital formation and to promote entrepreneurialism, Geertz presumed the desirability of the capitalist path to industrialism. "Unless the basic savings habits of the people of a country can be altered," Geertz explained, "the prospects for sustained economic growth are dim indeed" (1962:241). Altering these habits would require nothing less than a complete restructuring of the society: "An effort to change the [savings/income] ratio would demand an effort to change the general pattern of mores and social structure" (Geertz 1962:242). The goal of the development process, according to Geertz, was to push or pull tradition-minded peasants into modernity. "The agricultural cooperative," he suggested,

> may be seen as an "intermediate" institution which links traditional motivations to modern functions, serving at the same time to transform those

motivations to a more rationalistic basis; it "facilitates the learning of new skills, patterns of behavior, and value orientations, and makes possible some changes in the structural principles in the general direction of modernization, without undermining the basic cohesion and solidarity of the group." [Geertz 1962:259–260]

Geertz closed his description of the sociological impact of the rotating credit association with a burst of Parsonian jargon, noting that it was "an institution which acts to change the whole value framework from one emphasizing particularistic, diffuse, affective and ascriptive ties between individuals to one emphasizing—*within economic contexts*—universalistic, particularistic, affectively neutral and achieved ties between them" (Geertz 1962:260). He celebrated the progress of his Indonesian village "toward an increased segregation of economic activities from noneconomic ones, a freeing of them from traditional restraints" (Geertz 1962:261). Although he remained pessimistic about Indonesia's prospects for industrialization, Geertz's emphasis on entrepreneurship as the critical variable in promoting development indicates yet again the latent normativity in his thinking of narratives about Western (and especially American) historical change.

Even though Geertz focused on entrepreneurialism as the main mechanism for promoting development, his discussion of shared poverty implied that involution tended to quash entrepreneurialism. The argument thereby coincided with the interests of those who believed that any sustained economic growth would have to be state-led. According to Benjamin White, Geertz's denial that Indonesia contained a stark division between haves and have-nots echoed the view of both the former colonial elites and the postcolonial indigenous elites, who believed in a "vision of the harmonious and peaceful village community, characterized by solidarity and mutual aid" (White 1983:28). Jennifer and Paul Alexander argued that Geertz's shared poverty thesis unwittingly reproduced the dominant Javanese ideology. As they put it, Geertz's thesis provided " 'scientific' justification for the view that the major barrier to 'modernization' is the culturally based, obstructive values of the peasantry and that the way to overcome these is by education and greater technical expertise" (Alexander and Alexander 1982:597).

The idyllic vision of Indonesian *Gemeinschaft* justified the repression of landless and impoverished peasants organizing workers' collectives and agitating for land reform by allowing their efforts to be labeled the work of an outside "non-Indonesian" influence. This notion of happy, cohesive Indonesian village life, which the argument of *Agricultural Involution* helped buttress, made such organizational effort seem not only fundamentally unnecessary, but also fundamentally antithetical to the "true nature" of Indonesian culture. As took place just three years after the publication of *Agricultural Involution*, the repression of Indonesian leftists could thus take place under the guise of a national purity campaign.[3] If poverty resulted from cultural backwardness rather than from contemporary economic organization, it obviated the need for radical changes in the distribution of power or wealth.

It is difficult to separate the meaning of *Agricultural Involution* from the context of its reception. Although as we have seen, Geertz had developed the major premises of *Agricultural Involution* in the 1950s, the book's reception took place in the late 1960s and 1970s, because of its delayed publication. When it appeared to enthusiastic reviews, *Agricultural Involution* seemed the definitive statement on how peasant agriculture in densely populated rice-growing regions worked. It seemed to provide answers to several important policy questions regarding those regions. Two particular historical conjunctures crucially informed the reception of *Agricultural Involution*: the Vietnam War and the Green Revolution.

The importance of the Vietnam War for the reception of *Agricultural Involution* resides in the explanation it gave of peasant behavior. Involution made apathy or inactivity the norm of peasant behavior—virtually all progressive political-economic change in Geertz's writings descends from above, in the form of technocratic meddling or nationalistically oriented political leadership. Broadly seen, the U.S. government's official line was that insurgency in South Vietnam resulted from intrusion by disciplined North Vietnamese cadres bent on stirring up the primordial feelings of an otherwise passive peasantry of the sort apparently described by involution. Insofar as it could be seen as justifying wars against insurgent peasantries on the grounds that their radicalism had to come from without, Geertz's narrative of recent Indonesian economic and cultural history fit the ideological needs of those justifying the Vietnam War. In the eyes of his critics, Geertz's reluctance to condemn the authoritarian solution to the Southeast Asian "peasant problem" heightened the apparent affinities between his views and the views of the proponents of the war in Vietnam.

By the late 1960s, studies of peasant politics had moved away from involution's suggestion of peasant passivity. Eric Wolf's (1969) *Peasant Wars of the Twentieth Century* and James C. Scott's (1976) *The Moral Economy of the Peasant* traced the origins of peasant activism not to outside agitators, but to class resentments exacerbated by the process of social modernization and peasant subjugation to new forms of rent extraction. Both books attacked the idea of a politically passive or nonrational peasantry.[4] Insofar as they stood as subterranean historiographic critiques of the Vietnam War, they also implicitly lumped Geertz in with the faction of social scientists whose writings had helped justify the Vietnam War.

The second conjuncture to inform the context of *Agricultural Involution*'s reception was the Green Revolution, the common name for the augmented agricultural production stemming from the introduction of bioengineered high-yield seeds and chemical fertilizers to peasant agricultural economies. *Agricultural Involution* supplied a cultural explanation for the reasons behind development economist Arthur Lewis's famous assumption that the marginal productivity of peasant labor was often equal to zero (Lewis 1954), the basis for so many models in development economics.

Those seeking to make technological innovation rather than social reform the salient variable in development tacitly embraced Geertz's view of an economically stagnant and culturally involuted peasantry. Because it downplayed the national and international power relations binding the Indonesian peasantry, Geertz's thesis was susceptible to a protechnocratic interpretation by those eager to promote the Green Revolution. In the absence of social reforms to accompany the application of Green Revolution technology, however, most of the economic benefit from the Green Revolution ended up going to large landholders and agribusinesses, rather than to the peasants themselves (Perkins 1997).

The involution hypothesis implied that the peasants were never going to initiate development on their own; that is, they would never produce the agricultural surplus necessary for industrialization to take place. Even though Geertz himself might have reached a pessimistic conclusion about Java's development opportunities under any circumstances, the engineers and technocrats stood ready to appropriate his thesis as grounds for implementing their own schemes. Paraphrasing Nancy Fraser, it could be said that the involution hypothesis posited an objectified, predictable, and manipulable peasant, "thus effectively opening the door to the behavioral engineers and welfare technologists" (Fraser 1996:28).

The notion of involution served the vested interests of Western development advisors, who could point to its argument as evidence of the need for planning to overcome involution, which meant more jobs for social scientists, including anthropologists. As Geertz put it, "the mentalities of the peddler and the prince must be abandoned, and in their place must come that of the professional manager" (1963b:140). Geertz's historical account of the reasons for Javanese involution implied that the major political problem, namely Dutch imperialism, had already been solved. With the political issue squared away, development planners could get on with the "scientific" business of reforming the local culture toward modern, achievement-oriented values. Indeed, the durable fame of the book must in part be attributed to its amenability to this kind of appropriation by development enthusiasts. As James Ferguson has noted, "An academic analysis is of no use to a 'development' agency unless it provides a place for the agency to plug itself in, unless it provides a charter for the sort of intervention that the agency is set up to do" (1994:69).

Geertz nowhere made his political position explicit, of course. Indeed, he probably believed that his social science was value free and objective. Nevertheless, his work helped provide ostensibly scientific support for top-down industrialization (much as some scientific socialists provided support for Stalinist top-down development). His analyses thereby sanctified the main aim of Southeast Asian state agrarian policy, namely to forestall a political mobilization of the peasantry that might call for decentralization of political power. Although Geertz did not explicitly sanction these interpretations of his work, the policies followed by proponents of the prosecution of the Green Revolution and Vietnam War did follow logical paths made available by Geertz's arguments.

INVOLUTION AND INTERPRETIVE APPROACH

A final question concerns the relationship between Geertz's early work in economic anthropology and his later elaboration of interpretive anthropology. Broadly, two hypotheses may be advanced. First, we can understand Geertz's later work as based on or relying on his earlier economic work on involution. In this interpretation, Geertz's hermeneutic approach assumes the validity of his earlier economic analyses, and his specific analyses of Indonesian culture (if not his methods) are predicated on the invo-lution hypothesis. For example, essays like "Notes on the Balinese Cock-fight" (Geertz 1973) seek to answer the cultural questions left underdeveloped in *Agricultural Involution* but assume that these sorts of rituals are to some degree manifestations of involution.

A second reading of Geertz's post-1963 work is that it represents a departure from, and in some ways a revision of, his earlier economic work. Here, two further subpossibilities present themselves. On the one hand, perhaps Geertz felt as if the analysis in *Agricultural Involution* were misguided. After later consideration, Geertz may have decided that he had been wrongheaded to presume the normativity of social evolution. If this is correct, the interpretive method could be taken as seeking to undo the damage done by the incorrect arguments advanced in *Agricultural Involution*, albeit inexplicitly. On the other hand, it is also possible that Geertz did not so much think of the analysis in *Agricultural Involution* as "wrong" per se, but rather as merely misplaced.

Geertz, in making the interpretive turn, may have been trying "to understand the logic of events in [Javanese villages] from the inside, and not simply according to the parameters supplied by modernization theory, or for that matter any other type of generalizing development theory" (Austin-Broos 1987:156). *Agricultural Involution* basically came up with the right answers to the questions it asked, but unfortunately it did not ask the right, or at any rate the most interesting, anthropological ques-tions. The interpretive methodology, in this reading of Geertz's oeuvre, represents an attempt to develop a way of asking and answering the right kinds of questions. In other words, the interpretive method represents a way to think beyond involution, but is not an abandonment of the involu-tion hypothesis.

My own sense is that this last reading is most likely the right one. Geertz would probably reject the first possibility as too base-superstruc-ture in its understanding of his overall project. While many moderniza-tion theorists considered cultural matters epiphenomenal to economic and social matters, Geertz himself never believed this, although his work prior to 1963 is ambiguous on the question. The second possibility is almost certainly off the mark, because Geertz himself has gone out of his way to defend his findings and analyses contained in *Agricultural Involu-tion* (Geertz 1984). (Recently asked what, if anything, he would change about *Agricultural Involution*, Geertz replied with uncharacteristic bluntness: "Not one word.") Moreover, he had already begun to develop the interpretive method in the years he was publishing *Agricultural Involution* and its related works. *The Religion of Java*, written almost simultaneously with *Agricultural Involution*, foreshadows the interpretive methodology that would become famous with the publication of *The Interpretation of Cultures* (Geertz 1973). I think the right answer to the question of the relationship between the "early Geertz" and the "late Geertz" is that Geertz simply lost interest in the economic questions, perhaps because he felt he had "solved" that problem, and moved on to methodological and epistemological questions that he (and the rest of the profession, I might add) found more interesting.

NOTES

Thanks to Clifford Geertz for an interview conducted on 11 December 1997. Thanks also to Gillian Hart, Antonio Gilman, and Andrew Lakoff for their helpful readings.

1. This anthropological doublet can be traced to Malinowski's simultaneous denunciation of the "white savage" and call for anthropology to help mobilize intellectual resources "for the task of assisting colonial control" (quoted in Escobar 1991:661). The literature on postcolonial development anthropology, as typified by Escobar, has generally failed to emphasize the continuities between postwar discourses and earlier anthropological collaborations with colonial authorities, thus treating the break with colonialism as decisive for the formation of development discourse, including development anthropology discourse. Two exceptions are Little and Painter (1995) and Cowen and Shenton (1994).

2. Geertz took the concept of shared poverty from J. H. Boeke, though he made sure to distinguish his use of the term from Boeke's: "What Boeke regarded as an intrinsic and permanent characteristic of the Indonesian (or "Eastern") economic life, 'a primarily spiritual phenomenon,' was really an historically created condition; it grew not from the immutable essence of the Eastern soul as it encountered the incarnate spirit of Western dynamism, but from the in no way predestined shape of colonial policy as it impressed itself upon the traditional pattern of Indonesian agriculture" (Geertz 1963a:62).

3. I do not mean to suggest that Geertz intended to justify the sanguinary politics of the post-Sukarno Indonesian elite. However, it is worth observing that the Central Intelligence Agency (CIA), which actively supported Suharto during the 1965

massacres, funded much of CENIS's activity. CENIS was set up by Max Millikan following his tenure as assistant director of the CIA with funding from both the CIA and various private foundations. The anti-Communist agenda of modernization theory, in general, and CENIS, specifically, has been well documented (Gendzier 1985; Needell 1998). The main point in this context is that, regardless of Geertz's protests about his ignorance about the CIA side of things at CENIS, the modernizing norms embedded in the concept of involution validated the discourse of modernization adopted by post-1965 Indonesian elites to justify their rule. Geertz's insistence that his reasoning was purely scholarly or scientific represents a rather lame attempt to short-circuit discussion about this unfortunate coincidence. For a scathing indictment of the political context of Geertz's work, see Ross (1998).

4. Interestingly, Wolf's one explicit foray into Javanese anthropology (Wolf 1957) also relied heavily on Boeke's notion of shared poverty, but in a manner very different from that of Geertz. Geertz explained poverty in Parsonian terms as an extrarational value-orientation or an ideology of equality. Although Geertz stressed the historical nature and origins of this value-orientation, it was not mutable by rational choice on the part of the peasantry. By contrast, Wolf emphasized that shared poverty constituted a rational form of social insurance "to diminish the inequalities of risks" for peasants operating on the subsistence margin. Wolf's version of shared poverty implied that if material conditions changed, the peasantry would revise its calculations and adopt a different risk-sharing strategy.

REFERENCES

Alexander, Jennifer, and Paul Alexander
    1982 Shared Poverty as Ideology: Agrarian Relationships in Colonial Java. Man 17(4):597–619.

Austin-Broos, Diane J.
    1987 Clifford Geertz: Culture, Sociology, and Historicism. *In* Creating Culture: Profiles in the Study of Culture. Diane J. Austin-Broos, ed. Boston: Allan and Unwin.

Benda, Harry J.
    1965 Decolonization in Indonesia: The Problem of Continuity and Change. American Historical Review 70(4):1058–1073.

Boeke, J. H.
    1953 Economics and Economic Policy of Dual Societies, as Exemplified by Indonesia. Haarlem, The Netherlands: H. D. Tjeenk Willink.

Boomgaard, Peter
  1989 Children of the Colonial State: Population Growth and Economic Development in Java, 1795–1880. Amsterdam: Free University Press.

Clifford, James
  1988 The Predicament of Culture: Twentieth Century Ethnography, Literature, and Art. Cambridge, MA: Harvard University Press.

Cowen, M. P., and R. W. Shenton
  1994 Doctrines of Development. London, New York: Routledge.

Engerman, David
  1998 America, Russia, and the Romance of Economic Development. Ph.D. dissertation, Department of History, University of California-Berkeley.

Escobar, Arturo
  1991 Anthropology and the Development Encounter: The Making and Marketing of Development Anthropology. American Ethnologist 18(4):658–682.

Ferguson, James
  1994 The Anti-Politics Machine: "Development," Depoliticization, and Bureaucratic Power in Lesotho. Minneapolis: University of Minnesota Press.

Fraser, Nancy
  1996 Michel Foucault: A "Young Conservative"? In Feminist Interpretations of Michel Foucault. Susan J. Hekman, ed. Pp. 15–38 . University Park: Pennsylvania State University Press.

Geertz, Clifford
  1955 Religious Belief and Economic Behavior in a Central Javanese Village: Some Preliminary Considerations. Cambridge, MA: MIT Archives, Center for International Studies working paper E/55–C.
  1956a The Development of the Javanese Economy: A Socio-Cultural Approach. Cambridge, MA: MIT Archives, Center for International Studies working paper C/56–1.
  1956b The Social Context of Economic Change: An Indonesian Case Study. Cambridge, MA: MIT Archives, Center for International Studies working paper E/56–18.
  1960 The Religion of Java. Glencoe, IL: Free Press.
  1962 The Rotating Credit Association: A "Middle-Rung" in Development. Economic Development and Cultural Change 10(3):241–263. [First draft written in 1956. Cambridge, MA: MIT Archives, Center for International Studies working paper C/56–30].

1963a Agricultural Involution. Berkeley: University of California Press.
1963b Peddlers and Princes: Social Change and Economic Development in Two Indonesian Towns. Chicago: University of Chicago Press.
1973 The Interpretation of Cultures. New York: Basic Books.
1984 Culture and Social Change: The Indonesian Case. Man 19(4):511–532.
1995 After the Fact: Two Countries, Four Decades, One Anthropologist. Cambridge, MA: Harvard University Press.

Gendzier, Irene L.
1985 Managing Political Change: Social Scientists and the Third World. Boulder, CO, and London: Westview Press.

Gordon, Alec
1992 The Poverty of Involution: A Critique of Geertz's Pseudo-History. Journal of Contemporary Asia 22(4):490–512.

Higgins, Benjamin
1989 All the Difference: A Development Economist's Quest. Montreal: McGill-Queen's University Press.

Hüsken, Frans, and Benjamin White
1989 Java: Social Differentiation, Food Production, and Agrarian Control. In Agrarian Transformations: Local Processes and the State in Southeast Asia. Gillian Hart et al., eds. Pp. 235–265. Berkeley: University of California.

Kroeber, A. L., ed.
1953 Anthropology Today: An Encyclopedic Inventory. Chicago: University of Chicago Press.

Lewis, W. Arthur
1954 Economic Development with Unlimited Supplies of Labour. In The Economics of Underdevelopment. A. N. Agarwala and S. P. Singh, eds. Pp. 400–449. London: Oxford University Press, 1958.

Little, Peter D., and Michael Painter
1995 Discourse, Politics, and the Development Process: Reflections on Escobar's "Anthropology and the Development Encounter." American Ethnologist 22(3):602–626.

Mair, Lucy
1957 Studies in Applied Anthropology. London: Athlone Press.
1968 Applied Anthropology. In Encyclopedia of the Social Sciences, vol. 10. David Sills, ed. Pp. 325–330. New York: MacMillan Inc.

Michaels, Walter Benn
1992 Race into Culture: A Critical Genealogy of Cultural Identity. Critical Inquiry 18(4):655–685.

Murphy, Robert F.
1967 Culture Change. Biennial Review of Anthropology 5:1–45.

Nash, Manning
1965 Economic Anthropology. Biennial Review of Anthropology 4:121–138.

Needell, Allan A.
1998 Project Troy and the Cold War Annexation of the Social Sciences. *In* Universities and Empire: Money and Politics in the Social Sciences during the Cold War. Christopher Simpson, ed. Pp. 3–38. New York: The New Press.

Ortner, Sherry B., ed.
1997 The Fate of "Culture": Geertz and Beyond. Representations 59. Special Issue.

Perkins, John H.
1997 Geopolitics and the Green Revolution: Wheat, Genes, and the Cold War. New York: Oxford University Press, 1997.

Ransom, David
1975 Ford Country: Building an Elite for Indonesia. *In* The Trojan Horse: A Radical Look at Foreign Aid. Steve Weissman, ed. Pp. 93–116. Palo Alto, CA: Ramparts Press.

Ross, Eric B.
1998 Cold Warriors without Weapons. Identities 4(3–4):475–506.

Rostow, Walt Whitman
1960 The Stages of Economic Growth: A Non-Communist Manifesto. Cambridge: Cambridge University Press.

Rubin, Vera
1961 The Anthropology of Development. Biennial Review of Anthropology 2:120–172.

Scott, James C.
1976 The Moral Economy of the Peasant: Rebellion and Subsistence in Southeast Asia. New Haven, CT: Yale University Press.

Utrecht, Ernst
1973 American Sociologists in Indonesia. Journal of Contemporary Asia 3(1):39–45.

White, Benjamin
 1983 "Agricultural Involution" and Its Critics: Twenty Years After. Bulletin of
 Concerned Asian Scholars 15(2):18–31.

Wolf, Eric
 1957 Closed Corporate Peasant Communities in Mesoamerica and Central
 Java. Southwestern Journal of Anthropology 13(1):1–18.
 1969 Peasant Wars of the Twentieth Century. New York: Harper and Row.

2

The Evolution of Market Niches among Oaxacan Wood-Carvers

Michael Chibnik

The commercialization of craft production is an integral part of development programs in many rural areas of Africa, Asia, and Latin America. State agencies and nongovernmental organizations (NGOs) promote handicrafts in an attempt to provide economic aid to rural residents whose agricultural earnings are limited by small plots, low crop prices, and poor soils. Craft sales can enable households to meet subsistence needs and increase incomes even where land is scarce or unevenly divided. Artisanal production may provide rural men and women with an economic alternative to migration to crowded urban areas.

Economic anthropologists studying craft commercialization have usually focused on changes in work organization associated with new commodity chains linking rural artisans, development organizations, wholesalers, and store owners (e.g., Nash 1993b; Steiner 1994:40–60; Tice 1995). Entrepreneurs making and marketing crafts have set up workshops with hired laborers and established putting-out systems where pieceworkers at home use materials provided by merchants. Such changes have led anthropologists (e.g., Cook 1993; Kearney 1996:165–169; Stephen 1991) to write about the extent to which rural artisans are able to maintain autonomy as they become increasingly integrated into a global economy.

Few economic anthropologists, however, have carefully examined the product differentiation that ordinarily accompanies craft commercialization. Rural artisans selling crafts typically innovate and develop specialties in their attempts to establish niches for themselves in a complex economic environment. Specialization aids economic development by allowing numerous artisans to prosper. The market segmentation associated with increased artisan sales resembles the later stages of product life cycles described in the business literature and is somewhat analogous to the proliferation of equilibrium species in mature or climax stages of ecological succession.

This chapter examines the evolution of market niches in the trade in wood carvings in the state of Oaxaca, Mexico. Since 1985, artisans have developed specialties in their efforts to appeal to a diverse clientele. Some make expensive, labor-intensive carvings for collectors; others churn out cheap pieces for gift shops in the United States and tourists seeking souvenirs. Artisans vary in their painting and carving styles and the size of their pieces. They make animals, human figures, devils, angels, frames, chairs, tables, and ox carts. I have seen carvings of Benito Jurez, *subcomandante* Marcos (the Zapatista leader), *chupacabras* (imaginary beings who eat goats), Martians, mermaids, and helicopters. The diverse economic strategies that carvers have pursued in recent years are the result of a segmented market in the United States and Mexico that promotes novelty and rewards specialization. Artisans do not, however, have total freedom in their initiatives. They are constrained by their skills and the labor and capital they are able to mobilize.

MARKET DEVELOPMENT, PRODUCT
DIFFERENTIATION, AND EVOLUTION

Almost by definition, economic development in capitalist societies involves attracting customers to new products and expanding the market for existing products. Makers and sellers of an increasingly popular product often develop specialties in their efforts to gain a share of the market. Models from two very different fields, market research and ecological succession, may improve our understanding of why such product differentiation sometimes accompanies economic growth. Neither of these models precisely fits the evolution of market niches in the trade in Oaxacan wood carvings. Nonetheless, an examination of these models provides insights into the reasons why many carving households have become increasingly specialized in recent years.

Product Life Cycles

Market researchers (e.g., Capron 1978; Onkvisit and Shaw 1989) have shown that successful products such as automobiles, cameras, and audio-tapes ordinarily have certain life cycles. These business-oriented writers usually assume that their units of analysis are the firms making these products. The applicability of the product life-cycle model to Oaxacan wood carvers, therefore, depends in part on the extent to which the various groups making pieces can be regarded as analogous to firms. The product life-cycle model has five stages. Sales build slowly during the first stage of product *introduction*. The second stage is *early growth*, characterized by rapidly increasing sales. Sales continue to increase during *late growth*, but at a lower rate. The final two stages are *maturity*, when sales are relatively constant, and *decline*, where sales decrease until the product is finally withdrawn from the market.

During the introduction phase, there are usually only a few pioneers making the product. The increased sales that mark the end of this phase attract competitors, who continue to enter the market through the early growth stage. Because sales come from the growth in the market, this is not a stage of intense competition. During the late growth phase, competition heats up as the market begins to stabilize. The number of firms selling the product decreases as the strong force out the weak. The late growth period is characterized by product differentiation and market segmentation:

> In contrast to the imitative product strategy of early growth, extensive product modification occurs as competitors seek differential advantage through product design. Typically, product variations proliferate as competitors adapt their products to specific customer requirements. . . . In contrast to the early growth phase, price becomes a major competitive weapon in late growth. [Capron 1978:5]

Market segmentation is an attempt to divide markets into groups of potential customers with similar characteristics with respect to purchasing (Berrigan and Finkbeiner 1992; Weinstein 1987). By making products designed to appeal to particular types of customers, segmenters hope to increase their sales.

The maturity stage begins when sales cease to grow. During this phase, most sales are to repeat users and prices are competitive. Although the maturity stage may last many years, sales eventually decrease. Two common reasons why declines occur are technological obsolescence and changing consumer tastes.

Ecological Succession

Suggestive parallels can be drawn between product life cycles and stages of ecological succession as plants invade open fields (Burrows 1990:420–464; Colinvaux 1973:549–572). The first plants in such fields are *opportunists*, selected for their unspecialized behavior, plastic physiology, and expensive means of widespread dispersion. In the absence of significant disturbances, opportunists are gradually replaced by *equilibrium species* with specialized physiologies and stereotyped responses. As the environment becomes more crowded and more predictable, natural selection favors specialized adaptations to small econiches. This leads to a great increase in the number of species in the later stages of succession.

Comparisons of the changing economic strategies of Oaxacan artisans and the ecological succession stages of plants occupying an open field are clearly limited in scope. The applicability of a succession model depends, in part, on the extent to which analogies can be drawn between the selection pressures on production units making wood carvings in an expanding market and those affecting plant species in a recently formed ecosystem. Such analogies have at least surface plausibility. The development of specializations by Oaxacan wood-carvers and many other artisans is a textbook example of a cultural evolutionary process (Chibnik 1981; Durham 1990). Artisans continually try out new styles in their efforts to increase sales. Some experiments are unsuccessful (do not attract buyers) and are abandoned. Other innovations are "selected for" (attract customers) and replicated and become part of the cultural repertory of particular families and communities.

The ecological succession and market research analogies both suggest that artisans will adopt opportunistic or generalist economic strategies in the introductory and early growth stages of a product life cycle. The models also both imply that artisans will specialize in the late growth stage as they compete for customers in a crowded, more predictable market. The analogies diverge, however, in their implications concerning the number of competitors in the late growth stage. The market research model suggests that there will be fewer competitors as slower growth leads to more intense selective pressures. The succession analogy, in contrast, implies that there will be more competitors as niches are established in a stable economic environment.

CRAFTS AND DEVELOPMENT IN MEXICO

Mexico has long been known for the diverse crafts made by indigenous artisans living in rural areas. The state has energetically promoted handicraft production since the Revolution in the early twentieth century. Politicians and intellectuals in the 1920s and 1930s encouraged folkloric crafts as part of their efforts to develop symbols of national identity (García Canclini 1993:43). Postrevolutionary ideology aimed at the creation of a mestizo Mexico that incorporated indigenous groups into the state and emphasized both Amerindian and European roots of national culture. The state established museums of popular arts and industries and sponsored traveling craft exhibitions. To this day, the government regards crafts as serving an important ideological function. In parts of Mexico with large numbers of speakers of indigenous languages, the state encourages an ethnic identity based on craft sales in national museum outlets and bazaars sponsored by regional artisan institutes (Nash 1993a:11).

Since the 1940s, the Mexican government has incorporated craft promotion into economic development programs. The state sponsors contests for artisans and runs stores that buy and sell crafts from all over the country. Tourist offices prominently display the products of local artisans in their brochures. Regional and national agencies aid the production and marketing of crafts.

Transportation improvements in Mexico since 1950 have led to a great increase in foreign tourism. Although many visitors seek what they regard as traditional crafts, merchants have learned that tourists are also willing to buy "folk" arts that do not have long-standing cultural significance. Pre-Columbian motifs appear on pottery, jewelry, and wallets. Skirts, jackets, and blouses made from local textiles bear patterns invented in the twentieth century. Some merchants design new items and hire urban workers to make them. Others encourage innovation among the many talented artisans in the countryside.

The promotion of handicrafts in rural areas has been spurred by worsening agricultural conditions in much of Mexico. Many families are unable to earn significant incomes from farming their small plots. García Canclini (1993) nicely summarizes the appeal of crafts to development agencies:

> Given the impoverished and seasonal nature of agricultural production, crafts emerge as a suitable additional resource, and in some villages they become the major source of income. Without requiring large investments in raw materials, machines, or the training of a skilled labor force, they increase the earnings of rural families through the employment of women, children, and men during periods of economic inactivity. [39]

The state also regards the development of crafts as a way to stem the flood of emigrants from rural areas.

Because most crafts have a limited market, artisanry in rural Mexican communities is ordinarily not a particularly profitable supplement to agriculture and wage labor. In a few places (Stephen 1991; Stromberg 1976), the sales of crafts have been high enough to allow families to improve their standard of living significantly. In such cases, many people have abandoned farming and wage labor and now work full time as makers or sellers of crafts.

OAXACAN WOOD CARVING

I examine here the development of specializations in Arrazola, San Martín Tilcajete, and La Unión Tejalapan, three well-known wood-carving communities near the city of Oaxaca. About 1,700 people live in San Martín; Arrazola and La Unión each have approximately one thousand inhabitants. Many households in these communities have prospered by selling brightly painted, whimsical pieces to wholesalers and store owners from the United States. Wood carving in Arrazola, San Martín, and La Unión does not fit the stereotypical portrait of a Mexican craft in two important respects. First, the carvers are monolingual in Spanish and are not identified by themselves or others as "Indians."[1] Second, the wood carvings are novel creations without long-standing cultural significance.

The wood-carving boom originated in the activities of Oaxaca-based shop owners and three particular carvers—Manuel Jiménez of Arrazola, Isidoro Cruz of San Martín, and Martín Santiago of La Unión.[2] Jiménez, born in 1919, began carving wooden figures as a boy to pass time while tending animals. He sold a few carvings in the Oaxaca marketplace over the years. In the late 1950s and early 1960s, owners of craft shops in Oaxaca began buying Jiménez's carvings and showing them to folk art collectors such as Nelson Rockefeller. By the late 1960s, Jiménez was exhibiting in museums in Mexico City and the United States. Tourists and collectors started to visit Jiménez's workshop in Arrazola during the 1970s (see figure 2.1). The master kept his techniques secret, and for a long time the only carvers in Arrazola were Jiménez, his sons, and a son-in-law. In the early 1980s, however, other carvers in Arrazola began offering pieces for sale to people visiting Jiménez.

Isidoro Cruz was thirteen years old when he learned to carve during a long illness in 1947. While Cruz was working as an oxcart maker in the city of Oaxaca in 1968, he met Tonatiúh Gutiérrez, who worked for the National Council of Expositions. Gutiérrez hired Cruz to buy pieces for the council and encouraged him to sell his own carvings, which included animals, clowns, and masks. Cruz did not hide his methods, and about

FIGURE 2.1
Display room in home of Manuel Jiménez, the first and most famous Oaxacan wood-carver, Arrazola, Mexico. Photograph by Fidel Ugarte.

ten men in San Martín began to carve various types of wooden figures. In 1970, Gutiérrez became head of a government agency aimed at increasing craft sales. He named Cruz head of the agency's buying office in Oaxaca in 1971. During the four years Cruz ran the buying office, he was able to purchase many carvings from his friends and neighbors.

Between 1952 and 1967, Martín Santiago made seven different trips to the United States, where he worked as an agricultural laborer in California, Arizona, and Texas. After the U.S.-Mexican agreement (the bracero program) that had sponsored Santiago's seasonal agricultural migration ended, he found that wage labor and subsistence farming provided meager support for his growing family. In 1967, Santiago began selling wood carvings to a shop owner in Oaxaca who had stopped buying from Jiménez after a complex, bitter dispute. Santiago taught his four brothers how to make wood figures, and for many years the only carvers in La Unión were members of his large extended family.

In the 1970s and early 1980s, carvers in the three communities sold their pieces mostly to store owners in Oaxaca. Only Jiménez supported his family primarily by making wood figures; other carvers earned more from farming and wage labor. Wood carving during this time was a part-time occupation for a few adult males; women and children only occasionally worked on pieces. In the mid-1980s, wholesalers and store owners from the United States began to buy directly from carvers in Arrazola, San Martín, and La Unión. The weakening peso had made trading Mexican folk art more lucrative for dealers in the United States. By 1990, most households in Arrazola and San Martín earned part of their income from the sale of carvings. Because artisans in La Unión were less successful in attracting dealers and tourists, wood-carving households remained a minority.

As sales from wood carvings soared, the organization of work changed (Chibnik 2001). Male carvers asked their wives and children to help with painting and sanding.[3] Carving quickly became a family activity in which adult men contributed less than half the total labor. Some families in Arrazola and San Martín found that they could not fill large orders using only household labor and they hired one or two workers to help with carving, painting, and sanding.[4] In Arrazola, there are several *fábricas* (factories) that produce wood carvings with hired workers. In San Martín, a growing number of households buy unpainted carvings trucked in from elsewhere.

After these figures are painted, they are sold to local intermediaries and international wholesalers (see figure 2.2).

Although I often refer here to individual carvers, most artisans make their pieces in work groups. While these groups usually consist of related family members living together in a household, other forms of work organization involving hired laborers and piecework are also common. Unfortunately, everyone in the wood-carving trade—artisans, wholesalers, shop owners, and tourists—ordinarily refers to pieces as the work of a single person, typically an adult man. This is exemplified by the signatures on pieces, which usually carry only the name of the principal male carver.

REASONS FOR SPECIALIZATION

Specialization in the wood-carving trade is the result of both market demands and the initiative of artisans. Buyers of wood carvings include collectors seeking original, beautifully painted pieces, tourists purchasing inexpensive souvenirs, merchants stocking ethnic art shops, and wholesalers searching for items that can be sold in enormous gift shows. These different kinds of buyers, who have their own individual tastes, seek both items they know about and those they have never seen before. Therefore, the wood-carvers try to increase their sales by doing something distinctive that is attractive to some, but not all, buyers. In so doing, they hope to create a demand for new types of carvings.

The increased specialization in carving over the years cannot be neatly separated from overall changes in styles. Prior to 1980, most carvings bore clear relevance to the natural, cultural, and spiritual world of the artisans. Many carvings were of human figures (e.g., farmers, old men), ox teams, animals from the Oaxaca region, devils, angels, and skeletons. These pieces, which are now referred to as *rústico* (rustic), were carved and painted in a simple, albeit charming manner. As more dealers visited the wood-carving villages, artisans developed new styles in their efforts to attract clients. Animal carvings—sometimes of nonindigenous fauna such as zebras, lions, and elephants—sold the best and came to dominate the trade. Water-based aniline paints gave way to house paints that did not run as much and were less likely to fade in the sun. Carvings became more complicated and paint jobs more ornate as families competed to show their skills. Because some buyers prefer the older styles of carving and painting, a significant market remains for rustic pieces. Most contempo-

FIGURE 2.2
Miriam Gómez painting wood carvings, San Martín Tilcajete, Mexico. Photograph
by Fidel Ugarte.

rary artisans in La Unión specialize in modified versions of these simpler carvings, sometimes painted with aniline. Moreover, many buyers—especially those interested in Day of the Dead motifs—still seek out saints, angels, devils, and skeletons. Thus, some specialization is actually the continued production of "traditional" (twenty-year-old!) pieces.

The diversification of wood carvings in Arrazola, San Martín, and La Unión began with experiments by Manuel Jiménez, Isidoro Cruz, and Martín Santiago. These early wood-carvers attempted to increase their overall sales by selling a variety of pieces. Before 1970, however, the small number of wood-carvers and buyers limited the development of market niches in which individual artisans and wholesalers specialized in the production and purchase of particular types of pieces. Specialization did not really get under way until the early 1970s, when various state agencies promoting crafts held wood-carving contests in Oaxaca and bought the pieces of many entrants. These contests encouraged wood-carvers to try new pieces in efforts to win prizes and sell their pieces to the state. This stimulated a florescence of new styles in San Martín, in particular, because of Isidoro Cruz's connections with state bureaucracies promoting handicrafts. The establishment of some new crafts stores in the city of Oaxaca at this time also encouraged wood-carvers to innovate.

The astonishing diversity of pieces and styles that characterizes the contemporary wood-carving trade did not develop until the mid-1980s, when increasing numbers of wholesalers, store owners, and tourists from the United States visited Arrazola and San Martín. Many residents of these communities who previously had shown little interest in crafts began to make wood carvings. These neophyte carvers needed some way to attract dealers and tourists on their way to the houses of established artisans such as José Hernández in Arrazola and Epifanio Fuentes and Justo Xuana in San Martín. The obvious solution was to make something different that would appeal to potential buyers.

The lack of long-standing traditions in the wood-carving trade encourages experimentation. Some Oaxacan crafts such as embroidered wedding dresses from San Antonino (Waterbury 1989) are so well established that variability is restricted to rather fixed, culturally defined limits.[5] Buyers search for craft items that they consider to be typical of a particular place. Because there are no long-established wood-carving styles, buyers have fewer preconceived notions about what they are looking for and are more receptive to new types of pieces. Wholesalers and store owners want to diversify their stock; tourists like having something unique that will impress their friends and relatives.

In recent years, certain styles of carving and painting have come to be regarded as typical of particular families and communities as wholesalers and store owners seek out pieces and artisans that have sold well in the past. Margarito Melchor of San Martín has prospered for years by selling cats similar to those found on the cover of a popular book about the wood-carvers (Barbash 1993; Chibnik 1999). María Jiménez and her brothers make spectacular saints and angels in San Martín, while Juan Carlos Santiago of Arrazola is sought out for his penguins. Arrazola carvers are known for their elaborately curved, one-piece iguanas; La Unión artisans make multipiece rodeos, fiestas, and nativity scenes.

The fundamental appeal of the carvings, however, is still based on characteristics that encourage experimentation by artisans. Craft dealers, whom I have interviewed in the United States and Mexico, agree that customers especially appreciate the whimsy, color, and imagination of the carvings. When artisans are successful with particular kinds of carvings (e.g., frogs reading books, parrot musicians, reclining cats), some of their neighbors copy their styles in cheaper, less technically proficient knock-offs. A type of figure once regarded as original, whimsical, and imaginative may come to seem hackneyed.

Successful artisans are well aware of this process and sometimes complain bitterly about copiers. Their realization that the market can become saturated with particular kinds of pieces forces them either to innovate or develop specialties (e.g., difficult painting or carving styles) that cannot be easily copied. Even Margarito Melchor, who is an archetypal example of an artisan with a recognized, long-lasting specialty, was experimenting in the summer of 1998 with rustic-looking devils, angels, and witches that are quite different from his well-known, ornately painted cats, deer, goats, and squirrels.

The cheapness of materials also encourages experimentation. Artisans spend no more than two or three pesos for the paint and wood needed for a medium-sized carving that can be sold to a dealer for thirty or forty pesos (US$3–US$4 in 2001). Because several such pieces can be completed in a day, making something new requires minimal expenditures of time and money. If an experiment fails (a new type of carving does not sell), little is lost.

Carvers' abilities limit their freedom to experiment. Skilled, imaginative artisans typically innovate by making expensive, elaborately carved pieces with complex painting designs. Less-talented carvers are more likely to experiment by making smaller, cheaper, simpler, slightly different versions of other people's already successful ideas. Innovation is also constrained by the labor and capital available to particular carvers. Artisans with large families or the money to hire workers can afford to experiment with several new pieces while simultaneously making carvings that have sold well in the past. This economic strategy is not available to an impoverished artisan couple with young children. Because of their precarious economic circumstances and small labor pool, such a couple may be reluctant to innovate much.

TYPES OF SPECIALIZATION

Although Oaxacan wood carvings most obviously differ in what they represent, they also vary in size, color, painting style, materials, price, and a host of other characteristics. Carvers' specializations typically encompass some combination of these variables. A carving family might, for example, make many expensive iguanas painted with particular decorations. Most artisans have several specializations. Coindo Melchor of San Martín carves elaborate ox teams (two bulls, a driver, and a cart filled with animals and crops) and unique creatures that one writer (Barbash 1993:31) has described as "bird-headed-women." Aguilino García of La Unión sells fairly expensive skunks, crocodiles, armadillos, and palm trees. Antonio Aragón of Arrazola makes medium-priced, small, finely carved, realistic deer, dogs, lions, and cats. Despite such specializations, all carvers can and do make a wide variety of pieces and will readily change their product mix if what they are focusing on declines in popularity.

In the discussion that follows, I mention only the most important ways in which carvings vary. These are (1) representations; (2) physical characteristics; (3) carving and painting styles; and (4) price.

Representations

Carvings can roughly be classified into five categories—animals, religious or folkloric beings, humans, plants, and inanimate objects. Some carvings (e.g., trees with birds, drunks sitting on chairs around a table) include items from two or more of these categories. A few (e.g., skulls, masks) do not fit neatly into my classificatory scheme.

Animals are by far the most common carvings. An examination of the purchases of a large-scale dealer between 1995 and 1998 revealed that he had bought more than seventy different types of animals. The dealer spent the most money on cats; other frequent purchases included armadillos, frogs, iguanas, porcupines, donkeys, and giraffes. Animals are often painted with bright colors and designs and carved with exaggerated features that bear little resemblance to what occurs in the natural world. Anthropomorphism is common, and carvings of animals playing musical instruments, golfing, fishing, and engaging in other human pursuits are very popular.

Many carvings depict religious or folkloric beings important in Mexican popular culture. Angels, saints, and virgins tend to be somber pieces, often brightly painted, depicted alone. Devils and skeletons, in contrast, are often parts of lively scenes. There are, for example, oxcarts filled with skeletons, devils riding dogs, and skeletons drinking with witches.

Artisans often make mermaids and occasionally carve other mythical figures such as centaurs and Pegasuses. The most common carvings of imaginary beings, however, are *alebrijes* (sometimes spelled *alebriges*). These fantastic figures, frequently described as "space age," are modeled on the papier mâché sculptures of the Linares family of Mexico City.[6] Because many buyers now use the word alebrije to refer to any Oaxacan wood carving, artisans are beginning to refer to the "space age" pieces as *marcianos* (Martians). Carvings of human beings evidently do not sell well since they are made only occasionally. I have seen striking carvings of old men, farmers, drunks, mariachis, fruit vendors, cooks, lovers, and prostitutes. Despite the originality and charm of such carvings, they are made mostly by older artisans in La Unión and seem much less popular than they once were.

The artisans carve many trees and cacti. The only other plants that artisans commonly make are foods such as avocados, chiles, watermelons, and carrots. Carvings of inanimate objects include those that are purely decorative (e.g., bicycles, wheels of fortune) and those that have some practical use (e.g., jewelry boxes, refrigerator magnets, napkin holders). The most commonly made inanimate objects are picture frames decorated with raised carvings of animals and plants. Brightly painted miniature chairs and tables are also popular and are often sold to Mexican tourists as children's toys.

Physical Characteristics

Most carvings are made from copal (*Bursera*), a light wood that is easily cut when wet and hard after drying. Some carvers specialize by making some or all of their carvings out of other types of wood. Chairs, tables, frames, and magnets are usually made from pine. Zompantle (*Erythrina coralloides*) is used by a few carvers in San Martín, notably Isidoro Cruz. In recent years, Manuel Jiménez and his sons have carved only in cedar. Carvers in the late 1980s could be divided into those who used aniline and those who were switching to vinyl-acrylic house paints. Currently, aniline is used only by Isidoro Cruz and some carvers from the extended Santiago family of La Unión.

Aside from materials, the most obvious physical way that carvings vary is in their size. While big carvings are more striking, smaller pieces have the important advantage of being more easily transported by tourists. Big pieces ordinarily take longer to make and can be sold for higher prices. They are typically bought by collectors and store owners wanting something flashy to highlight a shop area. Smaller pieces, which comprise the bulk of the trade, are sold to diverse types of buyers—tourists, shop owners stocking cheap gift items, and wholesalers selling to retailers in the United States. Skilled carvers, whose reputations and contacts attract buyers willing to spend some money, tend to spend most of their time on medium-sized and big pieces. Most, however, make some small pieces (e.g., pigs by María Jiménez and her brothers) and a few (e.g., Sergio Aragón of Arrazola) specialize in miniatures.

Carvings can be subdivided into individual pieces and multipiece sets. Although every carver makes individual pieces, some specialize in particular types of sets such as animal musician bands, Nativity scenes, rodeos, fiestas, kiosks, and anthropomorphic animals sitting on chairs around a table filled with food and drink. Artisans are usually willing to sell parts of a set to an interested customer. The only reason that they will refuse to do this is if the set has already been ordered by someone else and the buyer is expected to pick it up soon.

Carving and Painting Styles

Artisans often attempt to develop unique styles that demonstrate technical ability, attract prospective customers, and cannot be copied easily. This may entail cooperation and consultation between a husband and wife since the most common division of labor involves men carving and women painting. Carvers and painters, however, have considerable autonomy in their creative efforts. Moreover, stylistic specialization does not occur only at the individual and family level. Some carving and painting styles are now characteristic of related households or even entire communities.

Carvers' technical abilities can greatly increase the value of their pieces. Carvings of animals ordinarily include a body and some attachments. The body of the carving of a lion, for instance, includes its torso, head, and legs, with ears and a tail as attachments. Artisans often demonstrate their skill by making complex bodies out of one piece of wood. This is most evident in the curving iguanas characteristic of numerous Arrazola carvers. Conversely, the rusticity of some La Unión cats can be seen in their multipiece bodies with legs nailed onto torsos.

When carvers judge the skill of one another, they most often look at the details in a figure. Some rustic animal carvings—which often have considerable charm— represent legs only crudely and do not indicate posture realistically. Talented carvers will accurately show an animal's movement and carefully delineate toes and claws. A carving I bought of a "woman of the streets" by Gabino Reyes of La Unión illustrates well what a skilled artisan can do. This small piece includes painted fingernails, a decorated short skirt, and a precisely rendered purse.

Painting offers more opportunity for specialization than carving, and artisans vary greatly in the colors and designs that they use. Some painters can be readily identified, for example, by the types of eyes on their animal carvings. Both low- and high-end artisans have developed characteristic painting styles. La Unión rustic pieces are often painted simply with one or two colors and few decorations. Equally cheap pieces from workshops in Arrazola are elaborately painted with a particular design that is readily identifiable. The painting styles of the La Unión rustic pieces and the Arrazola workshop carvings are easy to learn. The decorations used by Mariá Jiménez of San Martín on her expensive pieces, in contrast, indicate a remarkable talent (see figure 2.3). María, the best-known painter in the

FIGURE 2.3
Mariá Jiménez, the best-known painter of Oaxacan wood carvings, San Martín
Tilcajete, Mexico. Photograph by Fidel Ugarte.

carving villages, uses minute, detailed, repetitive decorations on saints, angels, toucans, and pigs carved by her five brothers. María says that she has about thirty designs that she has developed for painting carvings. These designs are related to decorative patterns María learned some years ago when making embroidered dresses.

Price

The wood-carving market is segmented by price into three general categories. Artisans sold their cheapest pieces for 50 pesos or less in June 1998, when the exchange rate was 8.8 pesos per dollar. Medium-priced pieces sold from 50 to 200 pesos; expensive pieces mostly cost between 200 and 1,000 pesos. The most expensive carvings regularly sold are made by high-end Arrazola carvers such as José Hernández, Miguel Santiago, Francisco Morales, and Manuel Jiménez. Although a collector paid 9,000 pesos in Arrazola for a carving in summer of 1998, only a few other pieces sold locally for more than 2,000 pesos. The highest priced piece sold in a carving village that I know of took place in 1995, when a doctor from Mexico City paid Isidoro Cruz the equivalent of US$3,000 for a "carousel of the Americas." Cruz spent three months working on this spectacular carving.

Price differences reflect a segmented market in the United States and Mexico (and less significantly Canada, Europe, and Japan), where some buyers seek out inexpensive carvings for gifts and souvenirs, others clever, medium-priced pieces, and still others expensive, one-of-a-kind carvings. This differentiated market could easily be seen when I visited Santa Fe, New Mexico, in May 1998. An enormous store called Jackalope sold hundreds of cheap carvings at prices ranging from $15 to $100. The front window of a smaller shop on the main square displayed a $755 lion carved by Maximiliano Morales of Arrazola (Francisco Morales's son). A clerk in the store told me that they had no problem selling carvings at this price.[7]

Although all artisans make pieces that vary considerably in cost, most focus on a certain price range. The most extreme example is Manuel Jiménez, whose cheapest pieces (priced only in dollars) sell for US$100. A more typical case is Aguilino García of La Unión, who slowly makes pieces that sold for between 100 and 400 pesos ($12–$45) in the summer of 1998. There are many artisan families whose business comes primarily from small animal carvings sold to dealers for about $3 apiece.

Artisans can only choose to a limited extent whether they will specialize in cheap, medium-priced, or expensive pieces. Obviously, not all artisans are able to command high prices for their work. Because expensive pieces—which are often large—generally take a long time to make, carvers can specialize in them only if they are sure to be able to find buyers. This depends on artisans' ability to make original, technically proficient pieces and whether or not they have an established reputation. Nevertheless, a certain amount of specialization with respect to price is possible. The owners of the workshops in Arrazola have decided, for example, to make inexpensive pieces aimed at tourists. Some skilled artisan families in Arrazola and San Martín who have the ability to make expensive pieces have chosen instead to mainly make medium-priced pieces. They prefer the quicker, surer returns that these smaller carvings provide.

EXAMPLES OF SPECIALIZATION

The four brief case studies that follow show some of the ways in which Oaxacan wood-carvers specialize. The artisans profiled vary in the types of carvings they make, the prices of their pieces, and the kinds of customers they have. The case studies also illustrate the diverse types of labor organization used to make pieces. They include one artisan working mostly alone, two families, and a workshop with hired laborers.

Expensive Pieces for Collectors

Miguel Santiago of Arrazola, born in 1966, sells perhaps forty wood carvings a year to about thirty-five different customers. Some of these sales are of individual pieces; others are multipiece sets with both human and animal figures (e.g., Frida Kahlo surrounded by monkeys). Miguel's carvings (or sets) typically cost between $300 and $800. Although Miguel has sold to buyers from Mexico, Europe, and Japan, most of his customers come from the United States. He is a versatile artisan who can and will make almost anything a client requests. His specialty can best be described as "exceptionally well-made, original, expensive carvings." Miguel works slowly and carefully and often spends more than a month on an order for a multipiece set (see figure 2.4).

Miguel, whose work methods resemble those of an architect, has orders for two years in advance. After potential customers suggest ideas for a carving, Miguel makes several sketches of possible pieces. Eventually, an agreement is reached about what will be made and the delivery date.

FIGURE 2.4
Miguel Santiago at work on a wood carving, Arrazola, Mexico. Photograph by Fidel
Ugarte.

Miguel sends a price estimate to his client about five months before the carving is due. The price may be raised later if Miguel decides to modify his original idea.

Miguel is unusual in his willingness to discuss the aesthetics of wood carving. His strong ideas about what is good work have made it difficult for Miguel to cooperate with others in craft production. He once made pieces with a talented brother, but they parted company because of artistic differences. Miguel later took on an eighteen-year-old nephew as a quasi-apprentice, but they, too, had a falling out. Today, Miguel carves alongside his father. José Santiago learned to carve in the mid-1980s after a motorcycle accident and a bout with appendicitis forced him to quit working as a mason. Miguel's pride in his work has led to an unusually explicit division of labor between father and son. The Santiagos are an enterprise with three product lines—ultraexpensive pieces designed, carved, and painted by Miguel; expensive pieces ($80–$100) carved by José and painted by Miguel; and moderately priced pieces ($35–$50) carved and painted by José. Signatures on these pieces indicate the carver and painter.

Inexpensive Pieces for Intermediaries

Reynaldo Santiago and Elodia Reyes have made carvings together in La Unión since their marriage in the mid-1970s. Reynaldo is from an artisan family and has always supported himself by carving and small-scale farming. He is the nephew of Martín Santiago, the first carver in La Unión. Elodia and Reynaldo have two daughters in their twenties and two sons, a teenager and a toddler. Although many teenagers and young adults work in the wood-carving trade, Elodia and Reynaldo receive no help from their children. One daughter works as a domestic servant in Mexico City; the other is married and is busy with her own family in La Unión. The teenage son works in the city of Oaxaca and has so far shown no interest in carving. The limited labor available to Reynaldo and Elodia forces them to work slowly. Reynaldo does all the carving, while Elodia is responsible for most painting. Reynaldo says that he helps with painting when he has the time.

Reynaldo and Elodia make some expensive pieces such as bandstands and ox teams that sell for $45. They also make some medium-sized (twenty-centimeters high) animals that cost about $7. The family specializes, however, in miniature (seven-centimeter) dogs, cats, giraffes, rabbits, and goats that sell for about $3. Elodia once used aniline paints, but switched to house paints around 1985 at the request of Henry Wangeman, a dealer who bought many of the family's pieces at that time. Because few tourists visit La Unión, Elodia and Reynaldo sell most of their pieces to Oaxaca store owners and wholesalers from the United States. They have always been dependent on only a few buyers. Elodia and Reynaldo's first pieces were sold to Casa Victor, a store in Oaxaca. When Henry Wangeman began coming to La Unión in the 1980s, he was by far their most important customer. Nowadays, they sell the majority of their carvings to two clients, a wholesaler in California and a store owner in Texas.

Inexpensive and Medium-Priced Pieces for Tourists and Wholesalers

The wood-carving trade has created a niche for female entrepreneurs in Arrazola. Olga Santiago, born in 1969, is one of four women in that community who runs workshops in which hired laborers paint and carve pieces. All of these businesses have considerable turnover, as the mostly young carvers and painters leave to work on their own. Two of these women are married and work independently from their husbands. Olga is one of two single female entrepreneurs. Although Olga's workshop is one of the newest and smallest in Arrazola, she is having considerable success.

When Olga was twenty-one, she began working as a painter in the first wood-carving factory in Arrazola. This business, run by Olga's cousin Pépe Santiago and his wife Mercedes Cruz, employs teenaged painters and carvers who are paid a weekly salary. In 1995, Olga and an older sister stopped working for Pépe and Mercedes and established their own business in which they paid painters and carvers by the piece. Olga has run this workshop alone since her sister left for the United States in the summer of 1997.

The workshop, near the house that Olga shares with her parents, is a large cement room packed with shelves of wood carvings. In February 1998, there were three women who painted in the workshop—Olga, her seventeen-year-old niece Anali Rodríguez, and her twenty-year-old friend and neighbor Lourdes Morales. A fourth woman painted for Olga at home. Many pieces sold in the workshop were carved by twenty-four-year-old Pedro Hernández of Arrazola, who worked almost full-time for Olga. Others were carved by artisans from nearby communities.

Because Olga's workshop is located a few blocks away from Arrazola's plaza, tourists visiting Oaxaca are unlikely to find her place on their own. Olga, therefore, pays commissions to boys from Arrazola and guides and taxi drivers from Oaxaca who take tourists to her workshop. The prices Olga charges, while much cheaper than those of comparable pieces in the United States, are high by local standards. A small piece of less quality than Reynaldo and Elodia's $3 miniature animals sells for $5; medium-sized pieces of middling quality cost as much as $20. Prices are negotiable, and tourists can pay considerably less if they are willing and able to bargain. Although tourists comprise a sizable part of Olga's business, wholesalers are more important customers. One particular Mexican wholesaler buys more from Olga than all tourists combined. On a May 1998 trip to the Arizona-Mexico border, I saw many pieces signed "Olga Santiago." Prices in both Mexico and the United States were double or triple those in Arrazola.

Pine Carvings for Mexican Wholesalers

Alba Matías, born in 1969, is from a large carving family in San Martín that specializes in pine frames, chairs, tables, and magnets. Alba learned to carve and paint at an early age and worked in the family business until she married Victor Victoria in 1995. Victor's family at that time was one of relatively few in San Martín not involved in carving. His father Luis is a building contractor and Victor worked in construction in the city of Oaxaca before his marriage.

After Alba and Victor were married, they moved in with Victor's parents and his teenage sister Leticia. The couple quickly established a successful family wood-carving business, making pieces similar to those of the Matías family. Alba taught Victor how to carve and paint and is still more knowledgeable about techniques than he is. The family makes pine crosses and (decorative, nonfunctional) machetes as well as frames, chairs, tables, and magnets. They also make ox teams in which the animals are copal and the oxcart is pine. Alba and Victor carve and paint, Leticia paints, and Victor's mother Francisca sands.

Because Alba knew many wholesalers through her family, she and Victor had no trouble finding customers when they began working together. Their pieces range in price from $4 for a small frame to $100 for a small table with two chairs. They sell many medium-sized frames for $6 and also do well with $30 chairs. Perhaps because transporting chairs and tables to the United States by air is costly, most of the wholesalers buying from Alba and Victor are Mexican. Although these Mexican dealers account for the bulk of the couple's sales, they occasionally sell to tourists and high-end Oaxaca shops.

DISCUSSION

Several aspects of the Oaxacan wood-carving trade encourage innovation and specialization. Because wood carving is a new craft, buyers have few preconceived notions about what pieces should look like. The low cost of materials makes it easy for artisans to experiment without losing their livelihoods. The existence of a sizable high-end market enables some skilled carvers and painters to earn substantial incomes by spending considerable amounts of time on commissioned, individualized pieces.

Despite these particular features of the wood-carving trade, general theories about the causes of specialization are clearly relevant to the evolution of market niches in the workshops of Arrazola, San Martín, and La Unión. The product life-cycle model fits well most of the changes in wood-carvers' economic strategies. After a long introductory stage involving a few pioneers (1950–1984), many families began carving during an early growth phase (1985–1990). The wood-carving trade is now at either the end of late growth or the beginning of maturity. As sales have leveled off and the market has become more predictable, carvers have developed niches. This specialization has reduced competition among artisans and allowed them to capture parts of a segmented market.

The number of carvers has not diminished during late growth, as the product life-cycle model would predict. There are three principal reasons why prosperous wood-carvers have not driven their less successful neighbors out of business. As noted earlier, the product life-cycle model assumes that the units of analysis are firms. Most carving production units, however, are family workshops that can survive economically in situations where labor costs would lead to the failure of capitalistic firms using paid employees (Chayanov 1966). Further, the absence of attractive economic alternatives makes struggling artisans reluctant to abandon wood carving. Finally, wood-carvers can easily change specializations if their initial efforts to find a market niche are unsuccessful.

While the product life-cycle model clearly applies in part to the wood-carving trade, the relevance of theories about plant succession stages is less obvious. An ecological analogy, however, has the merit of drawing attention to the selective pressures affecting the evolution of market niches. Specialized plants proliferate when their ecosystem becomes crowded and predictable. Although I would not wish to push this analogy too far, the wood-carvers seem to be creating more market niches as the number of artisans increases and their economic environment becomes more stable.

Recent trends in the wood-carving trade may lead to further specialization and innovation. In the past several years, a number of carvers have prospered by selling expensive pieces to dealers. Many low-end specialists working with wholesalers have been able to earn steady, if unspectacular incomes. Some artisans who sell unoriginal, inexpensive pieces to tourists, in contrast, have suffered economically as the number of visitors to the wood-carving communities has leveled off. Most carvers, therefore, understand that they must sell to dealers in order to be successful. Wholesalers and store owners, unlike tourists, are familiar with many different types of pieces. The dealers' never-ending quest for originality should continue to foster the artisans' creativity.

Anthropologists examining economic development might focus more on who can take advantage of the market niches accompanying the commercialization of particular products. The Oaxacan wood-carving trade allows artisans within particular communities to innovate and specialize in their attempts to take advantage of such niches. The conditions of trade for certain other products (perhaps bananas and coffee), in contrast, favor standardization on the local level and regional specialization. In such cases, intermediaries can easily specialize in attempts to establish market niches, but producers have much less autonomy than the Oaxacan wood-carvers.

NOTES

This paper is based principally on fieldwork carried out during the summers of 1995, 1996, 1997, and 1998 and in January–March 1998. I have also made several other short-term research trips to Oaxaca. I thank Holly Carver and Rafael Ricárdez for introducing me to the wood-carvers and Saúl Aragón for his assistance throughout this ongoing project.

1. Many of the carvers had grandparents who spoke Zapotec or other indigenous languages and were identified by others as "Indians." Ethnicity in the Central Val-

leys of Oaxaca in both the past and present is too complicated to be examined in depth here. Many speakers of indigenous languages in the region self-identify primarily as residents of a particular community and do not think of themselves as belonging to a pan-Indian collectivity. They often secondarily self-identify as speakers of a particular indigenous language and as "Mexicans."

2. I do not use pseudonyms for the artisans. Many carvers have asked me to use real names where possible. They like the publicity for their pieces.

3. There are today perhaps half a dozen female carvers in Arrazola and San Martín.

4. Carvers in La Unión have never used hired labor.

5. The very successful Teotitlán-based textile industry is characterized by almost as much variability as the wood-carving trade.

6. The word alebrije was made up by someone in the Linares family (Masuoka 1994:97).

7. The price of a carving in a store in the United States is typically four or five times what the maker is paid by a dealer.

REFERENCES

Barbash, Shepard
    1993 Oaxacan Wood Carving: The Magic in the Trees. San Francisco: Chronicle.

Berrrigan, John, and Carl Finkbeiner
    1992 Segmentation Marketing. New York: Harper Collins.

Burrows, Colin
    1990 Processes of Vegetation Change. London: Unwin Hyman.

Capron, Noel
    1978 Product Life Cycle. Boston: HBS Case Services, Harvard Business School.

Chayanov, A. V.
    1966[1920s] The Theory of Peasant Economy. Homewood, IL: R. Irwin.

Chibnik, Michael
    1981 The Evolution of Cultural Rules. Journal of Anthropological Research 37:256–268.
    1999 Popular Journalism and Artistic Styles in Three Oaxacan Wood–Carving Communities. Human Organization 58:182–189.

2001 Oaxacan Wood Carvers: Global Markets and Local Work Organization
In Plural Globalities and Multiple Localities: New World Borders. M. Rees and
J. Smart, eds. Pp. 129–148. Monographs in Economic Anthropology 17. Lanham, MD: University Press of America.

Colinvaux, Paul
1973 Introduction to Ecology. New York: Wiley.

Cook, Scott
1993 Craft Commodity Production, Market Diversity, and Differential
Rewards in Mexican Capitalism Today. *In* Crafts in the World Market. J. Nash,
ed. Pp. 59–83. Albany: State University of New York Press.

Durham, William
1990 Advances in Evolutionary Culture Theory. Annual Review of Anthropology 19:187–210.

García Canclini, Néstor
1993 Transforming Modernity: Popular Culture in Mexico. Austin: University
of Texas Press.

Kearney, Michael
1996 Reconceptualizing the Peasantry. Boulder, CO: Westview Press.

Masuoka, Susan
1994 En Calavera: The Papier Máché Art of the Linares Family. Los Angeles:
UCLA Fowler Museum of Cultural History.

Nash, June
1993a Introduction. *In* Crafts in the World Market. J. Nash, ed. Pp. 1–22.
Albany: State University of New York Press.

Nash, June, ed.
1993b Crafts in the World Market. Albany: State University of New York
Press.

Onkvisit, Sak, and John Shaw
1989 Product Life Cycles and Product Management. New York: Quorum.

Steiner, Christopher
1994 African Art in Transit. Cambridge: Cambridge University Press.

Stephen, Lynn
1991 Zapotec Women. Austin: University of Texas Press.

Stromberg, Gobi

1976 The Amate Bark-Paper Painting of Xalitla. *In* Ethnic and Tourist Arts. N. Graburn, ed. Pp. 149–162. Berkeley: University of California Press.

Tice, Karin

1995 Kuna Crafts, Gender, and the Global Economy. Austin: University of Texas Press.

Waterbury, Ronald

1989 Embroidery for Tourists: A Contemporary Putting-Out System in Oaxaca, Mexico. *In* Cloth and Human Experience. A. Weiner and J. Schneider, eds. Pp. 243–271. Washington, DC: Smithsonian Institution Press.

Weinstein, Art

1987 Market Segmentation. Chicago: Probus.

3

Tourists as a Common-Pool Resource: A Study of Dive Shops on Utila, Honduras

Lee Cronk and Shannon Steadman

A common-pool or common property resource (CPR) is characterized by high subtractability, meaning that one individual's use of it detracts significantly from another person's ability to use it, and by low excludability, meaning that it is difficult to prevent any particular individual from using it. The classic example of a CPR is a plot of grazing land shared by a group of farmers: The addition of new livestock to the common land diminishes its usefulness to the rest of the farmers, but it is hard to exclude any particular farmer's animals from the land. CPRs differ from three other types of goods: (1) public goods, such as national defense services, which share with common-pool resources the feature of low excludability but also have low subtractability; (2) toll (or club) goods, such as toll roads, which have low subtractability but high excludability; and (3) private goods, such as most consumer products, which have both high subtractability and high excludablity (Ostrom et al. 1994:67).

Ever since Garrett Hardin's (1968) seminal essay on "The Tragedy of the Commons," CPRs have been a central concern of social science in general and economic development studies in particular. In brief, Hardin pointed out that CPRs are inherently prone to overexploitation. Although the best thing for all concerned might be for the individuals using a particular CPR to restrain themselves, each individual's own ends are best served by exploiting it to the fullest. For many years, Hardin's model of the tragedy of the commons, combined with Olson's (1965) insights about the difficulty of getting groups to act collectively to solve problems, gave the study of CPRs a distinctly pessimistic air. A common view was that the only solutions to CPR problems were either to eliminate the CPR itself by dividing it up and turning it into a private good, thereby giving each individual an incentive to conserve the resource for the future or to use the central power of the state to enforce conservation of the resource.

More recently, it has become clear that another solution to CPR problems may be possible in some circumstances. Specifically, given the right conditions and institutional supports, it is possible for the users of the resource themselves to develop procedures and protocols for exploitation of the resource that allow its fair use and encourage economic development while minimizing the risk of overexploitation. Ostrom (1990:90; see also Low and Heinen 1993; Ostrom et al. 1994; Ridley and Low 1993) has identified a number of characteristics that contribute to the success of locally managed CPRs. For example, they must have clearly defined boundaries, sanctions for rule violations, procedures in place for changing rules, the ability to monitor members' use of the resource, and procedures for resolving conflicts between members. Successful examples of self-governed CPRs given by Ostrom (1990) include water resources and irrigation schemes (e.g., Glick 1970; Maass and Anderson 1986) and grazing lands (e.g., McKean 1986; Netting 1981).

Anthropologists have made major contributions to the literature on CPRs, which may reflect the fact that successful organizations for CPR governance typically exist on a small scale that is amenable to study by existing anthropological field methods. Anthropological contributions to this literature include not only Netting's study of grazing land management in the Alps (Netting 1981) but also studies of fisheries management schemes (e.g., Acheson 1998; Berkes 1987; Durrenberger 1997; Kurien 1995; McDaniel 1997; McCay 1987) and irrigation schemes (e.g., Baker 1997; Gragson and Payton 1997; Uphoff et al. 1990).

The existing literature published under the rubric of CPRs is limited in three ways:

1. *Exclusion of failures.* The existing literature on CPRs mostly concerns relatively successful examples of local CPR governance. For the further development of our understanding of what leads to cooperation in

some circumstances but not in others, however, it is also worth spending some effort to understand situations in which efforts to organize groups to manage CPRs have failed.

2. *Exclusion of nonnatural resources.* Virtually all existing studies of attempts to manage CPRs locally concern natural resources, mainly fisheries, grazing lands, and water. However, there is nothing in the definition of CPRs that limits them to natural resources. Any resource that has the key characteristics of high subtractability and low excludability is, by definition, a common-pool resource. Money provided by customers to a particular class of businesses is an example of an artificial resource that is nevertheless a common-pool resource. Such money has the characteristic of high subtractability in the sense that money spent by a customer at one business is not available to any other business, and it has the characteristic of low excludability in the sense that it is often hard to prevent either new firms from entering a market or existing firms from lowering their prices in order to attract more customers.

3. *Exclusion of collusion.* Although the problems faced by CPR management schemes are very similar to those faced by firms trying to form cartels and fix prices, the study of cartels is often explicitly excluded from the analysis of CPRs. Ostrom, for example, excludes from her consideration CPRs "in which a group can form a cartel and control a sufficient part of the market to affect market price" (1990:26). This choice seems clearly to be based on normative rather than theoretical concerns. The exclusion of collusion from CPR research seems particularly inappropriate in contexts in which the goal is the alleviation of poverty; the ostensible victims are tourists and other consumers from relatively wealthy countries, and the goods in question are luxuries, not necessities. Furthermore, excluding such schemes from our consideration seems not in keeping with the spirit of anthropology. It is ethnocentric to allow Western economics' biases against price-fixing agreements to prevent us from studying what those from other cultural backgrounds might see as perfectly legitimate arrangements among producers.

As many anthropologists have documented, one of the most negative side effects of market-based development around the world has been the breakdown of existing patterns of cooperation within communities (Black 1999:18). To the extent to which cooperation among local producers, even if it involves price fixing, can accommodate both market-based development and maintenance of previously existing patterns of cooperation within communities, it seems worthy of consideration. Even if the desire of policymakers is to discourage the formation of cartels and price-fixing arrangements, it seems worthwhile to use our best intellectual tools, including those developed for the study of CPRs, to study them. This chapter, which deals with the failed attempts of Utilian dive shop owners to form a cartel and fix prices, helps balance the literature in all of these three ways.

ETHNOGRAPHIC BACKGROUND

Located in the Caribbean Sea off the northern Honduran coast, Utila is the third largest of Honduras's predominantly English-speaking Bay Islands (Roatán and Guanaja are, respectively, the largest and second largest). Existing social science research on Utila is limited to some economic anthropology (Lord 1975), medical anthropology (Miller 1974), historical geography (Davidson 1974), and linguistics (Doran 1954; Lipski 1986; Warantz 1983). The ancestors of the island's current inhabitants, who reached the island mainly by way of the Cayman Islands, were chiefly of British and African descent. In recent years, a large number of mainland Hondurans have also come to the island in search of work. The population of the main settlement of East Harbor is about 2,000, with an additional 400 or so on a series of cays just off the island's southwestern tip.

Although Utilians at one time had a key role in the Central American fruit trade, since World War II, Utilian men have made a living mainly by leaving the island and working in the merchant marine and, especially in recent years, in the oil industry around the world. Commercial fishing has also been an important source of income for many Utilians. Particularly since Hurricane Fifi devastated the island in 1974, many Utilians have moved to the United States, most settling in the New Orleans area, and today most Utilian families have strong social and cultural ties to the U.S. Utilian culture has been described as highly individualistic and acquisitive with a strong ethic of consumerism (e.g., Lord 1975). Although a few Utilian households fit the Caribbean stereotype of matrifocality, by and large Utilian household heads are male, marriages are formal rather than common-law, and divorce is uncommon.

Tourism developed rapidly during the 1980s in the nearby nation of Belize and on the neighboring Honduran Bay Islands of Roatán and Guanaja, but on Utila it lagged behind due mainly to the island's relative isolation and unattractiveness. Although in recent years both boat and plane service to the island have become quite regular and reliable, in the past they were both somewhat erratic. With its severe insect problems at some times of the year and lack of good beaches, the island's only real attraction to tourists is its collection of coral reefs, which offer some very fine scuba diving and snorkeling opportunities. As Roatán, Guanaja, and Belize have grown more crowded and expensive for dive tourists, Utilians have seized the opportunity to expand their tourist operations, and now the island is the home to a large number of small inns, guest houses, restaurants, and dive shops. A small number of resorts catering to well-heeled tourists have opened or are planned for Utila, but for the most part visitors to Utila are young, low-budget travelers from Europe and North America in search of inexpensive scuba diving.

Utila's Dive Shops

The present study was conducted during the summer and fall of 1996 as part of a broader examination of Utilian culture and social life. All of the eleven dive shops that were open on the main island in early 1996 were parties to an agreement to fix prices, and all of those shops agreed to respond to a simple questionnaire about each shop's history, operations, and involvement in agreements to fix prices. In addition, the questionnaire was administered to the former owner of the oldest shop on the island, to the island's mayor, who is part owner of one of the shops, and to the owner of one of the two shops that opened on the island after the agreement was made. Only the owner of the other new shop refused to participate. A dive shop on the Utila cays was not included in the study because it was never a party to any agreement among dive shops and because it is in such a different competitive position from the rest of the shops due to its isolation.

The first commercial diving operation opened on Utila in 1969. Three more dive shops opened their doors during the 1980s, and the rest of the twelve shops on the main island of Utila opened in the 1990s. Five of the shops are wholly owned by Utilians, five are owned by non-Utilian foreigners, and two are owned by partnerships of Utilians and foreigners.

Broadly speaking, all of the shops are fairly similar to one another in terms of their sizes and resources, with anywhere from ten to thirty diving sets (i.e., all of the gear needed for one diver) and one to three boats. All of the shops employ between five and ten people, about half of whom are dive instructors, the rest being boat captains, office staff, cleaning staff, and people to run air compressors. Almost all dive instructors are non-Utilians, and all of the shops offer diving certification through the Professional Association of Diving Instructors (PADI).

Although a few experienced divers do visit Utila, the majority of the dive shop business on Utila is in teaching people how to dive. Utila has a reputation among tourists as a very inexpensive place to learn how to dive. Shops occasionally charge as little as $100 for a few days of instruction leading to the first level of certification with no additional charges for equipment rental, or, as is common among dive shops in the United States, requirements that students purchase their own "personal equipment," such as masks, snorkels, and fins. Certified divers can pay as little as $10 for additional "fun dives," tanks and equipment included, though a charge of about $25 per dive is more typical.

The dive shops on the island report a wide range of numbers of customers, with one shop reporting fewer than 200 certificates awarded per year and only 48 fun divers, while another shop reports more than 1,400 certificates awarded per year and 5,200 fun dives. These numbers do not necessarily represent the number of tourists on the island, because many visitors stay long enough to earn 2 or more certificates and take many fun dives after certification. Nevertheless, the size of the market is impressive. Assuming that each certificate costs the diver an average of about $140 dollars and each fun dive costs about $25, then between $1 million and $2 million per year are being spent on Utila on diving, and, of course, this does not include all of the money the divers and their friends spend on lodging, meals, and souvenirs.

The variation among the shops in terms of their numbers of customers probably reflects their attempts to gain extra market share through specialization and a variety of advantages and disadvantages each shop has in the competition for customers. For example, shops compete to offer classes in a variety of languages, with classes routinely being available at one shop or another not only in English but also in Spanish, French, Italian, Dutch, German, Danish, Norwegian, and even Indonesian and

Hebrew. Some shops attempt to gain an advantage by offering their customers package deals that include not only dive instruction but also lodging and food for the time it takes to complete a course. A few shops offer specialized classes in underwater photography and in deep diving using special gas mixtures. Many shops see themselves as being disadvantaged by their locations, which are either too far from the airstrip and dock where most tourists arrive or too close to them, causing tourists to pass them by in search of other deals. Virtually all shops expressed pride in the quality of their staffs and equipment and their focus on safety, although a common complaint was that such quality means little to tourists intent on finding the least expensive deal possible.

The shops make little effort to advertise off the island apart from a very few small adverstisements in publications aimed at tourists and a few fliers occasionally handed out to tourists as they leave the mainland for Utila or as they arrive on the island. Shop owners report that between 80 and 95 percent of their customers are walk-ups. One owner explained that although the normal way to reach dive tourists would be through diving magazines, those coming to Utila are typically on tight budgets and have little or no previous diving experience and so would be unlikely to have ever looked at such a publication. As of 1996, one dive shop had also set up a Web site, but the cost of doing so was negligible.

The owners uniformly describe the flow of tourists to the island as steady and reliable with only minor increases in two vaguely defined high seasons, one in the winter, when presumably tourists are trying to escape cold weather at home, and one in the summer, when college students are not in classes. The minor seasonality in Utilian tourism was not a major problem for any of the dive shop owners. Although most shops reported that they did need a few customers each month in order to pay basic overhead and stay in business, when business falls off most can either lay off instructors or rely on other sources of income. As one dive shop owner put it, "I can always live on bananas and land crabs."

The History of Agreements among Dive Shops

Hotel owners and restauranteurs on Utila often complain about the low prices that they are forced to charge due to all the competition and the extreme price sensitivity of the tourists they are able to attract to the island. But attempts to organize have usually met with either apathy or resistance. For example, the senior author of this chapter was present at an informal meeting of the island's tourist business owners in August 1994. Attendance at the meeting was poor, and the discussion quickly moved from the topic of how to organize so as to reduce competition among local businesses and get more money out of the tourists coming to the island to other concerns, such as the island's drug problem, its trash disposal problem, and complaints about the behavior of tourists.

Dive shop owners also have complaints about the effects of competition among the rapidly growing number of dive shops on their profits, sometimes observing that competition may force shops to cut corners to such an extent that safety is compromised. The shops have occasionally made a few informal verbal agreements to fix prices, particularly for the basic dive courses they offer. For instance, most of the island's shops agreed verbally during the summer of 1995 to fix the price for the basic open water course at $139. Although one dive shop owner was so irked by an attempt by other dive shop owners to pressure him into going along with this agreement that he immediately and spitefully dropped his price to $99, most of the shops stuck to the $139 price from June until September of that year. When the number of tourists began to drop in September, however, some shops began to bend the rules by offering two free dives to anyone earning a certificate at their schools. Soon the whole agreement fell apart, and many shops began to cut prices in order to compete.

Shortly thereafter, in November 1995, an owner of one of the dive shops began a more formal effort to organize. He sent a letter to all of the dive shop owners outlining the problems as he saw them and inviting them all to a meeting. The meeting was attended by representatives of all of the existing shops on the main island. They agreed to form the Association of Utila Dive Shop Operators (AUDSO) in order to maintain a relatively high price for their services and to ensure the maintenance of safety standards, protection of the reef environment, and good relations with the Utilian community. They agreed on prices of $149 for basic and advanced diving courses, $30 for a two-tank fun dive, $125 for a ten-tank package of dives, and $25 for a night dive. They also agreed that the courses would not include any additional free dives and that a safety committee would be formed to monitor the shops' compliance with basic safety standards regarding equipment and dive practices.

Because of a widespread perception that tourists were being pressured to choose a dive shop before they had a chance to learn about all of the shops, the group agreed that their instructors would not hustle for customers at the airstrip or the dock. On the other hand, the group encouraged its members to pass out brochures on the Honduran mainland to encourage more tourists to visit Utila rather than, say, Roatán or Guanaja. Each shop agreed to pay a membership fee of 400 lempiras (about $30) per month to the association and to limit their number of dive instructors to five. The association was to issue certificates of membership to be prominently displayed in each shop and to be removed if it were decided that a particular shop was not adhering to the association's guidelines.

Arguing that the island's reef was already overrun with dive boats, the association also asked the municipal government not to issue more permits for dive shops on the island. The mayor, who was part owner of one of the shops, agreed to this arrangement and threatened to use the power of the local government against any shops that failed to adhere to the pact, mentioning a Honduran law that requires businesses to publish price changes one month prior to the date of the change. Some shop owners believed that dive shops that violated the agreement would have their permits lifted for one or more weeks, but as far as any of the owners remembered, no sanctions were ever actually imposed on anyone and no sanctions of any kind were specified in the formal written agreement.

No formal procedures were ever established for monitoring the agreement or for settling any disputes that might arise among association members, and no meetings of the association were held after January 1996. Monitoring the agreement was left up to individual shops, which intensified the already existing feelings of suspicion and distrust among many of the dive shop owners who suspected nearly everyone (including, at first, the authors of this study) of being spies for the other shops. Despite the lack of monitoring, most shops adhered to the prices stipulated in the agreement for the first few months of 1996.

The shop owners we interviewed had a wide variety of opinions about why the agreement did not last more than those few months, with almost every shop on the island being blamed for its failure by the owner of some other shop. Some owners remember that some shops bent the rules by offering free rooms at inns they also owned. Others blame particular shops for cutting their prices, while still others blame the mayor for not penalizing shops that cut prices and for giving permits to new shops that were not parties to the agreement. The mayor defended himself by saying that he has too much to do and too few staff people to do it already and so could not be expected to monitor the behavior of so many dive shops. Owners of the new dive shops, for their part, pointed out that agreements to fix prices are not legal under Honduran law and thus that the legal status of the association was, at the very least, ambiguous. Although mainland Honduran law has traditionally not been vigorously enforced on Utila, the island has begun to attract more attention from Honduran authorities, particularly tax assessors, as the local tourist industry has grown.

DISCUSSION

One way to understand the difficulty in establishing successful arrangements for the local management of CPRs is through the Prisoner's Dilemma game. In this game, although both parties would benefit from cooperation, there is also a strong temptation to defect from an agreement to cooperate. However, if both parties defect, they both receive lower payoffs than they would had they both cooperated. The trick in avoiding overexploitation of a CPR is to restructure the payoffs in such a way that defection is less tempting and cooperation is more attractive (Ostrom 1990). For Utila's dive shop operators, the temptation to defect from the pact (i.e., to lower prices in order to attract more customers) was never effectively lowered and the incentive for cooperation was never effectively increased.

In other situations, people have been able to overcome this dilemma by creating agreements and institutions that do change the payoffs to appropriators of particular CPRs. Ostrom (1990:90) identifies the following elements as essential to successful CPR arrangements, many of which were not part of the AUDSO agreement:

1. *Clearly defined boundaries.* Ideally, for the success of a group like the AUDSO, it would be impossible for additional shops to open on the island without the approval of the group itself. This was left up to the mayor, who, despite being part owner of one of the shops, quickly gave permits to two new dive shops.
2. *Congruence between appropriation and provision rules and local conditions.* In short, the rules governing the management of the CPR should

be tailored to its characteristics. No single set of rules will work for all CPRs and not even for all CPRs of a particular type, such as water resources or fisheries. In the case of the Utila dive shops, there was an attempt to tailor the rules of the group to fit the characteristics of the CPR in question: tourists. In particular, the group's members appear to have understood that their prospective customers shared a number of attributes, such as a general ignorance about diving combined with a desire to learn and a keen awareness of their travel budgets. Thus, the practice of hustling for customers at the airstrip and dock, seen by many as an unethical practice that preyed on the tourists' ignorance about diving and about Utila, was banned by the agreement, and the price agreed on by the group was still quite low in comparison with that charged elsewhere in the world.

3. *Collective-choice arrangements.* Ideally, most of the individuals affected by the rules governing a CPR should be able to take part in changing them. Although all members of the AUDSO had equal voices in the group, because the AUDSO's founding charter included no procedures for changing the group's operating rules, this cannot be said to have been true.

4. *Monitoring.* The AUDSO agreement included no provisions for monitoring shops' compliance with the agreement.

5. *Graduated sanctions.* Apart from some vague hopes that the mayor would use his power to sanction shops that violated the agreement, the AUDSO agreement included no sanctions at all, graduated or otherwise.

6. *Conflict resolution mechanisms.* The AUDSO agreement included no procedures for conflict resolution.

7. *Minimal recognition of the rights to organize.* Powerful organizations outside the local community, such as national governments, must not interfere with the rights of the appropriators of a CPR to organize. As pointed out by the individuals who wanted to open dive shops on Utila after the AUDSO was formed, this was always a potential problem for the group. A group formed for the sole purpose of fixing prices ran the risk of attracting the attention and disapproval of Honduran authorities, although the AUDSO did not itself last long enough for this to be a problem.

Another way to approach the failure of the AUDSO is through the theory developed by economists to analyze cartel formation. Interesting and quite logical, much of that theory is similar to the theory developed for the analysis of CPR management. For example, many works on collusion and cartels follow the same tack as Ostrom's (1990) book in approaching the issue through the prisoner's dilemma game (e.g., Brown et al. 1976; Phlips 1995; Spar 1994; see also Axelrod 1984). Despite this formal similarity, the two bodies of theory appear to have been developed in isolation from one another and, at least in the case of Ostrom's analysis of CPRs, this isolation is deliberate. Overlap between the two bodies of theory is minimal, with cartel formation being examined as a collective action problem (*sensu*, Olson 1965) only occasionally (e.g., Bowman 1989). Although customers, like any class of CPR, have their own distinctive characteristics, and although the appropriators of a CPR are rarely under the severe restrictions regarding overt cooperation experienced by colluding capitalist firms, there is no reason why the formal theories regarding collusion and cartels, on the one hand, and CPR management schemes, on the other, should not converge at some point. In some small way, this study of collusion among Utilian dive shops may at least point at such a convergence.

People familiar with Utila, such as Utilians themselves, were not at all surprised by the AUDSO's rapid demise. While Utilians are proud of their island and its culture, they are also highly critical of it and eager to talk about its problems. One of the main themes that comes through in conversations and interviews with Utilians is a widespread frustration with the general lack of cooperation on the island. Attempts like that of the dive shop owners to organize group and community activities on the island nearly always fail. Even efforts to organize sports teams and leagues on the island tend quickly to fall apart in mixtures of apathy and bitterness. This lack of a sense of community has been noted elsewhere in the Caribbean, as well, and it has been compared to the behavior of crabs in a barrel, which could escape if they were to cooperate but which instead continually pull one another back down into the barrel (Wilson 1975).

Although many dive shop operators are not Utilian, they do tend to be independent and individualistic; one of the attractions of the dive shop business itself is the opportunity to be one's own boss while doing something one loves to do. Indeed, given that so many of the Utilian dive shop owners are non-Utilians, this absence of a sense of community may be even more of a problem for the dive shop owners to overcome than it would be for a group consisting of all native Utilians. This supports the argument made by McCay and Jentoft (1998) that CPR issues should be analyzed not solely from a "thin" or theoretically formal perspective but also from a "thick" or ethnographically informed perspective, one that takes into account the social and cultural context of the CPR problem. Although it would be easy to diagnose the AUDSO's failure simply as a result of the poor design of its charter, the shortcomings of the charter may themselves best be seen as reflections of the Utilian milieu. For example, the lack of any formal procedures for group decision making or for the imposition of sanctions may reflect a fear on the part of the organizers that too formal and powerful an organization might lead some dive shop operators not to join the association in the first place.

RECOMMENDATIONS

Dive tourism can develop in a variety of ways. Elsewhere in the Caribbean, its development has often been in the hands of large, foreign-owned hotels and resorts. Although such resorts may employ local people, the fact that they are not locally owned or controlled gives locals little incentive to get involved in environmental preservation (see Olsen [1997] for an interesting case study on Jamaica).

On Utila, in contrast, dive tourism has developed on a very small scale, involving many small dive shops, inns, and restaurants, most of which are owned by Utilians themselves. This style of development has the potential to accomplish several important goals simultaneously, including maintaining a high degree of local control over the island's economy, enhancing Utilians' incomes, and, like ecotourism elsewhere, giving locals a strong incentive to try to maintain the local ecosystem (see Nelson et al. 1993). In short, Utila's dive industry may provide a good foundation for sustainable development for the island for some time to come provided that the small shops continue to dominate. Their success in this regard may be enhanced by a certain amount of cooperation among the shops of the sort envisioned by the AUDSO. Furthermore, part of the reason all but one of Utila's dive shops agreed to answer our questions was that they all hoped that it might help them resolve their differences and come to some sort of lasting agreement. With these practical goals in mind, we would like to offer some suggestions about how they might go about redesigning their organization not only for the benefit of the shops themselves but also for the safety of their customers, the health of the reef, and the sustainable development of the island's economy.

For the AUDSO to avoid having problems with the Honduran legal system, it should incorporate formally. With the aid and advice of a Honduran attorney, it needs to become an organization devoted primarily to preserving the Utilian reef ecosystem and to maintaining safety standards among Utilian dive shops and only secondarily to regulating the prices charged. A new charter should include specifications about the groups' formal structure, including its officers, how long they will serve, and how they are chosen, how group decisions will be made, and how the charter itself will be changed, if necessary. It should include provisions for the settlement of disputes among group members and between group members and the association, perhaps including the specification of some disinterested party not from Utila as an arbitrator. An English-speaking attorney or judge from elsewhere in the Bay Islands might be a good candidate for that sort of role. A safety committee should be established, and the charter should include rules about safety inspections and a detailed list of sanctions for violations of safety rules, culminating in expulsion from the AUDSO.

Judging from the mayor's willingness to give out permits to new shops and his unwillingness to monitor shops' behavior, it would be unwise for the AUDSO to rely on the mayor or any other Honduran government official to restrict entry into the market or to help it enforce its charter. Rather than trying to restrict entry into the Utila dive shop market as a whole, the shops need to restrict membership in the AUDSO itself. This would require making AUDSO membership an attractive and profitable thing for which new Utilian dive shops must strive. In order to do this, the AUDSO itself must provide services for its members beyond its efforts to maintain a basic price level and an awareness of safety and conservation issues. In particular, the AUDSO might make itself useful to its members by advertising its member shops in international travel publications and on the World Wide Web. Because such advertisements may also attract customers to Utilian dive shops that are not members of the AUDSO, it might be wise to include in them some encouragement, such as a price break, for customers to make reservations with the AUDSO, including a deposit, before coming to Utila. In addition to the price break, the customers could be guaranteed a date for the beginning of a dive class on Utila while still retaining the right to choose among the members of the AUDSO after arriving on the island.

Such an arrangement would put the AUDSO in the position of collecting money on behalf of its members, and that might be a good step in terms of enhancing cooperation among the members. Because it is so easy for member shops to cheat on price agreements by making bargains with individual tourists, we recommend that the members of AUDSO turn the collection of all funds for dive classes over to the AUDSO. Cheating could be prevented by simultaneously making the AUDSO and not its member dive shops the clearinghouse for all of the paperwork involved with PADI certification. The paperwork involved in issuing PADI certificates makes the dive classes different from all of the other goods and services offered by the dive shops, and for the long-term success of the AUDSO, it would probably be wise for it to abandon the idea of regulating what member shops charge for activities like fun dives and night dives.

Although reorganizing the AUDSO in these ways would be expensive for the shops concerned and would require them to relinquish some of their autonomy, it would also achieve the dive shops' main goal of maintaining the profitability of the dive business on Utila. Further, both the dive shops and the tourists would be served by the association's efforts to preserve the reef that attracts the tourists in the first place and to keep diving safe. Although price competition would be reduced among member shops, tourists would be served by the maintenance of other forms of competition among the shops and by competition of all kinds between member shops and nonmember shops.

NOTE

This research was made possible by a grant from the Program to Enhance Scholarly and Creative Activities of the office of the Vice President for Research and Associate Provost for Graduate Studies at Texas A&M University and by a Faculty Development Leave for the senior author. We thank all of the Utila dive shop operators who so generously cooperated with this study and the following individuals who commented on the manuscript: Jeffrey Cohen, Norbert Dannhaeuser, Keith Hollinshead, Beth Leech, and Bobbi Low. Of course, we retain responsibility for any errors or shortcomings.

REFERENCES

Acheson, James M.
1998 Lobster Trap Limits: A Solution to a Communal Action Problem. Human Organization 57(1):43–52.

Axelrod, Robert
1984 The Evolution of Cooperation. New York: Basic Books.

Baker, J. Mark
1997 Common Property Resource Theory and the *Kuhl* Irrigation Systems of Himachal Pradesh, India. Human Organization 56(2):199–208.

Berkes, Fikret
1987 Common-Property Resource Management and Cree Indian Fisheries in Subarctic Canada. *In* The Question of the Commons. Bonnie J. McCay and James M. Acheson, eds. Pp. 66–91. Tucson: The University of Arizona Press.

Black, Jan Knippers
1999 Development in Theory and Practice: Paradigms and Paradoxes. 2d ed. Boulder, CO: Westview.

Bowman, John R.
1989 Capitalist Collective Action. Cambridge: Cambridge University Press.

Brown, Michael E., John J. Mearsheimer, and Walter J. Petersen
1976 A Model of Cartel Formation. Santa Monica, CA: The Rand Corporation.

Davidson, William V.
1974 Historical Geography of the Bay Islands, Honduras: Anglo-Hispanic Conflict in the Caribbean. Birmingham, AL: Southern University Press.

Doran, E.
1954 Notes on an Archaic Island Dialect. American Speech 29(1):82–85.

Durrenberger, E. Paul
1997 Fisheries Management Models: Assumptions and Realities or, Why Shrimpers in Mississippi Are Not Firms. Human Organization 56(2):158–166.

Glick, T. F.
1970 Irrigation and Society in Medieval Valencia. Cambridge, MA: Harvard University Press.

Gragson, Ted L., and Frederick V. Payton
1997 The Institutional Context of Irrigation in the Bajo Yaque del Norte Project, Dominican Republic. Human Organization 56(2):153–157.

Hardin, Garrett
1968 The Tragedy of the Commons. Science 162:1243–1248.

Kurien, John
1995 Collective Action for Common Property Resource Rejuvenation: The Case of People's Artificial Reefs in Kerala State, India. Human Organization 54(2):160–168.

Lipski, John M.
1986 English-Spanish Contact in the United States and Central America: Sociolinguistic Mirror Images? *In* Varieties of English around the World, vol. 8. Focus on the Caribbean. Manfred Görlach and John A. Holm, eds. Pp. 191–208. Amsterdam: John Benjamins.

Lord, David G.
1975 Money Order Economy: Remittances in the Island of Utila. Ph.D. dissertation, Department of Anthropology, University of California at Riverside.

Low, Bobbi S., and Joel T. Heinen
1993 Population, Resources and Environment. Population and Environment 15:7–41.

Maass, A., and R. L. Anderson
1986 . . . And the Desert Shall Rejoice: Conflict, Growth and Justice in Arid Environments. Malabar, FL: R. E. Krieger.

McDaniel, Josh
1997 Communal Fisheries Management in the Peruvian Amazon. Human Organization 56(2):147–152.

McCay, Bonnie
1987 The Culture of the Commoners: Historical Observations on Old and New World Fisheries. *In* The Question of the Commons. Bonnie J. McCay and James M. Acheson, eds. Pp. 195–216. Tucson: The University of Arizona Press.

McCay, Bonnie, and Svein Jentoft
1998 Market of Community Failure? Critical Perspectives on Common Property Research. Human Organization 57(1):21–29.

McKean, M. A.
1986 Management of Traditional Common Lands (*Iriaichi*) in Japan. *In* Proceedings of the Conference on Common Property Resource Management, National Research Council. Pp. 533–589. Washington, DC: National Academy Press.

Miller, William L.
1974 Etiology of Hypertension: An Anthropological Study in Utila, Honduras. Master's thesis, Department of Anthropology, Wake Forest University.

Nelson, J. G., R. Butler, and G. Wall, eds.
1993 Tourism and Sustainable Development: Monitoring, Planning, Managing. Waterloo, Ontario, Canada: Heritage Resources Centre.

Netting, Robert McC.
1981 Balancing on an Alp. Cambridge: Cambridge University Press.

Olsen, Barbara.
1997 Environmentally Sustainable Development and Tourism: Lessons from Negril, Jamaica. Human Organization 56(3):285–293.

Olson, Mancur
1965 The Logic of Collective Action. Cambridge: Harvard University Press.

Ostrom, Elinor
1990 Governing the Commons. Cambridge: Cambridge University Press.

Ostrom, Elinor, Roy Gardner, and James Walker
1994 Rules, Games, and Common-Pool Resources. Ann Arbor: University of Michigan Press.

Phlips, Louis
1995 Competition Policy: A Game-Theoretic Perspective. Cambridge: Cambridge University Press.

Ridley, Matt, and Bobbi S. Low
1993 Can Selfishness Save the Environment? Atlantic Monthly 272:76–78, 80–84, 86.

Spar, Debora L.
1994 The Cooperative Edge: The Internal Politics of International Cartels. Ithaca, NY: Cornell University Press.

Uphoff, Norman, M. L. Wickramasinghe, and C. M. Wijayaratna
1990 "Optimum" Participation in Irrigation Management: Issues and Evidence from Sri Lanka. Human Organization 49(1):26–40.

Warantz, E.
1983 Bay Islands English of Honduras. In Central American English. J. Holm, ed. Pp. 71–94. Heidelberg, Germany: Julius Groos.

Wilson, Peter J.
1975 Crab Antics. New Haven, CT: Yale University Press.

4

The Interstices of Urban Development: An Economic Anthropological Approach to Development in a Midwestern U.S. Community

Rhoda H. Halperin

This chapter is part of an ongoing case study in local economic development and community preservation in a long-standing working-class Cincinnati neighborhood on the Ohio riverfront. Our university-based research/advocacy team began its work in 1991, just as neighborhood grassroots leaders were beginning to gain voice in a city-generated development-planning process. From the outset, our role had been defined by the various stakeholders (the city, a citizens' advisory board, community leaders, and developers) as strengthening the community's voice in the planning process. Most people thought that we would go into the community, collect our data, report our results, and leave in a year—two at most. But our research/advocacy efforts have continued right up to the present and rather long implementation phase of the development plan (Halperin 1990, 1994a, 1994b, 1998).

Here I focus on the tensions between market and nonmarket forces as grassroots leaders and developers jointly plan and carry out economic development (Bruyn and Meehan 1987; Halperin 1988, 1994a; King and George 1987; Polanyi 1944). To say that the environment is contentious is probably one of the most extreme understatements in the development literature. The tensions between market-driven developers and development processes on one hand, and the nonmarket community-oriented grassroots leaders on the other, reflect not only different views of the world, but different versions of modernity and community. Developers' version of modernity is based on rational choice—getting the most for the least inputs. Grassroots leaders' version of modernity is not opposed to change or to community revitalization, but is based on what I call local (community-based) communitarianism, a multidimensional set of cultural economic processes that simultaneously uses combinations of market and nonmarket institutions in innovative ways. The goal of local communitarianism is to preserve and revitalize the community through affordable housing, provision of health services, and dedication to preserving community heritage. In contrast, the goal of market-driven development is the replacement of the original community with upscale housing and accompanying amenities—parks, bike paths, restaurants, and the like.

In many respects, East End, as the community is called, is a classic case of community economic development. That is, it is undergoing rapid, market-driven changes: displacement and dislocation, escalating property values (with related tax increases), and gentrification. In other respects, especially from the point of view of the local grassroots leaders, the situation is unique. The struggle to maintain the community for its residents is proceeding albeit in fits and starts, and with many steps forward and backward. Local institutions such as churches, schools, and other non-profits are being created and re-created as well as strengthened and reinvented. Some affordable rental housing has become available and there are plans for owner-occupied housing. A new health center opened in 1998.

ECONOMIC ANTHROPOLOGY AND COMMUNITY URBAN DEVELOPMENT

The following considerations are important for economic anthropology: (1) the role of the market in allocating land and other resources for housing; (2) the role of nonmarket institutions, especially local nonprofits and city government departments in allocating resources and supporting institutions for the maintenance and revitalization of the community; and (3) the relationships between market and nonmarket institutions, especially the actual and potential conflicts of interest that arise when a single individual is involved in working in both nonprofit and for-profit sectors (e.g., local banks and community-based nonprofits and/or the local community council and market-driven real estate companies). For several years, the president of the community council was not only a developer and slumlord, she also worked as a real estate agent for a large corporate firm.

As I use it here, local communitarianism is related to, but not the same as other communitarian movements (see Etzioni 1993). In the East End, its character is distinctly local both in origin and in orientation. I intend local communitarianism to be viewed here holistically as part of the small-scale social movement aimed at ensuring a place for working-class people in a rapidly deindustrializing city. It involves resisting the market takeover of the community and its goals address the many related needs of working-class community residents. In this context, education and recreation are just as important, and, in fact, must be built coterminously with housing and infrastructure. Grassroots leaders work to provide free lunches for children at the recreation center in the summer when the city announces that it is cutting the lunch program for lack of funds. This includes raising the money to buy, prepare, and serve food. Turning an old grade-school building long closed to the community into a viable East End school for East End children is something community leaders will work on tirelessly.

There is no question that the market-driven forces of development threaten the community as East Enders have known it. Developers and some city officials are not subtle in their attacks on the community, although some stabs at the community are more direct than others. When the flood hit in March 1997 and much of the community was underwater; even visiting federal officials like Al Gore argued that people should not live on or near the river. Some argued that affordable housing could never be built substantially enough to withstand the river's force. In fact, the newest affordable rental housing, built right on the river, held up and was not affected by the flooding because the living space had been built above garages. The teamwork of grassroots leaders who had grown up dealing with the vagaries of the river combined with the efforts of socially conscious architects to create a river-proof design. It was the upscale housing, with furnaces and appliances in family room basements that were most damaged by the floods. East End leaders took some delight in the damage done to this very expensive market-rate housing that had been built without the benefits of local knowledge.

THE COMMUNITY

Located along the Ohio River between the downtown and the eastern suburbs of Cincinnati, the East End is an eight-mile strip of land. People are ethnically urban white Appalachian, black Appalachian, and African American, with a ratio of whites to blacks of 2:1. The grade-school children of the 1990s are sixth- and seventh-generation East Enders. Families in the community maintain ties to kin in the rural hinterland—Ohio, Kentucky, and Tennessee.

In this region, the country is very close and still has small tobacco farms with subsistence gardens and livestock. In fact, the city of Cincinnati can be viewed as an urban island in the midst of a rural sea. In every direction, Cincinnati is surrounded by rural counties, some more rural than others (see Halperin 1990). When resources are stretched to the limit in the city (cash runs out for food, rent, telephone), families return to the country for varying periods of time. A long weekend often turns into several weeks. Children may stay even longer, even though they become truant from school (Halperin and Slomowitz 1988).

Although the population has declined from a high of 15,000 in the mid-1970s, all population figures are somewhat problematic because of daily and seasonal population movements. Many children, whose parents were displaced from the East End and have taken up residence in nearby communities, spend their days with grandparents in the East End. In summer, whole segments of extended families may move back to the country. It is also not uncommon for families to maintain bilocal residence patterns, moving back and forth between country and city as often as a dozen times per year (see Halperin and Slomowitz 1988). Roughly, though, the population of the entire East End is approximately 5,000 to 6,000 people. The segment targeted for development planning has declined to about 1,200 people.

Third World qualities, some more tangible than others, can be found in the East End. Local colonialism, a highly structured and institutionalized informal economy with many components, and an elaborate set of kin and neighborhood networks that stretch around the region (Halperin 1998) are some of the most striking. By local colonialism, I mean the processes of domination and control that have a local, city of Cincinnati, origin. Processes of local colonialism operate to control local labor as well as local housing resources. Several landlord/developers who reside in the community own not only substantial amounts of residential property (houses and small apartment buildings), but also small businesses. This means that their tenants are also often their employees and, therefore, subject to manipulation by the landlord bosses. If a tenant complains too much about a leaky roof, he or she may be in danger of losing a job in the landlord's business establishment. This situation is irritating to East End tenants, many of whom have resided in the community for thirty years or more. East Enders constantly disperse resources throughout a network of kin and neighbors and thus could never accumulate a down payment to purchase a house.

Residents understand they are living in investment properties that will eventually be condemned and then torn down to make room for upscale, market-rate housing. Several landlord/developers have taken positions on community boards and organizations so that they can better look out for their investments and future profits. This colonialist presence means that East End leaders must combat development and developers on a daily basis. The closeness of East Enders to the local ecology, especially the river, is important as a source of both identity and subsistence. East Enders tell time by the sounds of the riverboats; historically, the river has been a source of work and pleasure. One elderly man used his boat, which he kept docked in front of his East End house, to travel to work every day. The boat dock was part of a family boat-hauling business and still is. Family is the strongest metaphor for community.

PLANNING FOR DEVELOPMENT

In the late 1980s, the city of Cincinnati stepped up its efforts to plan for the development of the eastern riverfront. In 1987, the city set up a citizens' advisory board, composed of retired corporate executives, wives of executives, and other local elites, to develop a renewal plan for the East End. As part of its commitment to preserving the community, the advisory board mandated a study of the community to "strengthen the voice of the community in the planning process." Our university-based research team became part of a complex research/advocacy process, some of which involved working with citizen elites, but most of which was devoted to working with grassroots leaders. In many instances, we worked as culture brokers to negotiate the power relations between and among elites, city officials and community leaders.

In the spring of 1992, the city of Cincinnati passed a development plan that included many community-maintaining provisions, among them: a mandate for affordable housing, the Pendleton Heritage Center building, and the provision of an autonomous implementation team to oversee the step-by-step processes needed to see that the plan's provisions would be met. Knowing how vulnerable local politics and especially grassroots-run institutions were to developer takeover, grassroots leaders were sophisticated enough to create a Plan Implementation team that would stand apart from the East End Area Council (EEAC), the local community council. The separateness of the implementation team did not last long, however. As soon as the developers took over the EEAC, they put the team under EEAC control.

Since I have documented the planning issues rather thoroughly in my recent book, *Practicing Community* (1998), I focus here on a few points that highlight the tension between market-driven development efforts and the nonmarket-driven community preservation efforts on the part of the grassroots nonprofits. I want to do this with a special focus on housing and heritage. My own role in the community has been and remains complicated. I have been a member of the Neighborhood Development Corporation and Heritage boards for several years. One cannot conduct in-depth research in an urban community without taking on an advocacy role.

I also want to emphasize that the project of strengthening the community's voice in the planning process was viewed by the city and the developers alike as counterhegemonic. That is, by arguing for restrictions on heights and densities of buildings and for maintaining the existing character of the neighborhood, the community voice was, and still is, viewed as antidevelopment. A strong community voice not only reduces profits for developers, but also reduces the city's tax base. In order to increase the revenues to the city, heights and densities had to be maximized. Maintaining community is not consistent with these market-driven plans.

MAINTAINING COMMUNITY

It is in the context of this small-scale, kin-dominated, local, face-to-face community that the efforts of grassroots leaders to resist market domina-

tion must be understood. Community leaders work hard to maintain resi-
dent-dominated nonprofit institutions devoted to maintaining and building community. In addition to the community council, the EEAC, which
is currently under the control of the developers, there are three main nonprofit corporations in the East End. They are dedicated to housing, health,
and heritage preservation.

Housing, affordable rental housing and owner-occupied single-family
housing, is the focus of the neighborhood development corporation
known in the community as EERCURC, which stands for East End Riverfront Community Urban Redevelopment Corporation. A group of neighborhood leaders started EERCURC in the late 1980s with the help of a
dedicated city staffer who participated in crafting by-laws and Articles of
Incorporation. Over the last ten years, the leadership of EERCURC has
remained in the hands of East Enders, but not without the conflicts and
jealousies that often go along with accomplishments and accolades from
powerful outsiders. Keeping EERCURC "up and running" is almost a full-
time job. Board members must be kept active, meetings must be scheduled, hearings attended at City Hall, etc.

The East End Health Center is part of a consortium of federally funded
health centers in Cincinnati. Fees are on a sliding scale, and nobody is
turned away. Neighborhood leaders dominate the board, but grassroots
control and responsibility is eased by a highly competent administrative
staff for the health center, which is itself operated jointly with another center in a predominantly African American neighborhood several miles
from the East End.

The third nonprofit, the Pendleton Heritage Center (PHC), has as its
primary mission the creation of a community building where local nonprofits can have office space and hold meetings. Currently, the meetings
of nonprofits float around the neighborhood. They are held in churches,
recreation centers, and private homes. There is no place to keep files and
records, and until recently, grassroots leaders had no access to copier or
fax machines. The PHC is also planned as a community museum with
exhibits and programs devoted to "celebrating the diversity" that has historically been such an essential part of East Enders' experience.

HOUSING

Housing in the East End is probably the most essential piece of community building and maintaining economic development and it has always

been the major focus of local communitarianism. Bringing East Enders back to the East End is the keystone of community maintenance. But affordable housing is one of, if not the most, contentious issue in the East End. The more affordable housing units there are, the stronger is the neighborhood's foothold.

A Brief History of Housing

Historically, single-family dwellings and small apartment buildings predominated in the East End. Two-story, four-unit apartment buildings are common; elders always reside on the lower floors with children or younger relatives above. There are no high-rises or housing projects in East End. In the past twenty-five years, housing stock has deteriorated significantly, and many East Enders have been displaced. Nonetheless, several family compounds, composed of large, extended families, provide an urban version of the compounds in rural areas. Five or six houses in a single block, belong to members of one family. Some have apartments in them, others are smaller structures with only nuclear families. As parents age, they make sure that at least one or two of their grown children live within shouting distance.

Underground Wiring

From the outset, one of the most contentious issues in the planning process was that of underground wiring. Using aesthetics and unobstructed river views as their main arguments, developers argued that underground wiring was an essential element of the East End Plan. East End residents and grassroots leaders argued that the underground wiring was not a high priority issue on several grounds: (1) It was too expensive and would make affordable housing unaffordable. (2) Current residents with aboveground wiring might be forced to pay for placing wires underground, would not be able to, and would be forced to leave the East End. This would then be the source of further displacement of residents. Despite attempts to assuage grassroots leaders by promising assistance for placing wires underground, the issue remains contentious to this day. In fact, using humor as a typical grassroots weapon, the grassroots president gave the following critique of the importance of "views" over basics by quoting from Dr. Seuss's famous allegory, *Yertle the Turtle*, on social stratification. She did this in the grand chamber of the Cincinnati City Council on the day the vote on the plan was taken.

> Your majesty, please. . . . I don't like to complain,
> But down here below, we are feeling great pain,
> I know, up on top you are seeing great sights,
> But down at the bottom, we too, should have rights.
> We turtles can't stand it, our shells will all crack!
> Besides, we need food. We are starving! Groaned Mack.

After this speech, a rather unholy alliance was formed between two of the major stakeholders in the plan, stakeholders from opposite ends of the social structure. East End leaders allied themselves with a group of wealthy hillside residents who wanted to restrict the heights of new buildings in the East End so that their views of the river from their homes on the hillside would remain unimpeded. Since the "hillside people," as East Enders called them, included a rather powerful nonprofit corporation composed of lawyers and wealthy businesspeople, the voices advocating low-rise, low-density housing began to be heard.

Affordable Rental Housing

Two complexes of affordable rental housing have been built/rehabbed since 1994. One is a thirteen-unit apartment building with two- and three-bedroom units. The Betz Flats, as this building is called, was developed through a partnership between Fifth Third Bank and the Cincinnati Preservation Office, a for-profit and a nonprofit agency respectively. The other set of affordable rental housing units, known as Lewiston Townhomes, is a complex of three-bedroom townhouses, eleven units in all, one of which is designed for handicapped persons. It was developed through a partnership between EERCURC and another nonprofit, Family Housing Developers, Inc., a group led by attorneys from the Legal Aid Society.

In opposition to grassroots efforts, developers work to replace affordable housing either by tearing down existing structures and building new, market-rate housing, or by rehabbing and thereby upscaling old buildings. The developers are outsiders who are variously land-bankers and large-scale real estate moguls, small business developers, and slum landlords. The developers operate almost entirely in the for-profit sector, although, as noted above, they can skillfully use nonprofits to their advantage. They will almost always pay lip service to community preservation, since this is definitely the politically correct thing to say, but their actions convey a different message. The developers use a whole panoply of indirect techniques to sabotage the community maintaining and building efforts of nonprofits. They criticize the details of grassroots projects—rooflines, driveways, turnarounds associated with affordable housing; they filibuster at meetings and delay votes until most community members have gone home; they attempt to criminalize and colonize grassroots leaders and their home places; and they maintain the outer appearances of friendliness and dedication to the East End community.

Owner-Occupied Single-Family Affordable Housing

In a recent proposal to the city, the EERCURC board requested thirteen city-owned lots to build affordable, owner-occupied single-family units. Included in the submission were not only pro bono architectural plans, offered from the same architect who designed Lewiston Townhomes, but also a whole set of commitments from both the for-profit and the nonprofit sectors. Banks and foundations had to insure support that would keep mortgage payments on these $80,000 structures to payments that approximated current monthly rents (between $300 and $400 per month, depending on the size of the unit). In addition, another nonprofit, Community Design and Development Center, consisting of a university-based set of architects, designers, and engineers, had to commit to providing technical support for EERCURC's proposal.

The city views grassroots efforts with great skepticism, in part because developers pressure them to do so, but also because they have a difficult time believing that working-class people can, in fact, see a project through. This kind of class prejudice must be countered by grassroots leaders with allies from powerful quarters, including the university and other nonprofits.

HERITAGE

The Pendleton Heritage Center building was originally a carbarn for the storage and maintenance of the trolleys that once ran up and down Eastern Avenue, the main east-west thoroughfare that bisects the community. Referred to by old-timers as the Pendleton Club, this red brick building sits in the center of a predominantly African American section of the East End. In the 1940s, when the trollies stopped running on Eastern Avenue, the Pendleton Club became a social hall and recreation center for the East End's black community. Fond memories still remain. Recently, the city-owned building was used to store recreational supplies. It has been the dream of grassroots leaders, black and white alike, to bring the building back to the community.

One of the arguments used by the developers against the Heritage Center rehabilitation project was that it was simply too expensive to renovate such an old building. A new one, developers argued, would be much cheaper. Knowing that it would be virtually impossible for the community to obtain land and funding for such a project, the developers did not oppose the Heritage Center project directly; they merely argued, rather relentlessly and at great length, that there was a better way to do it. In reality, grassroots leaders knew that developers saw their property values as being eroded by the potential presence of a Heritage Center. A grass-roots stronghold was the last thing developers wanted in the central section of the East End development plan area.

It soon became clear that the Pendleton Heritage Center Board was not to be deterred by rational economistic arguments against the project. They saw the Pendleton as a monument to East Enders' central role in shaping a new East End in a way consistent with past practices and patterns of class culture. The board had already overcome many of the stumbling blocks placed before it by both the city and the developers (cleaning up an adjacent polluted site for the parking lot before obtaining a building permit, recruiting wealthy citizens to serve on the board and soliciting churches and local foundations for funds and volunteers). Every time it looked as though the city was ready to hand over the building and the accompanying allocated funds, another stumbling block appeared.

At one point, the developers tried to convince the city that only a small handful of East Enders were interested in the Pendleton project in the first place. East End grassroots leaders responded to this challenge by organizing the neighborhood to attend a large meeting (almost a rally). One of the senior leaders was recruited to videotape the meeting, just in case the city officials and staffers did not show up. Just as predicted, the city opted out at the last minute and not a single staffer appeared. The videotape created a permanent record of the enormous turnout, complete with eloquent speeches from lifelong East Enders testifying to the importance of the Pendleton building in their childhood memories—weddings, dances, and other social gatherings had been held there.

There is no question that progress on the Pendleton has been slow. But, in order to understand the development of the Pendleton, it is important to view it as more than a building. For, in fact, it is really a multidimensional social movement that encompasses many visions of community revitalization. The visions are different for each board member, but they share a common resistance to the market takeover. Some see the new Pendleton as a reincarnated version of the old Pendleton Club, a building that belongs to the community and that provides a home for all residents. Others see it as a political center and stepping-stone for future community projects such as a community-based school that focuses on East End heritage. In a community in which intergenerational ties are extremely important, some grassroots leaders see the Pendleton as a place where grandmothers, parents, and other family members can congregate in positive and productive ways. One leader talks about a room in the Pendleton where small children can use their imaginations, drawing on the walls if they wish.

In this context, well-intentioned outsiders who try to push the Heritage Center Board to make decisions before they are ready can damage relationships among board members. Even more damage can be done when do-gooders think they know what is best for the community. In one instance, a retired corporate executive became involved in the Pendleton project and immediately tried to bring in a contractor friend to give estimates and advice. He had decided that opening a room of the Pendleton was better than nothing and became determined to accomplish his goal. He was also quick to judge grassroots leaders who did not agree with him as "flying off the handle." The efficiency of corporate styles and the single-minded task orientation may have its place in the twin towers of Procter and Gamble, but these styles fly in the face of the much slower and more painstaking consensus building that was necessary for the project to reach beyond the Pendleton building to build community. From the grassroots viewpoint, the Heritage Center is not just a building, but a magnet and focal point for getting residents involved in rebuilding community. These are some of the subtleties of noncorporate institutions, subtleties that are often lost on the well-intentioned but narrow-minded outsider. Corporate

management styles have their own ways of creeping into nonprofit organizations and they create tensions that are not lost on East Enders.

As of this writing, the Pendleton Heritage Center is a major center in
the community. It opened its doors in November 1999, in time to provide
space for a team of local women to collaborate with community activists
and university professors in planning the East End Community Heritage
School. The school opened on Labor Day, 2000, and many other activities
have been planned jointly between the Heritage School and Heritage Center. Both the school and the center are run as nonprofit organizations.

SUMMARY AND CONCLUSIONS

The Commodification of the Community

The relationships between market and nonmarket institutions are both
complicated and tense in this case of urban development, especially when
market-driven developers have the support of the city power structure.
Gentrification—especially riverfront gentrification—generally wipes out
working-class communities. Witness the cities of Philadelphia, Boston,
and Baltimore, to name a few (Bridge 1995; Cybriwsky et al. 1986; Gans
1962; Sanjek 1998; Sieber 1993; Smith and Williams 1986). In the East
End, gentrification has been contained and prevented from proceeding in
certain areas. Valuable riverfront property has been used for affordable
rental housing units that are permanent and well built. But developers
control the community council and the East End's future is uncertain.

When the poet laureate of the East End begs the city not to take our
homes by urban renewal, she is serious. Before the thirteen-unit apartment building, Betz Flats, was reopened she wrote a poem analyzing class
and power relations in the East End:

> Since the Betz Flats has been made to close its door
> Most landlords are kicking out the poor
> Being thrown aside like an apple core
> So the rich can accumulate more
> The grabbing and snatching of our land by the rich
> Makes us feel we have a bad case of the poison ivy itch
> The cemetery is full of the poor and the rich
> When we all die, we'll go in the same type of ditch
> We know we live on priceless land

And it can be taken with the shake of a hand

· · · · · · · · · · · · · · ·

City planning we know you're not going by the "golden rule"
We the East End residents are not stupid and we're no fool
So please city council we're begging you don't be cruel
Please! Don't take our home by "urban renewal." [Eileen
Waters, September 1991]

REFERENCES

Bridge, Gary
   1995 Gentrification, Class and Community: A Social Network Approach. *In*
   The Urban Context. Alisdair Rogers and Steven Vertovec, eds. Pp. 259–286.
   Washington, DC: Berg Publishers.

Bruyn, Severyn T., and James Meehan, eds.
   1987 Beyond the Market and the State: New Directions in Community Development. Philadelphia: Temple University Press.

Cybriwsky, Roman A., David Ley, and John Western
   1986 The Political and Social Construction of Revitalized Neighborhoods:
   Society Hill, Philadelphia, and False Creek, Vancouver. *In* Gentrification of the
   City. Neil Smith and Peter Williams, eds. Pp. 92–120. Boston: Allen and
   Unwin.

Etzioni, Amitai
   1993 The Spirit of Community: Rights, Responsibilities, and the Communitarian Agenda. New York: Crown.

Gans, Herbert
   1962 The Urban Villagers: Group and Class in the Life of Italian-Americans.
   New York: The Free Press.

Halperin, Rhoda H.
   1988 Economies across Culture. London: Macmillan.
   1990 The Livelihood of Kin: Making Ends Meet "The Kentucky Way." Austin:
   University of Texas Press.
   1994a Cultural Economies Past and Present. Austin: University of Texas Press.
   1994b Appalachians in Cities: Issues and Challenges for Research. *In* From
   Mountain to Metropolis: Appalachian Migrants in American Cities. Kathryn
   M. Borman and Phillip J. Obermiller, eds. Pp. 181–198. Westport, CT: Bergin
   and Garvey.
   1998 Practicing Community. Austin: University of Texas Press.

Halperin, Rhoda H., and M. Slomowitz
1988 Hospitalized Appalachian Adolescents. *In* Appalachian Mental Health. Susan Keefe, ed. Pp. 188–205. Lexington: University of Kentucky Press.

King, Mel, and Samantha George
1987 The Future of Community: From Local to Global. *In* Beyond the Market and the State. Severyn T. Bruyn and James Meehan, eds. Pp. 217–229. Philadelphia: Temple University Press.

Polanyi, Karl
1944 The Great Transformation. New York: Holt, Rinehart.

Sanjek, Roger
1998 The Future of Us All: Race and Neighborhood Politics in New York City. Ithaca, NY: Cornell University Press.

Sieber, Timothy
1993 Public Access in the Urban Waterfront: A Question of Vision. *In* The Cultural Meaning of Urban Space. Robert Rotenberg and Gary McDonogh, eds. Pp. 173–193. Westport, CT: Bergin and Garvey.

Smith, Neil, and Peter Williams, eds.
1986 Gentrification and the City. Boston: Allen and Unwin.

II

DEVELOPMENT IN PRACTICE

5

Barriers to the Diffusion of Agricultural Knowledge: A Balinese Case Study

Nitish Jha

Since its inception, the term "development" has implied a constructive process induced in a population by an external human agency. In the past decade, however, local participation has become a central focus in the development endeavor. Anthropologists have been in the vanguard of the movement to involve the beneficiaries of development in the development process. Their advocacy of the cause of local participation is manifested in, among other things, their championship of local or indigenous knowledge. The ongoing work of anthropologists to highlight the relevance of indigenous knowledge is gradually resulting in an attitudinal shift in the strategy of development where the prevailing approach has been to emphasize the developer's expertise.[1]

As crucial as this is, anthropologists have concentrated on highlighting the value of local knowledge to the neglect and detriment of another equally important aspect. Given their preoccupation with protecting indigenous knowledge against the depredations of unsympathetic developers, anthropologists have, intentionally or unintentionally, avoided attempts to explain development impasses caused by factors within the communities that are undertaking or experiencing such development. In overlooking the systemic nature of knowledge and the existence of social or structural barriers to its diffusion, anthropologists have ignored issues that they are singularly well equipped to deal with. They have also ended up reifying what is simply a useful heuristic dichotomy in the characterization of knowledge.[2]

The compartmentalization of knowledge with the intent of endorsing only the local angle is inadvisable in actual development settings. Insisting on the primacy of indigenous knowledge over external knowledge may be wrongheaded. Rather, knowledge that has a bearing on development concerns must be viewed as a composite system resulting from a blend of what is useful in both local and external experience (see Agrawal 1995). The real culprit in cases where knowledge fails to disseminate properly lies elsewhere. As this study shows, the lack of diffusion of knowledge relevant for development can be due to social and structural barriers in a community.

In any community, knowledge is constantly being generated or acquired, assimilated, transmitted, tested, revised, adapted, and even jettisoned by its members. Each individual possesses only a subset of the overall stock of knowledge. None of the processes to which knowledge is subject are free of structural impediments. In addition, knowledge itself is a dynamic resource that is open to capture and contestation by various rival interests within the local population. Access to it is stratified as a result.

In Balinese agriculture, local knowledge has held its own, and much of the credit for giving it its due goes to an anthropologist (Lansing 1987, 1991; Lansing and Kremer 1993). Current agricultural technology draws from both local and external sources. In the case presented below, difficulties in the implementation of a particular strategy arose because of prevailing patterns of social organization and the motivations of individual actors, not because of the inappropriateness of one or the other branch of the knowledge dichotomy. It falls, therefore, to anthropologists to decipher the nature of barriers to knowledge dissemination and, thereby, enable the system to function more smoothly.

INTEGRATED PEST MANAGEMENT IN THEORY

The price and availability of rice have long been barometers of Indonesia's political equilibrium (Hill 1996:123). They explain the pro-food strategy followed by the Indonesian government since 1966, even during the oil boom decade when the agricultural sector languished in so many other petroleum-exporting countries. Before the current state of affairs, the cynosure of Indonesia's agricultural development was the success of its rice policy.

The Green Revolution (i.e., the spread of genetically engineered varieties—or High Yield Varieties (HYVs)—of staple cereals) was singularly responsible for altering the country's status from being the world's largest rice importer in the 1970s to becoming self-sufficient in rice by 1985. But this new technology came at a price; HYV cultivation needs expensive inputs that include frequent seed purchases, adequate irrigation, chemical fertilizer, and pesticides. Moreover, changes in cropping patterns to achieve the target of self-sufficiency led to disturbances in agricultural ecosystems. Droughts, as well as massive pest and disease outbreaks, posed ever-greater threats to self-sufficiency and the livelihoods of rice cultivators (Hill 1994:72–75, 1996:124–135).

In Bali, the country's most prosperous province, wet-rice production is an economic mainstay. Rice cultivation is not only an agronomic and economic process but is profoundly social and religious as well. Balinese rice farmers band together in associations called *subak*. A subak's complex social organization and corporate nature derive from its members' control over the water in an irrigation system. Each subak has its own irrigation temple, which sets a cropping schedule, determining what and when to plant given the amount of water in the system. This is replicated on a larger scale, with the main temple in a regional hierarchy coordinating water-sharing and cropping patterns among all the subak in a watershed. This traditional system of enforcing crop discipline within a subak, and staggering cultivation schedules across groups of subak, has the effect of keeping pest populations under control (Lansing 1991). With farmers synchronizing their cultivation schedules en bloc, pest populations are sharply reduced after harvest by using indigenous techniques of pest control and making it difficult for pests to migrate to nearby fields.

With the advent of the Green Revolution, however, the existence of this traditional system was jeopardized by the intervention of the government and the Asian Development Bank. In trying to promote the national objective of self-sufficiency in rice production, the state established a tripartite mandate: (1) that only HYVs be planted; (2) that cropping be continuous in all subak; and (3) that fallow be abolished. The threat of legal penalties backing up this mandate and the offer of easy agricultural credit, not to mention the prospect of mushrooming yields, led to more than 75 percent of Bali's terraces coming under HYVs by 1980. Thus, the government superseded the secular role played by the water temple hierarchy without even attempting to understand it (Lansing 1995).

The spread of HYVs on Bali was accompanied by rising pest populations, water scarcity, and falling crop yields—all direct consequences of the areal, temporal, and technological changes in crop discipline brought about by the government's ignorance of traditional farming practices. An anthropologist, Stephen Lansing (1991, 1995), realized that the temple system was critical in maintaining the ecological balance and a minimum level of agricultural productivity. It was his tireless exposition of the superiority of indigenous management to the authorities that finally resulted in a restoration of the temple system to its secular functions.

Despite the problems, farmers in Bali continue to plant HYVs because of their promise of high yields. Unfortunately, having sacrificed resistance at the altar of productivity, many HYVs are more prone to attack by pests and diseases than traditional rice varieties are. Additionally, and quite perversely, the overuse of pesticides in HYV cultivation has led to pesticide resistance. For farmers and scientists this has meant a constant battle against the latest pest species and disease strains in the rice fields.[3] In 1974, the brown planthopper (*Nilaparvata lugens*) became one of the most harmful rice pests as a consequence of the intensive use of chemical pesticides (Chadwick and Marsh 1993:23–24; Hill 1994; Shepard et al. 1995:172–177).

At about the same time, the realization that pesticides also pose public health risks and contaminate soil and water catalyzed research on an environmentally sound alternative to their use. This combinatory method—which draws from both indigenous knowledge and modern science—was called Integrated Pest Management (IPM). It encourages natural control of pests by using pest predators, planting pest-resistant crop varieties, adopting indigenous pest management practices, and, as a last resort, judiciously using pesticides (World Bank 1999).[4] IPM is a top-down strategy but, unlike the crop mandate in the early Green Revolution era, it was formulated as an advisory program.

In 1998, with substantial support from the World Bank and other donor agencies, the Indonesian government initiated one of the most ambitious IPM programs ever. Four years later, an IPM training project was added to support the national program. It envisaged training 800,000 farmers and trainers and providing policy support to strengthen the regulatory and environmental management of pesticides. The World Bank (1999) claims that "by 1997 the project had trained more than 600,000 farmers, including about 21,000 farmer trainers."[5] It trumpets this alleged success of IPM saying, "Trained farmers carry out their own field investigations while relying on local and traditional knowledge to adapt broad concepts and practices of IPM to local conditions. They use community mechanisms to diffuse knowledge and support the adoption of IPM practices by other farmers" (World Bank 1999:108).

In the following case study, I isolate the structural impediments and local interests that belied this claim for knowledge dissemination in the context of one farming community within which the IPM strategy was propagated.

INTEGRATED PEST MANAGEMENT IN PRACTICE

Indonesia today is still recovering from a monetary and social crisis that began in mid-1997. It started with the value of several Southeast Asian currencies, including the Indonesian rupiah, plunging on the world market. Combined with plummeting real incomes, skyrocketing food prices, and the government's inability to subsidize rice production and consumption, this sudden spiral into a recession sparked riots that brought an end to years of social, political, and economic stability (Asia Yearbook 1999:6, 26, 129; Brauchli 1998; ESCAP 1999:75, 79; Mallet 1999:256–262). The monetary crisis only aggravated the already dismal economic conditions resulting from widespread crop loss. It was against this backdrop that I conducted my field research.

I spent twelve months in 1997–98 studying a subak in central Bali. The subak is a relatively large one—spread over more than 200 hectares—and is divided into five parts. Each part, or *tempek,* functions more or less autonomously in terms of cultivation activities.

In early August 1997, district-level agricultural extension workers turned up at the monthly meeting of one of the tempek and announced that an extension program in IPM was to be conducted for farmers belonging to the tempek. Thirty volunteers were required to participate in thirteen weekly sessions provided they met three criteria: They should be literate, they should cultivate land, and they should be able to commit to attending every session. A nominal compensation would be paid to each person attending a session. The tacit expectation—expressed to me with some skepticism by an extension agent—was that farmers would teach their compatriots in turn.

When no volunteers were forthcoming, the tempek president arbitrarily selected twenty-four farmers, several of whom barely met the three criteria specified. It was a foregone conclusion that he would participate in his official capacity, although he himself did not cultivate any land. Moreover, IPM is supposed to instruct farmers about limiting pesticide use. The majority of participants did not even use pesticide because they could not afford it. The program, therefore, did not make it a point to target those farmers who did.

Over the next thirteen weeks, two sessions were canceled, once because an extension worker fell ill, and another time because most of the participants had ritual obligations to meet. Attendance for the remaining sessions varied between 60 and 85 percent. A couple of farmers were replaced by others midway through the program. Still others who had been nominated never showed up because they had paying jobs in the village or in distant towns.

Instruction in IPM involved theoretical and practical lessons in observing pest populations and disease and was combined with managerial games and simple mathematical problem solving. Some of the instruction imparted was too esoteric or too complex for most of the farmers, while some was plain ideology. The latter included listing the four principles of sound agricultural practice, which ended with the dictum "The farmer is the IPM expert."

The field staff was very clear about adopting a hands-off approach. They were present in an advisory role: local representatives of far-off agricultural research stations and the Indonesian government. Farmers, they told me, are free to plant whatever crops or rice varieties they choose. Farmers are the only decision makers, they said. This new sentiment reflects an about-face in state policy from the first decade of the Green Revolution when the government issued an agricultural fiat regarding crop discipline. I am inclined to believe that this is a case of "once bitten, twice shy."

In the course of the field school, information on fertilizer use, the availability of improved seeds, etc., was elicited by the farmers themselves. However, the central issue was the dissemination of IPM. While the farmers were very knowledgeable about certain types of pests and their predators, their knowledge of many insects and of bacterial and fungal diseases in their microenvironment was either incomplete or simply incorrect.

Although farmers can identify almost twenty-five varieties of rice, the main choice is between two of these: ketan and IR 64. Ketan is a tall, glutinous, slow-maturing, variety of traditional rice; IR 64 is a short, nonglutinous, fast-maturing HYV. Local farmers refer to the two as Old Rice (*padi lama*) and New Rice (*padi baru*) respectively.[6] Both are planted extensively by the subak, with the nonglutinous New Rice providing the daily staple and the more starchy Old Rice being used mainly in ritual preparations. Surpluses in both varieties are marketed by individual farming households, and prices fluctuate in response to demand as well as regional supply. The IPM field school taught farmers about the degree of pest resistance of different rice varieties.

If there was one specific piece of knowledge that these twenty-odd farmers came away with, it was that Old Rice is less susceptible to the brown planthopper than New Rice is, and that brown planthopper populations are typically much larger in the rainy season when the prudent choice of crop is Old Rice. In fact, in the rainy season preceding the IPM field school, the majority of farmers in the subak lost between 50 and 90 percent of their HYV crop to hopperburn as well as several viral infections for which these infamous rice pests are vectors.

Again, this lesson was handed down to them in the form of another dictum: "Rainy Season, Old Rice; Dry Season, New Rice." The next growing season—immediately after the field school program ended—happened to coincide with the annual rains. The directive from the subak priest and the subak high command was that all farmers should grow New Rice. That season—under a nationwide shroud of social and economic uncertainty—every farmer in the tempek, save one, obeyed the order and planted IR 64. In abiding by the priest's dictates, the farmers were—for the most part—knowingly endangering their own livelihoods.

In this specific instance, the much-touted friction between local and external knowledge proves to be a false dichotomy. After all, the IPM program itself is a syncretic blend of both types of knowledge. A comprehensive view of the matter illuminates various problems in the dissemination of information: organizational constraints on the transmission, assimilation, and application of knowledge, as well as local vested interests that have a stake in supporting some parts of this knowledge while disputing others. Hence, knowledge and the ability to apply it become functions of socially and politically selective factors, not just intellectual ones (see Stehr 1994).

KNOWLEDGE APPLICATION: STRUCTURAL BARRIERS AND LOCAL INTERESTS

There are two ways to make sense of the seemingly counterintuitive turn of events in the Balinese IPM case study. The first concerns social organization and the existence of structural barriers to knowledge diffusion throughout the subak. This includes the haphazard choice of participants; the decision of the agricultural extension workers to focus on a single tempek when few inter-tempek communication channels exist within the subak; the requirement of a fixed number of IPM participants not proportionate to the actual population of a tempek; and the reluctance of the agricultural extension staff to take a more active role in supervising the implementation of the knowledge they had imparted.

The structure of information flows within the subak is particularly important. For the field staff to have ignored the fact that tempek boundaries are often nonporous with regard to knowledge meant that the desire of the World Bank program—to spawn serried ranks of farmer-trainers—was doomed from the start.[7] Moreover, contrary to the bank's claim for the unmitigated success of IPM, landless sharecroppers who participated in the IPM program had little incentive to follow up on the instruction received, let alone teach other farmers in structured settings.[8]

The design of IPM has become progressively more farmer-friendly since 1980. IPM observation procedures are no longer as tedious or technical as they were and have been devised to mesh with routine agricultural task schedules (Waibel 1993:79). The primary reason for avoiding pesticide application, and the IPM that precedes it, has more to do with cost than with the labor involved. Despite agricultural subsidies continuing through the early part of the financial crisis, pesticides were the most expendable items on a long and increasingly costly list of expenditures incurred by farming households (see Poffenberger and Zurbuchen 1980). Only when pest infestations threatened to overwhelm already uncertain subsistence did farmers resort to using them. IPM is designed as a preventive measure; it teaches farmers to make periodic observations of the standing crop and to apply pesticides carefully when symptoms of serious infestation are first observed. The average farmer, however, used pesticides as a cure—and usually when it was too late to save the crop anyway. There was no follow-up to evaluate the impact of the IPM program. Extension officers were more anxious to meet quantitative goals in terms of the number of farmers trained than to ensure that the IPM knowledge was actually applied.

Furthermore, almost half the attendees at the IPM training sessions were proxies for the farmers who were actually selected. These young men, employed in the local handicraft trade, had little interest in farming but were not averse to exploiting the opportunity to earn an additional income. Their own work schedule was flexible, allowing them to attend the weekly IPM meetings. Since they were not the main income earners themselves, the remuneration paid out to them was not a bad deal. Meanwhile, the fathers and uncles they represented earned better money elsewhere in various trades and services.

The second and thornier of the two issues affecting knowledge flows is that of politics and factionalism within the subak, and its manifestation in this case. Not only is knowledge heterogeneous and differentially distributed at the level of the local community, but its possession is contested even here. The rebel farmer who went against the decree of the subak priest and planted Old Rice was a former president of the tempek. He had been accused of corruption and was removed in a coup engineered by the current tempek president barely a month before the IPM program began. The winner of the contest between priest and renegade farmer depended on who could muster a bigger show of strength.

The former tempek leader, although recognized as a good farmer, was now in disgrace and was shunned by his followers. The priest, on the other hand, held the moral high ground, but the majority of farmers did not have faith in either his ritual or agricultural abilities. His decision went against the recommendations of the agricultural extension workers but was ratified by the subak leadership, which includes the subak president, the priest himself, and all five tempek leaders. Ordinary members, including farmers who had attended the IPM field school, had no say in the decision about crop discipline. Save for one tempek president, no one in the subak leadership had had the benefit of participation in the field school. Moreover, the priest used the threat of religious sanction to enforce his decision: Farmers growing Old Rice were denied the goodwill of Dewi Sri, the Balinese Hindu goddess of rice and prosperity, and had to forfeit any recourse to petitioning her if something were to harm their crop.

The stands of both the priest and the rebel farmer were couched in terms of protecting against the risk of pests, but in different ways. The priest's primary concern was to synchronize the subak's cultivation cycle with those of neighboring subak so that pest migrations from the latter would cease. According to him, everything depended on timing and the necessity of coordinating the shorter cultivation cycle of New Rice with specific astral phenomena. The renegade claimed that the goal of harmonizing crop cycles across subak could be achieved without planting New Rice and contravening the IPM crop discipline principle. Many farmers said or insinuated that the priest was not an expert in traditional astronomy and that his knowledge of both the ritual and secular aspects of cultivation was flawed. They agreed with the renegade farmer's strategy and believed it was safer. Yet they were not willing to openly challenge the priest's authority as the rebel had done. Thus, even where IPM knowledge was disseminated, it seems to have been subverted by the priest's directive to plant New Rice in the rainy season.

The subsequent poor harvest, combined with the general economic conditions in the area at the time, pushed the price of New Rice up threefold, squeezing many farmers who then turned to the market for their own consumption needs. Notwithstanding the knowledge imparted at the IPM field school and the misgivings born of previous experience, the more or less unanimous—and largely coerced—decision to grow a rice variety susceptible to the brown planthopper at a time when this pest's population had been known to boom imperiled the subsistence of the majority of cultivators.[9] A lack of understanding of local risk assessment and, more importantly, ignorance of the sociology of knowledge and its application in local communities lie at the bottom of this development strategy gone awry.

CONCLUSIONS

In considering why the farmers made what was apparently a risky decision, one has to take into account a complex of factors. No normative explanation will clarify the circumstances adequately. Farmers assess risks on the basis of more than just pure economic rationality. Roumasset

(1976) and the various contributors to Barlett (1980) provide alternative analyses of risk assessment by farmers, but none deal satisfactorily with the aspect of decision making that may be termed moral suasion. The pyrrhic victory of the subak priest, for instance, was enabled by his purported religious knowledge.

Several subak scholars propose that religion is a glue; that the threat of divine sanction and the incentive of earning supernatural merit are the primary reasons why many Balinese farmers unite for the common good (Sutawan et al. 1990). While this is true, my findings reveal that behind the normative facade of a religiously homogeneous organization, ritual activity in the subak offers an arena for conflict—over physical assets, labor, time, control over decision making, and, not least, access to knowledge. Religious knowledge may thus be used to achieve unabashedly political ends.[10]

One must beware of the danger of treating a farming community as undifferentiated (see Nanda 1991:40, 47). A critical task should be determining what social, political, and economic factors underlie its diversity.[11] Little attention has been paid by anthropologists to the manner in which access to knowledge is structured within any such community. This analysis needs to get under way in order to unearth the patterns of social organization and behavior that determine the privileging of different segments of knowledge by different groups of people.

As in the case examined here, the classification of knowledge based on its provenance is a nonissue in many development scenarios; in IPM, for instance, scientists as well as farmers take the complementarity of modern science and traditional knowledge systems for granted. Instead, the focus should be on problems of the social organization of knowledge. For far too long, the participatory nature of local control has been entirely assumed by the people planning and implementing development programs. In the design of these interventions, the differentiated sociopolitical categories of the farming population—in terms of their knowledge, objectives, rights and obligations, and other operational endowments and constraints—have been altogether ignored.

Factors that, when played out, result in the overall welfare of the farming population need to be distinguished from ones that impede the spread of knowledge and, thereby, harm the community's general well-being. As evidence of whether a strategy is faring well or ill, one can measure vari-

ables that all participants in the development process agree on as consti-
tuting either desirable or undesirable outcomes.

Philosophers and political scientists were among the first to address the
issues of how knowledge is constructed and how this construction represents the interests of those involved (Habermas 1971; Mouffe 1979; Said
1978). More recent theorists propose that administrative ability has come
to rely on the specialized knowledge of the domains to be managed
(Campbell and Manicom 1995; Stehr 1994). Their commentaries are
located in the specific context of postindustrial societies, where scientific
and technological knowledge is the cornerstone of economic and social
action. However, their observations hold for small-scale communities as
well.

These authors point out that knowledge possession and political power
do not always go hand in hand. Stehr adds that a growing stock of knowledge, to which potentially all the members of a society have access, threatens existing power relations and creates more rather than less instability.
He asserts that the use, nonuse, or misuse of knowledge cannot be predicted and that there is "no linear trade-off between the increase in knowledge and the territory of 'irrational' politics" (1994:2). The fragility of
social structure is a direct consequence of the clash between multiple
sources of legitimacy for knowledge (Stehr 1994:166–167).

This is in keeping with the paradox posed by the IPM study, where a
growth in knowledge actually undermines order. New learning should
have empowered at least those who attended the field school. Yet, the
authority of the priest in determining crop choice prevailed despite being
weakened by widespread doubts about his wisdom. This may suggest that,
under the circumstances, there was little point to disseminating new
knowledge, but until the dynamics of its spread are investigated more systematically, such a conclusion is unjustified.

It suggests, however, that external knowledge should not be the unwit-
ting scapegoat in every development scenario. Instead, more attention
should be paid to the attributes of all knowledge at the local level, to determine whether such knowledge is limited or dispersed, priced or free, coer-
cive or noncoercive. Anthropologists interested in development should
heed the holistic nature of knowledge, and account for factors that determine its differential distribution and application within communities.[12]
They should act as facilitators, minimizing or alleviating structural prob-

lems related to the role of knowledge in development, and help design development strategies that have a greater probability of success. Hence, while knowledge is important for development, it is equally important for development agents to identify and comprehend the factors that create knowledge gaps or information problems, which hinder the implementation of strategies for socioeconomic advancement.

In distilling the moral of this case study, I expose myself to the criticism that I am merely reinventing the wheel. Were you Balinese, you would accuse me of adding salt to the sea. But if empirical cases are not documented methodically and knowledge is not treated comprehensively, we could end up dismissing out of hand the relevance of any external knowledge whatsoever in the development process. In the context of agricultural development, in particular, we would then be guilty of a grave and potentially harmful error of judgment. To twist the words of another familiar adage—in keeping with the experience of the Balinese farmers—we, quite literally, would be guilty of throwing out the paddy with the ditchwater.

NOTES

For their unstinting help and hospitality, I am beholden to the residents of my host village in Bali, especially Jro Mangku Dalem, his family and I Wayan Sukerta. In Denpasar, I Wayan Budha's family took me in as one of its own. At Udayana University, Professors I Wayan Ardika, I Gde Pitana, Pande Wayan Sudana, and Nyoman Sutawan aided and advised me. My fieldwork was supported by the Sachar Funds and the Department of Anthropology at Brandeis University as well as by the Henry Luce Foundation and the Association for Asian Studies. I am grateful to the Indonesian Institute of Sciences, Jakarta, and to Udayana University, Denpasar, for sponsoring my project. Robert Hunt, Daivi Rodima, Mark Seifert, and Amy Todd heard and critiqued the initial draft of this paper. Comments and questions from George Appell, Michael Chibnik, Gracia Clark, Antonio Gilman, James Hess, Robert Hunt, Deborah Winslow, Willem Wolters, and two anonymous reviewers helped me further refine this piece. Any faults in the final version are mine alone.

1. The literature in this area is vast and varied. Volumes of case studies compiled by Appell (1985), Brokensha et al. (1980), Dove (1988), Hobart (1993), and others provide growing testimony to the fact that local knowledge is vital to the process of development and is ignored only at the cost of creating serious social imbalance. These works also criticize the hubris and debunk the infallibility of outside agents who profess authoritative knowledge of local environments.

2. Some scholars like Shiva (1988, 1991) use this dichotomy as a basis for a pro-grammatic condemnation of all modern, science-based development projects, labeling them Western, oppressive of farming communities and indigenous peo-ples, and antagonistic to their knowledge. In contrast, they portray local knowl-edge as being timeless, self-contained, evenly distributed throughout the—invariably Third World—community in question, and a panacea for all development ills. See Nanda (1991) for a scathing critique of such radicalism.

3. There are numerous publications on this issue: handbooks for farmers and agricultural extension workers, scientific research updates, and reviews of pest management schemes (Mueller 1985; Oka 1997; Shepard et al. 1987, 1995). Sev-eral chapters of Chadwick and Marsh (1993) are relevant to the discussion here. There is even one early anthropological appraisal of IPM that contrasts the effi-cacy of top-down versus bottom-up implementation of IPM using empirical examples from the Philippines (Goodell et al. 1982).

4. IPM validates the knowledge of farmers, combining it with that of scientific researchers (Ou 1971). Some authors maintain that modern commercial agricul-ture could draw on the strengths of traditional pest management, that is, its self-sufficiency and environmental compatibility. But the available information on such indigenous practices is based on qualitative observations rather than detailed quantitative measurements and has yet to be systematically collated (Brown and Marten 1986; Fujisaka 1992).

5. There is no explanation of the difference between the categories of "farmer" and "farmer trainer." The way it was presented to me in the field, all farmers are expected to disseminate knowledge about IPM; thus, all farmers are trainers.

6. The official term for HYVs is *padi unggul* (superior or improved rice). This obscures the fact that farmers themselves have always experimented with tradi-tional varieties in attempts to breed better hybrid strains.

7. I learned later that another tempek has a long-standing rule that bans the car-rying of lanterns into the fields in order to guard against the danger of attracting insect pests after dark. The nonobservance of this rule is punishable by fines. Its origin is unclear, but the fact that most of the farmers in the other four tempek had never heard of this rule or instituted a similar one is partial evidence of the fact that some organizational features of the subak are not conducive to the spread of information.

8. The social organization of the subak has been a black box. Several eminent scholars have studied the subak but none have adopted it as the primary unit of analysis and studied it in any detail (C. Geertz 1980; Lansing 1991). It has long

been assumed to be a homogeneous corporate entity. My field data show that, in fact, it is split into two distinct, nonisomorphic groups (Jha 1999). The implications of this dichotomy for theory and concepts in irrigation studies and for the targeting of agricultural development assistance—including the IPM program in Bali—are important but are not investigated here. For a discussion of some factors affecting land-poor sharecroppers, see World Bank (1999:76–77).

9. Hunt (1995:183–186) discusses the issue of uncertainty in field research. I left the village before the end of the rainy season in question, so this analysis is unavoidably incomplete. A Balinese correspondent later wrote that most farmers in the subak lost between 5 and 80 percent of their standing crop to hopperburn but he gave no details about the comparative damage done to the two rice varieties. I cannot, therefore, conclude whether any party was in error. This does not, however, alter my contention that the farmers were compelled to take a risk.

10. The use of the term "local participation" in the context of development projects suggests that merely devolving decision-making powers to a community will lead to unalloyed, community-wide involvement in all aspects of project management. This is hardly the case here. Although decision making is supposedly consensual in nature, political, economic, and social relations that develop outside the subak manifest themselves in unequal power distribution among its members. Decisions benefiting the majority are co-opted by a minority. The submission of members to resolutions harmful to their own interests implies a peculiar mix of political and moral organization that falls somewhere between theoretical depictions of farming communities as either "moral" (Scott 1976) or "rational" (Popkin 1979).

11. Studies of local-level political organization and behavior are also relevant. A sampling in the Balinese case would include H. Geertz (1959), Hansen (1981), Hart et al. (1989), Hobart (1978), and Ravenholt (1974).

12. Much has been written regarding the anthropologist's role in development. I will not attempt to summarize these arguments here, but some of the more lucid and powerful ones include those by Cernea (1985, 1995), Dove (1988), Hoben (1982), Murphy (1990), and Robins (1986).

REFERENCES

Agrawal, Arun
    1995 Dismantling the Divide between Indigenous and Scientific Knowledge. Development and Change 26(3):413–439.

Appell, George N., ed.
   1985 Modernization and the Emergence of a Landless Peasantry: Essays on the Integration of Peripheries to Socioeconomic Centers. Williamsburg, VA: College of William and Mary.

Asia Yearbook
   1999 Asia 1999 Yearbook: A Review of the Events of 1999. 40th ed. Hong Kong: Review Publishing.

Barlett, Peggy, ed.
   1980 Agricultural Decision Making: Anthropological Contributions to Rural Development. New York: Academic Press.

Brauchli, Marcus W.
   1998 Indonesia's New Struggle Is Basic: A Shortage of Rice. The Asian Wall Street Journal XXIII (37): 21 October.

Brokensha, David, D. M. Warren, and Oswald Werner, eds.
   1980 Indigenous Knowledge Systems and Development. Washington, DC: University Press of America.

Brown, Becky J., and Gerald G. Marten
   1986 The Ecology of Traditional Pest Management in Southeast Asia. *In* Traditional Agriculture in Southeast Asia: A Human Ecology Perspective. Gerald G. Marten, ed. Pp. 241–272. Boulder, CO: Westview Press; Honolulu: East-West Center.

Campbell, Marie, and Ann Manicom
   1995 Introduction. *In* Knowledge, Experience and Ruling Relations: Studies in the Social Organization of Knowledge. Marie Campbell and Ann Manicom, eds. Pp. 3–17. Toronto: University of Toronto Press.

Cernea, Michael M., ed.
   1985 Putting People First: Sociological Variables in Rural Development. New York: Oxford University Press.

Cernea, Michael M.
   1995 Social Organization and Development Anthropology. Human Organization 54(3):340–352.

Chadwick, Derek J., and Joan Marsh, eds.
   1993 Crop Protection and Sustainable Agriculture. Chichester, UK: John Wiley & Sons.

Dove, Michael R., ed.
1988 The Real and Imagined Role of Culture in Development: Case Studies from Indonesia. Honolulu: University of Hawaii Press.

Economic and Social Commission for Asia and the Pacific (ESCAP)
1999 Economic and Social Survey of Asia and the Pacific 1999. New York: ESCAP, United Nations.

Fujisaka, Sam
1992 Farmer Knowledge and Sustainability in Rice-Farming Systems: Blending Science and Indigenous Innovation. In Diversity, Farmer Knowledge and Sustainability. Joyce Lewinger Moock and Robert E. Rhoades, eds. Pp. 69–83. Ithaca, NY: Cornell University Press.

Geertz, Clifford
1980 Negara: The Theater State in Nineteenth-Century Bali. Princeton: Princeton University Press.

Geertz, Hildred
1959 The Balinese Village. In Local, Ethnic, and National Loyalties in Village Indonesia: A Symposium. G. William Skinner, ed. Pp. 24–33. New Haven, CT: Yale University.

Goodell, Grace, P. E. Kenmore, J. A. Litsinger, J. P. Bandong, C. G. de las Cruz, and M. D. Lumaban
1982 Rice Insect Pest Management Technology and Its Transfer to Small-Scale Farmers in the Philippines. In The Role of Anthropologists and Other Social Scientists in Interdisciplinary Teams Developing Improved Food Production Technology. Pp. 24–33. Los Baños, Philippines: International Rice Research Institute (IRRI).

Habermas, Jürgen
1971 Knowledge and Human Interests. Boston: Beacon Press.

Hansen, Gary E., ed.
1981 Agricultural and Rural Development in Indonesia. Boulder, CO: Westview Press.

Hart, Gillian, Andrew Turton, and Benjamin White, eds.
1989 Agrarian Transformations: Local Processes and the State in Southeast Asia. Berkeley: University of California Press.

Hill, Hal
1994 Indonesia's New Order: The Dynamics of Socio-Economic Transformation. Honolulu: University of Hawaii Press.

1996 The Indonesian Economy since 1966: Southeast Asia's Emerging Giant. Cambridge: Cambridge University Press.

Hobart, Mark
1978 Padi, Puns and the Attribution of Responsibility. *In* Natural Symbols in South East Asia. G. B. Milner, ed. Pp. 55–87. London: School of Oriental and African Studies, University of London.

Hobart, Mark, ed.
1993 An Anthropological Critique of Development: The Growth of Ignorance. London: Routledge.

Hoben, Allan
1982 Anthropologists and Development. Annual Review of Anthropology 11:349–375.

Hunt, Robert C.
1995 Agrarian Data Sets: The Comparativist's View. *In* The Comparative Analysis of Human Societies: Toward Common Standards for Data Collection and Reporting. Emilio F. Moran, ed. Pp. 173–189. Boulder, CO: Lynne Rienner Publishers.

Jha, Nitish
1999 Water Subak and Ritual Subak: The Dualistic Social Organization of Irrigation in Bali. Paper presented at the 98th Annual Meeting of the American Anthropological Association, Chicago, 17–21 November.

Lansing, J. Stephen
1987 Balinese "Water Temples" and the Management of Irrigation. American Anthropologist 89:326–341.
1991 Priests and Programmers: Technologies of Power in the Engineered Landscape of Bali. Princeton: Princeton University Press.
1995 The Balinese. New York: Harcourt Brace.

Lansing, J. Stephen, and James N. Kremer
1993 Emergent Properties of Balinese Water Temple Networks: Coadaptation on a Rugged Fitness Landscape. American Anthropologist 95:97–114.

Mallet, Victor
1999 The Trouble with Tigers: The Rise and Fall of South-East Asia. London: HarperCollins.

Mouffe, Chantal
1979 Hegemony and Ideology in Gramsci. *In* Gramsci and Marxist Theory. Chantal Mouffe, ed. Pp. 168–204. London: Routledge & Kegan Paul.

Mueller, K. E.
    1985 Field Problems of Tropical Rice. Rev. ed. Los Baños, Philippines: IRRI.

Murphy, Josette
    1990 Farmers' Systems and Technological Change in Agriculture. *In* Social Change and Applied Anthropology: Essays in Honor of David W. Brokensha. Miriam S. Chaiken and Anne K. Fleuret, eds. Pp. 17–30. Boulder, CO: Westview Press.

Nanda, Meera
    1991 Is Modern Science a Western, Patriarchal Myth? A Critique of the Populist Orthodoxy. South Asia Bulletin XI(1&2):32–61.

Oka, Ida Nyoman
    1997 Integrated Crop Pest Management with Farmer Participation in Indonesia. *In* Reasons for Hope: Instructive Experience in Rural Development. Anirudh Krishna, Norman Uphoff, and Milton J. Esman, eds. Pp. 184–199. West Hartford, CT: Kumarian Press.

Ou, S. H.
    1971 Status of Crop Protection Activities and Crop Protection Problems in Southeast Asia. New York: The Asia Society.

Poffenberger, Mark, and Mary S. Zurbuchen
    1980 The Economics of Village Bali: Three Perspectives. Economic Development and Cultural Change 29(1):91–133.

Popkin, Samuel L.
    1979 The Rational Peasant: The Political Economy of Rural Society in Vietnam. Berkeley: University of California Press.

Ravenholt, Albert
    1974 Political and Economic Problems of Indonesia as Viewed from the Perspective of the Balinese Farmer. *In* Proceedings of a Seminar on Agricultural and Rural Development in Indonesia, 28–29 October. Pp. 5–18. East Lansing: Michigan State University.

Robins, Edward
    1986 The Strategy of Development and the Role of the Anthropologist. *In* Practicing Development Anthropology. Edward C. Green, ed. Pp. 10–21. Boulder, CO: Westview Press.

Roumasset, James A.
    1976 Rice and Risk: Decision Making among Low-Income Farmers. Amsterdam: North-Holland Publishing Company.

Said, Edward
    1978. Orientalism. London: Routledge & Kegan Paul.

Scott, James C.
    1976 The Moral Economy of the Peasant: Rebellion and Subsistence in South-
    east Asia. New Haven, CT: Yale University Press.

Shepard, B. M., A. T. Barrion, and J. A. Litsinger
    1987 Friends of the Rice Farmer: Helpful Insects, Spiders, and Pathogens. Los
    Baños, Philippines: IRRI.
    1995 Rice-Feeding Insects of Tropical Asia. Los Baños, Philippines: IRRI.

Shiva, Vandana
    1988 Staying Alive: Women, Ecology and Survival in India. London: Zed
    Books.
    1991 The Violence of the Green Revolution: Third World Agriculture, Ecology
    and Politics. Penang, Malaysia: Third World Network.

Stehr, Nico
    1994 Knowledge Societies. London: Sage.

Sutawan, N., M. Swara, W. Windia, W. Suteja, N. Arya, and W. Tjatera
    1990 Community-Based Irrigation System in Bali, Indonesia. *In* Irrigation and
    Water Management in Asia. W. Gooneratne and S. Hirashima, eds. Pp. 81–147.
    New Delhi: Sterling Publishers.

Waibel, H.
    1993 Government Intervention in Crop Protection in Developing Countries.
    In Crop Protection and Sustainable Agriculture. Derek J. Chadwick and Joan
    Marsh, eds. Pp. 76–93. Chichester, UK: John Wiley & Sons.

World Bank
    1999 World Development Report 1998/99: Knowledge for Development. New
    York: Oxford University Press.

6

The Common Sense of Development and the Struggle for Participatory Development in Sri Lanka

Mike Woost

Development has many faces. In this chapter, I explore the participatory face of development as it has taken cultural form in Sri Lanka. Participation as a development concept originally was part of a critique of development that took issue with the top-down character of most development undertakings. As Majid Rahnema (1992) has pointed out, advocates of a more democratic development process took up the concept of participation. It was supposed to provide a means for common folk, the usual targets of development, to make their mark on the kind of changes that would affect their lives. In its most direct form, it was supposed to turn development into a process that would be defined from below. Even here there are many faces, from small locally organized efforts to improve subsistence conditions, to Robert Chambers–like initiatives to enroll both experts and local folks together (see, for instance, Chambers 1983).

However, as Rahnema (1992) also has noted, participation fairly rapidly became mainstream discourse. Stirrat and Henkel (n.d.) have gone so far as to say that participatory approaches like that of Robert Chambers have done nothing but serve the interests of top-down development by providing a new discourse through which to impose centrally constructed development programs. In this guise, participation gives people the opportunity to discover that what they need are the very development programs the international agencies offer, whether savings schemes or rural improvement projects.

The question one must ask, however, of even the critiques of participation, is how this sort of incorporation into the mainstream is accomplished. It is easy to discern mainstream control of such activities. Few development projects allow local people the time to build a community of interests and formulate their own projects of renewal or change. It is thus easy to describe how the incorporation of alternative discourses of development ends up serving dominant interests in the development hierarchy. Yet it is a very different kind of endeavor to specify how this kind of incorporation is ideologically constructed in the cultural practice of development.

In the pages that follow, focusing on the Sri Lankan development context, I outline some of the ways in which the notion of participation is brought into line with mainstream development interests. The questions I ask of participatory development in Sri Lanka are similar to those James Ferguson (1994) asked of development generally in his book, *The Anti-Politics Machine*. Ferguson noted that development critics, such as Lappé and Collins (1977), often take for granted the process through which development actually fails to do what it intends and instead ends up serving the interests of power. Instead of merely pointing out development's failure, Ferguson argues that we need to see how this occurs despite the good intentions of those involved. To simply say that development is the devil's handmaiden implies a megalomaniacal scheme to forward the interests of the capitalist global economy. As Ferguson points out, it is unfair to say that all people who work in development share such interests. Nor are they simply dupes of a monolithic dominant ideology. We need, instead, to peer into the black box of development and find out what happened to all the good intentions that disappeared inside it.

In the case I am raising, the situation is somewhat different. Rather than look at specific development projects as Ferguson (1994) did, I examine the ways in which a particular conception of development is incorporated into mainstream development frames of discourse: the discourse of participation. As noted above, participation can be seen as a potential ground for framing a different, more democratic kind of development, or even postdevelopment view of the world. Yet, most development critics, as well as insiders, claim that participation is simply another buzzword within development discourse, a buzzword without real substance or potential for changing the way development works. Incorporation of this kind often remains a very mysterious process. It is as if new conceptualizations of development arise and then disappear inside a black box of incorporation and reappear magically transformed as mainstream discourse, with all their critical edges blunted from the journey. Incorporation of this sort is not a natural process. It involves an ideological transformation that has to be worked out in cultural practices within development.

In order to unpack this process, to make it more transparent, I argue that we need to recognize that development in the Sri Lankan social formation (the complex of social forces structured in dominance) is made up of many different groups and categories. They include International Development Organizations (IDOs), such as USAID and CARE, political parties, mid- and lower-level development nongovernmental organizations (NGOs) originating in Sri Lanka, as well as the competing groups and classes of people who eventually become development "beneficiaries." Each of these categories has their own interests. Yet they all come together in the effort to distribute and lay claim to the resources made available through development. It is in the confrontation, struggle, and negotiation among categorical interests that the transformation/incorporation of notions like participatory development can be observed. I should also point out that incorporation into the mainstream should not be seen as inevitable. It is the result of the kind of struggles I outline below. The outcome of any such struggle can never be certain, even though, as we will see below, some players in the game come with more resources to their advantage.

First, a few words about the notion of category interest that I am using here. I have borrowed this idea from Ferguson's (1994) analysis of the "Bovine Mystique" in Lesotho. Ferguson argues that class analysis alone fails to reflect either the complexity of interests to be found in rural society or the way these change over people's lifetimes. A young man working in a South African mine accumulates cattle at home to avoid having his earnings dissipated by his wife on daily household expenses. She, needless to say, resists such investments and the mystique that makes it all but impossible to sell cattle. Later, when he retires from the mines, he slowly sells off the herd, which has now become his retirement fund. The Bovine Mystique may end up serving dominant patriarchal interests in rural Lesotho and perhaps even the interests of the South African mine owners, but it does both in quite a circuitous way, as outcomes of an ongoing and protracted struggle among a variety of category interests. It is not simply the imposition of a dominant patriarchal ideology; nor can it be seen as merely a reflexive linear reproduction of tradition or the logical outcome of a rationally thinking peasant or in this case, mine worker. Rather, it is the result of conflict, negotiation, and struggle among all the category interests who would each like to see a different outcome.

I argue here that similar processes of conflict and negotiation are at work in the transformation of participatory development into yet another tool of the dominant construction of development. In the process of being reproduced, it has been transformed by the struggle among the many different interests to be found on the cultural and political terrain of development in Sri Lanka. The many different players in the Sri Lankan development game—NGO employees, government officials, villagers—clearly have different category interests. All of these come together as a complex imbrication of interests and practices, none of which is completely monolithic. But it is not merely a negotiation of interests; some players have more power to play the game effectively than do others.

My concern is with four category interest groups: the state and other dominant political forces, international NGOs, Sri Lankan NGOs, and rural villagers. My contention is that what is going on in the black box of incorporation is the struggle among these various positions and interests. The outcome of this struggle articulates development "common sense" (in the Gramscian sense, which I discuss below) at various levels of practice and power in ways that undermine more democratic articulations of development and thereby serves some interests more than others. Yet the marginalization of more democratic alternatives that is the outcome of this struggle cannot be seen as simply the imposition of the dominant position. I can better support this contention by first discussing each of the primary category interests in turn.

CATEGORY INTEREST #1: THE SRI LANKAN STATE

A more complete description of the transformation of participation would include a discussion of development ideology from the post-1977 open-economic reforms through the 1980s (see, for instance, Brow [1988, 1990] or Woost [1990, 1993]). Here I will confine myself to how the Sri Lankan government has constructed participation in the 1990s. The category interest of the Sri Lankan state might be distilled into one term: Newly Industrialized Country (NIC). Since the initiation of the open economy under the United National Party in 1977, the overriding economic goal of the state has been to transform Sri Lanka into an NIC. This goal has powerfully shaped the government approach to participation in development. The push for NIC status entails luring foreign investors seeking more flexible contexts for accumulation (Harvey 1989) with such offers as tax incentives, guarantees on cheap labor, and free trade zones.

Although this strategy does provide jobs for some sectors of the population (often women in garment and electronics factories), it can hardly be said to represent a democratization of development. In fact, I maintain that the strategy undermines dialogue on development, and the only way most people participate is to sell their labor. What is more, the drive for NIC status has gone hand in hand with welfare reforms that are perceived by many as an assault on the poor. Consequently, these development strategies create new contradictions for the state to address. For example, voices protesting the open economic strategy began to be heard more widely in the late 1980s.[1] Further, many critics, citing the outright failure of some massive development projects, argued that the promise of development had failed to materialize.[2] There was additional pressure on the government from international development organizations who increasingly wanted to see the government promoting some form of participatory development. Thus, it is no surprise that the implementation of the open economy went hand in hand with a repositioning of development ideology.

Overall, the main problem for the government was how it could promote a market-led development strategy, one that promoted capitalist expansion with all its attendant contradictions (class cleavages, cuts in welfare subsidies, curtailing union activity), and still maintain popular support. The government, in short, was in the contradictory position of promoting policies that would provide investors with the opportunity to turn a profit, while at the same time it had to worry about popular perception that these policies favor one class over another. There at least had to be ideological compensation for the lack of attention to the needs of the rural and urban poor. The ideological strategy adopted in the early 1990s was one dressed in the garb of "peoplization" and is exemplified in the 200 Garment Factories program initiated by the late President Premadasa.[3]

In the ceremonial complex that grew up around this program (see Tennekoon 1988; Woost 1990, 1993) we find the notion of participation ever present. The late President Premadasa appeared on television nearly every day, speaking at the opening of some garment factory. His testimonials on these occasions proclaimed an awakening of a rural society marked by the emergence of "textile villages" in which the factory, as a center of economic development, supposedly brought about an economic and social boom for everyone in its vicinity. The investment capitalist was typically constructed as a kind of guardian deity or patron of the village, who provided employment to villagers.[4] As a result, investment-led development was said to create a community of the rich and poor.[5] Within this discourse, villagers were seen not simply as factory workers, but as people working collectively with investors to make a product. Mass production itself had been replaced by "production by the masses" in league with the investor.[6] Therefore, it was argued that this peoplized economy was one in which "everyone will get the opportunity to realise his human potential and each will recognize the other's need and worth. The resulting mutual respect and goodwill will banish class hatred."[7]

Even so, this construction of development sets definite limits on people's participation. It does not give them the power to define development for themselves. Rather, development is a process in which the poor benefit from the patronage of the rich. The poor are not really empowered at all, but are ushered into a new form of dependency in which they lose their power to speak. Thus, the role of these voiceless "people" in development is not to participate in the construction of democratic alternatives to state-sponsored market-led development, but rather simply to produce for their patrons. They are not to decide what to produce or under what conditions they will do it, but simply to provide the labor needed to make the items that powerful investors deem marketable in the world economy. The people must remain silent until called on to speak.[8]

CATEGORY INTEREST #2: INTERNATIONAL NGOs

The second set of interests, the IDOs (such as CARE and USAID) also have a contradiction to maneuver. Many of these organizations have long been in the business of funding major development projects, building up the infrastructure, supporting in their own way the government's market-led initiatives in the drive for NIC status, even though this is often done in the name of community development. Yet ever since the 1970s, many international NGOs had concluded that they must work harder to promote popular participation in development among the rural and urban poor. Since at least McNamara's (1987) farewell address to the World Bank in the early 1970s, it has been recognized that not enough people have benefited from all the resources put into development. It is often admitted that few of the poor have actually reaped the benefits promised by development.

Thus, many IDOs have adopted programs that focus on increasing the participation of the "masses" in development. These programs are often viewed, however, as a supplement to large-scale projects, rather than a replacement for them. Consequently, participatory initiatives are limited in key ways. First, they tend to be globally oriented, more concerned with raising GNP and export production than with raising development consciousness and popular participation. For example, many IDOs are often at pains to promote and fund development projects that will support the agendas of the New World Order, namely, entrepreneurship, agribusiness, and market-oriented businesses. Second, they display an overriding concern for the bottom line that directly limits the kinds of alternatives that are posed to mainstream development. One IDO worker told me that many international organizations would like to increase funding to local NGOs concerned with social justice issues. Yet their hands are tied by budgetary concerns: They must fund projects that produce a product that can be counted, marketed, and sold. Only in this way can they demonstrate to donors that the funding provided to a local NGO was money well spent. Thus, despite the good intentions regarding participation, support of the new worldview and concern for the bottom line combine in contradictory ways that end up channeling funding in ways that rarely augment alternative notions of participation.

CATEGORY INTEREST #3: SRI LANKAN NGOs

Local NGOs are often said to play an important intermediary role in the effort to empower the people and gain their participation in development (see IRED 1991:v). However, they are part of the development hierarchy and are subject to the restrictions and agendas of both the state and the international NGOs on which they depend for funding. This dependency yields a rather precarious situation for local NGOs and the people who run them. To avoid conflict, some simply adopt the official version of participation, which emphasizes compliance more than local initiative. However, others continue to work on the basis of very different definitions that are often at odds with official development goals. Here we see more of the struggle over meaning. During the course of my research in the 1990s, I was able to interact with the personnel of nearly thirty NGOs at both ends of this spectrum and to document some of the ways the dominant interpretation of participation practically affected their activities.

NGOs that situate their activities squarely within the official discourse often provide some service, educational or otherwise, that is supposed to empower people to operate more effectively within the market system. The majority of the organizations of this type that I studied were involved with income generation and credit schemes. There were also efforts by a number of NGOs to teach budding entrepreneurs how to read the rapidly changing market in the era of flexible accumulation.

According to many of the NGO leaders I interviewed, these programs are popular with the government and with international donors because they fit well with the emphasis on market-led development and with the Sri Lankan government's slogan "trade not aid." Thus, NGOs involved in this type of activity are increasingly the ones that catch the donor's eye. For instance, one foreign donor agency gave me the names of several NGOs that were being funded for their participatory orientation.[9] Nearly all fit the above description. But even more interesting is the fact that when I visited these organizations, I was told that the credit schemes they sponsored were empowering because they taught individuals how to operate systems of credit successfully and how to start their own businesses. This would, in turn, create jobs, so those who work for these new entrepreneurs could also take control of their lives. The programs were said to be participatory because they encourage people's participation in the market-led development strategies.

However, the people who work in these organizations contend with ideological contradictions of their own. One NGO staff member confided to me that while he worked to implement strategies like this, he did not feel they were truly participatory. (This was not an isolated comment. Most of the NGO workers I interviewed made similar assessments of their situation.) Instead, such programs are funded because they resonate with the rhetoric of the open economy, rather than because of their participatory character. Furthermore, he maintained that such programs owed their limited successes to the fact that the poor already have a lot of experience working for the better-off members of their communities. In that sense, the majority of poor people's lives are not substantially changed. They simply take up work with new patrons: the emerging village entrepreneurs. The frustration for him was that he and other NGO workers were increasingly forced to adopt such strategies while using participatory rhetoric in order to get funding. So, while the intentions of most of these organizations are good, in the sense that most would really like to increase the level of democracy in development decision making, the overall effect of their activities was to bolster the dominant strategies of development, strategies that severely limit opportunities for participation.

At the other end of the spectrum are NGOs that are struggling over the interpretation of participation itself. For example, I encountered organizations engaged in efforts ranging from providing legal aid services for farmers and promoting environment-friendly community development, to those aimed at raising villagers' consciousness about development in more general terms. Some were, in fact, explicitly antidevelopment. As one might expect, there was great potential for conflict between these NGOs and the government, resulting in various forms of harassment. For example, the leaders and staff of one NGO were jailed on various charges under emergency regulations. They were released after a few days, but the incident clearly sent chills through the NGO community. More formally, in 1992 the government set up an official commission of inquiry to investigate corruption among NGOs.[10] Many members of the NGO community felt that this was simply an attempt to intimidate NGOs that strayed from the official development path. The most practical sanction was to cut off funding to any errant NGO. Since any international donor must get government clearance to give funds to an NGO, this could be rather easily accomplished.[11]

CATEGORY INTEREST #4: VILLAGERS IN SOUTHEASTERN SRI LANKA

In this final section, I outline some of views of development participation from the perspective of rural people. The views expressed here come from people who live in the region surrounding a village in southeastern Sri Lanka called Suduwatura Area Gamma (where I have done research off and on since the mid-1980s). The village is small. In the late 1980s, it was home to only about three hundred people comprising about forty or so households. The people who struggled for this frontier settlement's official establishment in 1985 are migrants from other areas in Sri Lanka. In this effort, the people have had so many encounters with official forms of development that it seems at times an all-consuming way of life (Woost 1990). One thing that emerges from this development experience is a historically tuned common sense about how development works.

Here, "common sense" alludes to Gramsci's concern with that realm of consciousness where practical knowledges, understandings, and dispositions about the world, from both past and present, are sedimented together in often quite contradictory and fragmentary ways (1971). It is in this arena of consciousness, for example, that local notions about improvement confront and vie with official versions of development and rural improvement. For instance, farmers in the village asserted that the way to improve their life is to work hard on the land, turn it into slash and burn plots or even paddy land if possible, and to build permanent homes. Yet these farmers constantly confront state-disseminated ideologies that belie their practical knowledge. Farmers are told that improvement comes through proper political party affiliation, contributing labor to development celebrations, building temples, and constructing irrigation facilities that will allow them to abandon the practice of slash and burn agriculture. That is how the farmers will become more "cultured." These opposing definitions may both be applied, but only in different contexts, and thus their contradictions are ignored or are not even apparent.

For these reasons, attempts to inculcate official versions of development and thereby reshape local frameworks of interpretation and practice may yield quite unexpected, even inexplicable results. Thus, as Gramsci argued, common sense is an important field of ideological struggle, since it provides people with their frameworks of interpretation and action in the world. In this case, the common sense of rural villagers with respect to development is shaped and ordered in the encounter with powerful category interests outlined earlier. As a result of this encounter, many alternative notions of development are wholly absent from rural folks' common sense vocabulary. In fact, I argue that the shape of development common sense among many rural peoples forms a contradictory ground upon which to even think about, let alone build, alternative and more participatory forms of social change. Any sense of alternatives to development is at its very weakest at this level of the development hierarchy. Rather than engage in a struggle to construct an alternative development, people at this level are most concerned with satisfying their subsistence needs and to find ways to access additional funds for modest consumer spending.

In order to pursue these interests, rural people have learned to monitor the comings and goings of various development projects, much as they monitor the onset of the monsoon winds. Through decades of experience, these folks have learned that development projects come from the outside (whether sugarcane scheme, cement factory, or tank project) and they simply have to decide whether their involvement is worth the risk or not. To think that they would have a real say in decisions regarding their own "development" is just not a part of their ideologically structured common sense.

Over the years that I have worked in this village, many development projects have come and gone. In every case, people indicated that they could make no predictions about the outcome. They had little information about the projects introduced from outside the village. Adding to their sense of disempowerment was the fact that such projects were organized by people from a different social class, people who had clout in a different political and economic world than poor farmers. Thus, the projects were never participatory in the critical sense of grassroots planning. The local people's only decisive input was whether or not they would get involved.

This, then, is common sense of development for most farming families. Development comes to them and they can choose only whether to participate and take the risks involved. It is a bit like the national development lottery (the official government lottery). One can never be sure that buying into a project is the right choice, but then, on the other hand, it might just pay off big, at least for now. As one man said, "It's all a gamble anyway." However, most villagers feel they would be foolish to turn down such opportunities. Even the people who complain about nepotism would most likely accept a project if they were to be the beneficiaries. But this is part and parcel of how they understand their relation to development. For most of the people living under this regime of common sense, it is very difficult to conceive of how development might work differently, or how it might be reshaped by them more directly. They simply wait and hope something is brought to the village and then attempt to make it work for their own families. This, then, exemplifies the outcome as well as the villager contribution to the process of incorporation. Their common sense of development is shaped by this experience, which, in turn, shapes how they act in the development context.

CONCLUSION

Rural villagers find it difficult to locate ideological terrain on which to construct a space for an alternative form of development rooted in participation. I argue that this is an outcome of the ongoing struggle among the category interests I have outlined above. The villagers' own interests are heavily shaped by their overriding concern over basic subsistence as well as their increasing desire for consumer items now available in the market. They are not completely powerless in this struggle. Though their common sense of development is clearly framed and thereby limited by previous struggles, their reading of the situation is, all the same, fairly accurate. Given their own experience of development and what they have heard about it through media and other sources, they have largely learned to take for granted that this is the way development works—it arrives from the outside as projects fully delineated by others. My questions to them about participatory forms of development most often brought nothing but looks of consternation, as if to ask me, "What are you talking about?" Participation was just not in the realm of possibility. And this is what Gramsci meant when he said that common sense was both framed and disorganized, making more penetrating critiques impossible. So participation never even materializes at this level except rhetorically (and many do know the English word "participation"). Rural folk can contribute little to the struggle over participation since, once projects arrive at their doorstep, the whole notion has already been watered down in the struggle among higher-level interests.

But in spite of the powerful transformation of the notion, I do not think the struggle for participation is over. As Raymond Williams argued (1977), no aspect of culture is ever made once and for all. I noted above that many local NGOs and activists still work to find ways around the process of incorporation. Yet, in order to produce a different, possibly more democratic interpretation and understanding of participation, we have to attend to what goes on inside the black box of incorporation, where interests of all sorts meet and attempt to shape common sense about participation. This is important, since the way that participatory development takes shape is a product of a confluence of interests in struggle, not a simple imposition from above or below. In short, IDOs attempt to maintain their control of development by allocating funds to projects in which participation is defined as teaching people to participate in the market. The government, for its part, defines participation as contributing labor to projects sponsored by the state and international investors. Local NGOs, while varying in their approach, have little power to change IDO or government strategies. To survive, they must conform to the more powerful forms of discourse in some fashion or risk losing access to funding. In the process, whatever interest they may have had in pursuing greater democracy in development is relegated to the background. To change this particular configuration of development process, to transform it into something more democratic in both discourse and practice, will require transformative struggles of many kinds within and between all the complex categories of interest involved. But it is at just such politically congested crossroads that culture and history are made.

NOTES

1. For example, there were protests in 1992 against the construction of a huge hotel complex near a Buddhist holy site at Kandalama and against the lease of large areas of land in the southeast to multinational agribusiness firms.

2. For instance, the massive irrigation system at Lunugamvehara in the south, which ran completely dry in 1992, while up in the highlands the Samanalawewa dam sprang very serious leaks.

3. *Daily News* (Colombo) 6 August 1992, p. 6: "Two Leading Manufacturers Say: Garment Factories Can Provide Solution to Rural Job Program" and 2 January 1992, p. 1: "Scientist Lauds President's Initiative."

4. *Daily News* (Colombo), 25 November 1992, p. 6: "Socio-Economic Revolution in Villages through Garment Factories"; *Sunday Observer* 15 November 1992, pp. 37–40: "Building New Centres of Economic Growth"; *The Island* 17 October, 1992, pp. i–iv: "Boom-Time for Garments Industry."

5. *Daily News* (Colombo) 3 July 1992, pp. 11–12: "Investor-Producer Link Paves the Way to Freedom."

6. *Daily News* (Colombo) 21 May 1992, p. 6: "Manpower Our Most Abundant Resource."

7. *Daily News* (Colombo) 29 October 1992, p. 15: "President Vows to Usher in New Order Bound by 'Spirit of Caring and Sharing.'"

8. Examples of this kind of participation are to be found in nearly every television or newspaper account of a factory opening (see *Daily News* [Colombo] 30 October, 1992, p. 6: "Mother, Father and Son in Garment Industry"; *Daily News* [Colombo] 17 November 1992, p. 21: Advertisement: "Today Dialtex Interweaves into Kuliyapitiya").

9. This individual also implied that as an international donor institution, there were certain restrictions on the type of NGO that they could fund. Not only did the funding of an NGO have to fit into the scheme of the international institution's development mission, more importantly, the Sri Lankan government also had to approve the funding of any NGO. Thus, the implication was that this individual was inclined to fund a wider range of "participatory" activities, but there were limits on what could be done.

10. See, for instance, an article by Jehan Perera in the Sri Lankan English daily, *The Island*, 8 November 1992, p. 12, "The Survival of NGOs in This Democracy."

11. One powerful NGO, the Sarvodaya Shramadana Movement, had been very vocal about its opposition to many of the government's development strategies. It had even been involved in some public protests. The leader of the organization subsequently became the object of a vicious, though anonymous, slander campaign associating him with the leaders of the outlawed Janata Vimukthi Peramuna party and those of the Liberation Tigers of Tamil Eelam. He was also called before the Commission of Inquiry in the latter part of 1992. At the same time, funding approvals were not forthcoming from the government, leaving many international donors who looked on the organization favorably unable to provide further funding even though they wanted to do so. Some international donor agencies I contacted indicated that they were told very explicitly that they could no longer gain approval to fund Sarvodaya. It is interesting that some of the first Sarvodaya projects to be denied funding were those involved in providing legal aid to rural farmers (see Perera et al. [1992] for more details on Sarvodaya's problems).

REFERENCES

Brow, James
    1988 In Pursuit of Hegemony: Representations of Authority and Justice in a
    Sri Lankan Village. American Ethnologist 15:311–327.

1990 The Incorporation of a Marginal Community within the Sinhalese Nation. Anthropological Quarterly 63(1):7–17.

Chambers, Robert
1983 Rural Development: Putting the Last First. London: Longman.

Ferguson, James
1994 The Anti-Politics Machine: "Development," Depoliticization, and Bureaucratic Power in Lesotho. Minneapolis: University of Minnesota Press.

Gramsci, Antonio
1971 Selections from the Prison Notebooks of Antonio Gramsci. Q. Hoare and G. Nowell-Smith, eds. and trans. New York: International Publishers.

Harvey, David
1989 The Condition of Postmodernity: An Inquiry into the Origins of Cultural Change. Oxford: Basil Blackwell.

IRED
1991 Development NGOs of Sri Lanka: A Directory. Colombo, Sri Lanka: IRED-Development Innovations and Networks.

Lappé, Frances Moore, and Joseph Collins
1977 Food First: Beyond the Myth of Scarcity. Boston: Houghton Mifflin.

McNamara, Robert
1987 Paupers of the World and How to Develop Them. In Peasants and Peasant Societies. T. Shanin, ed. Pp. 425–428. Oxford: Basil Blackwell.

Perera, Jehan, Charika Marasinghe, and Leela Jayasekara
1992 A People's Movement under Siege. Ratmalana, Sri Lanka: Sarvodaya Book Publishing Services.

Rahnema, Majid
1992 Participation. In The Development Dictionary: A Guide to Knowledge as Power. Wolfgang Sachs, ed. Pp.116–131. London: Zed Books LTD.

Stirrat, R. L., and Heiko Henkel
n.d. Unpublished manuscript.

Tennekoon, N. Serena
1988 Rituals of Development: The Accelerated Mahaväli Development Program of Sri Lanka. American Ethnologist 15:294–310.

Williams, Raymond
1977 Marxism and Literature. London: Oxford University Press.

Woost, Michael

1990 Rural Awakenings: Grassroots Development and the Cultivation of a National Past in Rural Sri Lanka. *In* Sri Lanka: History and the Roots of Conflict. J. Spencer, ed. Pp. 164–183. London: Routledge Chapman Hall.

1993 Nationalizing the Local Past in Sri Lanka: Histories of Nation and Development in a Sinhalese Village. American Ethnologist 20(3):502–521.

7

Culturally Sustainable Development

Gracia Clark

Within the international discourse on sustainable development, much concern focuses on the strains placed on natural resources and ecological systems by the current directions of economic development. But development is also a cultural process, carried out within and by human societies and cultures, whose structures of meaning can also be stretched to the point of collapse. Human cultural adaptability is impressive, but not infinite. Unless development paradigms also take the limits of human social and cultural resources into account and provide for their renewal, neither economic growth nor ecological survival can actually be accomplished.

Current globalization processes overvalue universal and technical criteria and undervalue local values, persons, and consequences, reducing local cultures to depoliticized remnants of local music, dances, foods, and design motifs, within which the legitimacy of ethnicity is then confined. This ornamentalization, as a specific form of marginalization, has triggered a cultural backlash that feeds into a wide range of fundamentalisms that are emerging on all continents, including Christian, Islamic, and Hindu variants (Sassen 1998). While often attacking each other, these movements all reassert the ideological coherence and veto rights of their own specific cultural systems, with serious economic as well as religious consequences. Rather than reviving actual historical practices, they often enforce an essentialized, timeless version of local cultures that suggests their primary mandate is to revive at least an illusion of historical continuity.

Development analysts have drawn attention to the positive benefits of integrating cultural and social considerations into projects and policies for many years. Unfortunately, even those most active and influential in international development agency circles still frame their proposals with comments on the continuing pervasive neglect of sociocultural factors in • design and implementation (Cernea 1991; Kottak 1991). More critical scholars argue that the dominance of financial issues over agency decision making is actually increasing under neoliberal policy regimes (Escobar 1995; Korten 1995). Studies of specific projects also point out that efforts to address cultural factors are often halfhearted or wrongheaded (Ferguson 1994; McMillan 1995). The challenges economic transformation pose to human cultural and social sustainability include reducing the capacity for negotiating change, individually or collectively. Older women traders from Kumasi Central Market in Ghana, West Africa, vividly reveal the limits of this negotiating capacity in life narratives they recorded in 1995. Far from rejecting sociocultural change out of hand, they continue an Asante tradition of finding comfort not in certainty, but instead in indeterminacy. The dramatic, sometimes catastrophic economic changes of past decades have underlined one lesson for them: In their continued ability to negotiate and renegotiate lies their best and only chance of survival or prosperity in the long term.

Kumasi was already established as a cultural and commercial center in the eighteenth century, and grew as the imperial capital of Asante in the nineteenth century. The Asante confederacy united a group of Akan city-states in the forest zone that controlled major gold-producing areas and the trade routes linking European forts on the coast with older trans-Sahara networks. Chiefs and commoners, men and women, all traded enthusiastically, although men had more access to the chiefly connections and unpaid family labor that speeded accumulation. Asante political and kinship relations had incorporated money, trading, and market production for so long that these were integral to local norms. Matrilineages held and assigned rights to land, houses, and other inherited property, underlining the bond between maternal brothers and sisters rather than spouses. Each adult member, male and female, was assessed for contributions to joint lineage expenses such as funerals and legal fees. Husbands and wives also kept separate budgets, contributing money and domestic labor for specific purposes. The option of duolocal residence, with both spouses in their respective lineage homes, is as common today as when Meyer Fortes did research near Kumasi in the 1940s (1949).

After colonial conquest in 1900, Kumasi's position as a railhead, high-way junction, and administrative center ensured its continued commercial dominance over the adjoining regions. It also developed thriving sawmills, furniture and shoe factories, automobile repair yards, and other large and small industries. Today, Kumasi's huge Central Market provides retail services in food crops, imported consumer goods, and local manufactures to an urban population of 800,000, and wholesale distribution for a hinter-land stretching beyond Ghana's boundaries. Some 20,000 traders sell daily in Kumasi Central Market, in a complex of open yards, lines of open and locking stalls, and a two-story cement building.

Seventy percent of these traders are Asante women, and they staff all levels of trade, from the smallest retailer to the largest wholesaler. Most commodities are thoroughly identified as belonging to them, with only a few stereotypically sold by northerners or Asante men. Shifts in the ethnic and gender division of labor by the 1920s sent Asante men into cocoa farming and waged work, so women took over the marketplace system. Subsequent declines in the incomes associated with these and other male-identified sectors fed intense conflict over the income levels enjoyed by wealthier market women, most of them uneducated. Class and gender ten-sions peaked with price controls in the 1970s and early 1980s, enforced by violent repression of traders and demolition of markets. Under continuing neoliberal austerity since then, unemployed young men have again filtered into these female-identified market locations to compete for shrinking consumer demand.

Asante relations of marriage, parenthood, and matrilineal descent have long preserved an unusually high degree of autonomy and individual agency that facilitates continual redefinition of gender and kinship norms. The resulting flexibility and negotiability, while frustrating for household analysts, has kept the Asante family system strong while the actual obliga-tions recognized shift wildly. Each individual's social position in the family and community affects their bargaining power, but their ability to negoti-ate effectively and reach the desired results is also subject to historical change through cumulative shifts in the expected range of outcomes.

Flexibility and autonomy in kinship and marriage are vitally linked to an individual's autonomy and flexibility within the local economy. With-

out an independent income, neither men nor women can function as normal adults in lineage or marital relations. Present economic conditions
make it increasingly difficult for young people to establish themselves as
autonomous Asante adults with independent subsistence incomes. Many
older women now support two or three generations of dependents and see
no way for these to maintain respectable family relations when the elders
themselves no longer can. To them, the future looks all too certain.

GLOBAL POLARIZATION

Increased polarization between rich and poor at the national and the community levels is widely reported in nations turning to neoliberal economic
policies, including our own (UNICEF 1987). The shapes and directions of
such social change vary widely between nations, and indeed between
regions and classes or other social categories within nations, as their historical legacies and contemporary circumstances create different bases of
inequality. Despite these divergent patterns of inequality, however, the
tendency remains highly consistent: Each such pattern intensifies in its
own way and its own specific socioeconomic cleavages develop greater
breadth and reduced permeability. Abstract indicators such as global and
national income distribution confirm qualitative reports of sharply perceived relative impoverishment.

Are these widening disparities an unfortunate side effect of incomplete
globalization, or an integral part of the current globalization process? Sassen (1991, 1998) portrays overvaluing the global and undervaluing the
local as the two sides of a coin. First, she analyzes the labor process of the
global elite of managers and consultants, especially the currently dominant sector of financial services. To maintain their elite status and to
accomplish their work of decision making and control, they require a rari-
fied social and technical environment from which all traces of the local
physical and social context have been meticulously removed by service
and security workers. For the globe-trotting expert to believe him- or herself a culturally neutral technocrat and to act as such, these continuing
erasures must be made invisible by systematically undervaluing them,
both financially and ideologically.

Decisions produced by the elite through this labor process must likewise be overvalued and decontextualized in order to be effective. Abstrac-
tion and quantification enable these to enter the development policy arena

with virtually absolute authority as neutral technical expertise. The decisions can then be insulated from their sometimes unfortunate or contradictory results through another stage of decontextualization. Because abstract principles like the free market are valued more than concrete local results, transnational agents and agencies can rely implicitly on devalued local populations and governments to repress and clear away any embarrassing messes. These groups thus remain an essential part of global spaces, but are cruelly repositioned within them.

Sassen based her analysis on one kind of global space—the central business districts of leading global cities. She draws parallels with free-trade zones and off-shore banking havens in peripheral locations, which are similarly stripped of local or national controls and accountability. The policy regime called structural adjustment provides the material and ideological discipline for establishing such global space in entire developing nations.

The overvaluation of top management functions described by Sassen within the global system reappears within the familiar international dynamics of the development industry now reconstructed as the Bank/Fund policy consensus. This technocratic neoliberal policy process replicates deference to the same global elite: consultant experts, private investors, and commodity buyers and the dismantling of regulations to facilitate the movement of capital along transnational circuits. Official calculations of comparative advantage in tradables treat risks and costs to local producers and consumers as invisible, implicitly devaluing them. Local currency devaluations explicitly lower the value assigned to local costs and benefits, while budget priorities lower the resources available for local needs. Nonelite groups participate in this undervaluation of themselves and others, however unwillingly, by absorbing more than their share of such burdens, thus feeding the corresponding overvaluation of the elite.

The process of devalorization of the local presented rather abstractly by Sassen thus translates quite directly into painfully concrete changes in economic and political constraints in Africa, including Ghana. Budgets for health and education, already inadequate by world standards, shrink further under the pressure of higher priorities placed on debt repayment and investment incentives. Negotiating room with foreign donors and lenders also shrinks when the prestige of universal technical criteria outweighs national and local goals or needs. Starved of resources and legitimacy, local populations see their leverage dwindle for resisting, renegotiating, or even surviving the low position constructed for them within these firmly globalized contexts.

Under such severe constraints, local populations cannot even cooperate with neoliberal reforms as energetically as predicted. In Ghana, for instance, the Structural Adjustment Program supposedly presented new, more accurate incentive structures after 1985 to local and global producers. The predicted rapid supply response, an expansion of investment and employment in sectors enjoying comparative advantage, remains disappointing today. While the defined boundaries of the legal economy did expand under deregulation, embracing much more of the real economy, its size did not. Employment levels shrank sharply in the private formal sector as well as in the public sector. The lack of a social safety net makes complete unemployment hard to sustain, but incomes in the informal sector also dropped sharply. Despite their enviable entrepreneurial skills and drive, the Asante had run short of the material and ideological resources needed to exercise their economic agency effectively. Without the effective ability to move between economic sectors or innovate, the proposed rewards of adjustment only reached those few with access to outside resources, and foreign investment levels have also been disappointing (World Bank and UNDP 1989).

CONTINUITIES IN NEGOTIATION

The need to renegotiate major social relations to adjust to changing economic and political configurations did not in itself shock Asante or contradict major cultural values or assumptions. As many observers note, Asante kinship and marriage relations are already structured as a shifting balance between opposing demands that can never be completely satisfied. Fortes warned, "But it must be remembered that attachment to the maternal home, the pull of conjugal ties, and the desire for independence are all active throughout a woman's and indeed a man's life" (1949:78). Intense negotiations within the lineage arenas so important to inheritance and financial assistance testify to their continued importance.

Because of exceptionally elastic definitions of the content of kin relations, commitment to lineage ties remains strong, even while actual capability to meet specific kinship obligations fluctuates dramatically over time and class divides. Asante still find kinship well worth contesting, because it establishes the right to ask for whatever they will need most desperately in the future and to refuse obligations that have become impossible or useless to meet. Both men and women invoke lineage solidarity for job referrals, school sponsorship, loans, housing, and domestic help, among other urgent needs. Women can claim subsistence support, food farmland, and housing with special legitimacy by arguing these are assets necessary for raising children for the matrilineage. Kumasi market women interviewed in 1995 were well aware of their active participation in historically negotiated changes in kinship and marriage relations. Their husbands and sons participate in the full range of blue- and white-collar occupations found in this large city, whose falling wages and incomes therefore impact the family budget very directly (Clark 1994). Both men and women feel keenly the need to accommodate changing economic constraints and opportunities as shrewdly and strategically as they can.

These older women traders had already adjusted during their lifetimes to a dramatic shift in the balance of payments between husband and wife. For urban Asante, the hallmark of marriage (even without the performance of customary or church rites) is the exchange of the man's daily or weekly "chop money" used to buy food for the woman's cooking and for other domestic services. In rural areas, the woman would also provide much of the food from her own farm. The man pays for his children's school fees, medical bills, and other expenses directly, as a father, and should do so whether the marriage continues or not.

Through the 1960s, wives clearly expected their chop money to cover the family's entire food needs and, with careful management, to provide cash savings. These funds could be used at the wife's discretion for increasing her trading capital, for small family emergencies, for clothes that enhanced her personal status or for helping her own relatives. One Kumasi trader who had been a policeman's wife explained to me in 1994 their finances when she first married him, around 1940: "He gives you two shillings, . . . and we come to cook it. It is enough for us. Sometimes, I even get a penny as a profit. The pennies, too, I save them, and after some time it becomes an amount which can buy something. But today, it is not like that."

By the late 1970s, Asante men and women could still recite the ideal standards of what a husband and father should pay for, but economic crisis had already transformed the support levels they expected and accepted. Wives no longer hoped to accumulate capital or buy head scarves from their chop money; with a good husband, at least they might save from their own earnings. They struggled to keep their business capital separate from subsistence, although they were quite willing to spend business income on daily expenses or school fees. The husband should pay enough to cover his own food, and for some of the children's expenses, but this Kumasi trader explained how a husband's income level should also be taken into consideration: "My husband is a government worker, and as for the government worker, how much is his pay? When the month ends, there are a lot of expenses. . . . Today, even if the man looks after the child all the time, you, the woman, will rather see that you get more tired than him." If the woman is understanding about his limited income, the man should also respect her need to devote time to earning money, and scale back his expectations for domestic services. The ensuing negotiations may be amicable, but may also lead to bitter mutual recriminations. These budget pressures only intensified during the 1980s and 1990s, as wages and incomes stagnated and prices continued to rise.

By the 1990s, parallel shifts were looming in relations between mothers and their adult children. Asante mothers consider their children the natural focus of their energies, and the future foundation for their own autonomy in late middle age. By investing as heavily as possible in their older children's careers, mothers could once rely on older children to assist their younger siblings financially, allowing the mother to move securely into active family and community leadership and eventually into frail old age. This model cycle assumes that both boys and girls will become financially independent by their late teens or early twenties, in time to support their own children. In the late 1970s, these expectations were still realistic. Able-bodied men and women of good character could still start work without significant capital and earn enough to feed a family, even if they could no longer build up substantial enterprises starting at the bottom, as their mothers had, or build a house.

It had become increasingly difficult for young people to establish themselves as autonomous breadwinners, with the personal incomes necessary to function normally as Asante adults in lineage and marriage relations. One elderly trader described how her hopes of support from her adult children had been disappointed: "None of these children have got any work to do which will bring comfort into my life. . . . All the trouble comes back to fall on the grandmother." Structural adjustment cutbacks in public sector employment and lending, intended to ensure wage restraint, demand restraint and credit restraint, lowered capital availability in informal trading while forcing new unemployed competitors into trading. Only those few mothers who had managed to educate their children through university level and placed them in the managerial ranks benefited from the new money flowing through international linkages.

Elderly women were interviewed who had themselves started out as capital-poor young women, but in an economy where they felt free to choose from a wide range of trading strategies and commodities and could build up substantial businesses using supplier credit and other forms of social capital. They see their children and grandchildren, both male and female, as much more tightly constrained because the same entry-level work has higher capital requirements and smaller profit margins today. If a young hawker, for example, cannot build up a more stable enterprise than hawking to support her future children, she faces a lifetime on the edge, economically and socially vulnerable. Supplier credits have disappeared from many city market locations where they had previously been common, just when massive inflation and devaluation raised capital requirements sharply. As one Kumasi mother said in 1995, "If the money is not there, then you get tired for nothing. . . . When you are going to find work for a child, or you want a child to work, there should be money. I don't have it, too." These older traders faced a severely rising capital and income needs for child sponsorship and for keeping their businesses viable. The same austerity policies, meanwhile, increased the reproductive burden for old and young alike, both in financial and labor terms, as costs of education, medical care, rent, water, and electricity escalated out of reach. They see none of the younger generation positioned to take over their role when they inevitably succumb to age and illness. One still vigorous Kumasi trader remarked on the pressures she felt:

Now I imagine that I am fifty years old. My children and grandchildren may be twenty-five now, and all of them depend on me. . . . And look at these people, about eight or ten of them sleep with us in one room, because of the difficulties. And I got a small room somewhere to rent it for some of them who are in it now. The oldest one, on top of all these, has been given

a room by my mother, since she has a house in this town. My mother's
children, too, we are four. She cannot give rooms to my children only, and
it will not be possible to share them for all our children. So what shall we
do now?

These same individuals have witnessed and enthusiastically participated
in a dramatic series of social transformations, in family roles among other
cultural arenas, and could discuss the pros and cons of those changes at
length. They were reporting current prospects for change in very different
terms, suggesting that a difference in degree has crossed over into a quan-
tum difference. Without any visible means of providing a viable subsistence base, their direct descendants cannot take over a recognizable Asante
adult position as autonomous agents. Their social reproduction remains
incomplete, not because of the degree of sociocultural transformation they
predict, but because they cannot see how to transfer responsibility for conducting this transformation to a new generation. It is this threatened dis-
continuity in the process of social negotiation and renegotiation, rather
than changes in the predominant aggregate results of individual negotiations, that threatens cultural sustainability.

CONCLUSION

This line of analysis takes even more seriously than usual the insight that
cultural processes involve constant contestation and reproduction. It is
not enough simply to acknowledge that every social relation is negotiated,
but to recognize real historical differences in the negotiating capability of
specific actors. The policy changes comprising structural adjustment represent significant alterations in the distribution of these capacities. Market
women are most aware of the material aspects of disempowerment, such
as the lack of food, shelter, and money that prevents them from taking
proper care of their families. These shortfalls mean not only physical suf-
fering for many, but social crisis for even more, who cannot reproduce the
personal agency central to their own family values.

These consequences link the ethereal realms of globalized finance very
directly to the concrete dilemmas facing the imagined unwed mother lying
awake on her grandmother's bedroom floor. Macrolevel budget priorities
reinforce the conditions that so harshly limit the range of individual
choice in poor communities. Macrolevel neoliberal ideological changes

delegitimize serious attention to the needs and interests of these communities. The carefully defined national arenas of financial negotiation include international agencies as stakeholders and enforcers, while excluding participation by and accountability to local populations. This exclusion not only directly reduces their collective negotiating positions but prevents them from effectively moderating those same budget priorities that are undermining their individual positions.

Just as genocide and environmental catastrophe threaten the physical reproduction of human societies, the threats to cultural reproduction posed by outpacing the capacity for negotiation and reconciliation of cultural changes risks a collapse of the system of meaning—a kind of cultural bankruptcy with serious economic and ethical consequences. In Ghana, the obsession with immigration overseas and the widespread acceptance of apocalyptic Christian beliefs has spread widely throughout lower- and middle-class society. Substantial numbers of the approximately seventy market traders interviewed in 1995 placed their hopes for the future in sending a child overseas or awaiting the end of the world. Both strategies encode an implicit despair of the economic and moral potential of contemporary national life.

Such economic despair has historically created conditions of ideological volatility and vulnerability to leaders who promise extreme solutions, for example in 1930s Germany. Today, racist and xenophobic movements such as Islamic fundamentalism, the Christian Right, and welfare reform often emerge from popular reaction against expert-led modernization programs and global media hegemony, whose fruits are neither economic satisfaction or cultural meaning. In the United States, France, Yugoslavia, Sudan, or Rwanda, the fastest shortcuts to revalorizing local cultural ideals and local accountability run through an even sharper devalorization of the closest adjacent group. Already weakened, such neighbors make a more realistic immediate target for attacks than the relatively unapproachable international elite. Ironically and tragically, these communalist attacks only echo the globalist devalorization of women, minorities, and immigrants within their inflammatory rhetoric and their brutal victimization tactics. Many of these backlash movements are nationalistic in name but transnational in organization, sparking violent repression in many parts of the world that has serious consequences for economic progress by any standards.

Recent dynamics in Asante family values show that a fierce pride in cultural identity can be rooted in the continuing capacity for cultural innovation as firmly as in myths of cultural superiority or of unchanging replication of the past. So far, this has prevented the occasional outbreaks of xenophobia among Asante from taking root to produce either ultranationalism or civil war, as experienced in nearby Liberia or distant Serbia, to mention only two examples. Asante bend every effort, not to preserve the past unchanged, but to survive the future as someone they can recognize as Asante. They count on a future they cannot count on, in which their continuing ability to improvise and renegotiate will be their best security. They value and nurture the skills and attitudes related to negotiation, which they continue to deploy with mastery and desperation in the face of unprecedented challenges today. Still, fundamentalist Christian and Islamic movements, both of which have been associated with political and cultural repression elsewhere in the world, have noticeably gained in strength in Ghana. The popularity of apocalyptic explanations of current hardships had extended to members of mainstream international denominations participating in my 1995 interviews.

Not only the amount of change, but the process of change may be critical indicators for monitoring the cultural sustainability of development trends, whether these changes are planned or unintended. Sustaining human cultures as systems of meaning requires preserving the continuity of the negotiation of change, by respecting and protecting the time, material resources and ideological space needed to participate meaningfully in the historical negotiation of significant changes involving them. McMillan (1995) documents the lengths to which Burkinabe farmers went to preserve their social assets of lineage and locality relations even when official policies in a resettlement project were designed specifically to disrupt them. Recent discussions by Berry (1993) of investment in social networks as a kind of accumulation of the means of negotiation and by Guyer (1996) of long-standing African traditions of invention suggest that such attachment to process rather than result may be more widespread than previously suspected.

Development strategies that aim to take local priorities seriously need to value these social and cultural assets as highly as the standardized universal and statistical measures like growth in yields per acre or the GNP. When deprived of the social means of negotiating or even meaningfully digesting the drastic changes they are living through, peoples threatened with cultural bankruptcy have demonstrated their willingness to take destructive and even catastrophic measures to reinstate their cultural agency. Development initiatives must therefore incorporate locally meaningful modalities of participation not only for equity reasons, but to provide a framework for renewing the cultural resources on which the long-term sustainability of local economies, communities, and ultimately ecologies depends.

REFERENCES

Berry, Sara
1993 No Condition Is Permanent. Madison: University of Wisconsin Press.

Cernea, Michael, ed.
1991 Putting People First: Sociological Variables in Rural Development. Washington, DC: World Bank.

Clark, Gracia
1994 Onions Are My Husband. Chicago: University of Chicago Press.

Escobar, Arturo
1995 Encountering Development. Princeton, NJ: Princeton University Press.

Ferguson, James
1994 The Anti-Politics Machine. Minneapolis: University of Minnesota Press.

Fortes, Meyer
1949 Time and Social Structure: An Ashanti Case Study. *In* Social Structure. Meyer Fortes, ed. Pp. 54–84. Oxford: Clarendon Press.

Guyer, Jane
1996 Traditions of Invention in Equatorial Africa. African Studies Review 39(3):1–28.

Korten, David
1995 When Corporations Rule the World. London: Earthscan.

Kottak, Conrad
1991 When People Don't Come First: Some Sociological Lessons from Completed Projects. *In* Putting People First: Sociological Variables in Rural Development. Michael Cernea, ed. Pp. 431–464. Washington, DC: World Bank.

McMillan, Della
    1995 Sahel Visions: Planned Settlement and River Blindness Control in Bur-
    kina Faso. Tucson: University of Arizona.

Sassen, Saskia
    1991 The Global City. Princeton, NJ: Princeton University Press.
    1998 Globalization and Its Discontents. New York: New Press.

UNICEF
    1987 Adjustment with a Human Face. New York: Oxford University Press.

World Bank and UNDP
    1989 Africa's Adjustment and Growth in the 1980s. Washington, DC: World
    Bank.

8

An Analysis of Risk Perceptions: Understanding Beneficiaries' Concerns in Sustainable Development Activities

Elizabeth T. Kennedy

Communities throughout the world seek to reconcile environmental conservation with development, yet a balance has not been achieved because the needs of local peoples, one of the pivotal issues for viable conservation efforts, are not being met (Castilleja et al. 1993; ECLAC 1991). People living near protected areas often reside on marginal lands commonly referred to as buffer zones.

Buffer zones are strips of land that surround national parks, reserves, and protected areas. They are intended to function as transitional areas between developed and protected areas (Miller and Lanou 1995). Buffer zones, in almost all cases, display various degrees of ecological deterioration that threaten the long-term sustainability of the core protected areas. Understanding the rationale for land use in buffer zones and exploring the alternative land-use possibilities in these zones is an important linkage in the conservation/development interaction.

Land-use decisions are influenced by external factors such as policies, prices, and access to resources (Wilson 1996). There are also important internal factors contributing to how we choose to manage land resources;

these include knowledge, priorities, and values. These internal factors shape our risk perceptions, and how we perceive the risks of our actions strongly influences our choice of action. If we wish to modify land-use decisions, we must understand the motivations that shape these decisions. We must better understand how individuals perceive and manage risks within the particular social, economic, and ecological context in which land-use decisions are made. The ultimate long-run solutions to a conservation and development alignment must involve the concerns, values, goals, and risk perceptions of the impacted communities. This chapter reports some preliminary results relating to perceptions of ecological, social, and economic risks from the perspectives of individuals associated with the AMISCONDE project, a conservation and development project implemented in Costa Rica and Panamá.

RISK PERCEPTION, DEVELOPMENT, AND CONSERVATION

Risks are culturally defined, and the perceptions of risks are influenced by socially embedded values and beliefs of a particular culture. How risk is conceptualized, identified, and ultimately measured has significant policy implications. There is a rich literature devoted to this discussion on risk, and the dialogue pivots, to some degree, on the contrast between an objective expert and a subjective pluralistic interpretation of risk.

In risk analysis, risk is often defined by contrasting it to a hazard. A hazard is something harmful or something that contributes to the probability of an undesirable outcome. Risk is the probability of some harm occurring. In these terms, the concept of risk is interpreted as a property of the physical world that can be objectively measured (Bradbury 1989). This constitutes a rationalist view of risk (Hornig 1993), and suggests that there is a correct, value-free measure of risk that can be obtained. An alternative view, referred to as a subjectivist interpretation of risk (Hornig 1993), asserts that multiple factors other than probability of harm influence the conceptualization of risk (Slovic et al. 1979), and that these factors evolve within a social context comprised of priorities and value judgments (e.g., defining the characteristics of an undesirable outcome).

Dake (1992) argues that while individuals perceive risks and have concerns, it is the culture that provides the systems of belief that are then reshaped and internalized by persons, becoming part of their worldview and influencing their interpretation of phenomena. When people reason and make decisions, they make causal connections between actions and outcomes and make value judgments about the possible outcomes by regarding them in a cultural context. In this framework, the processes of identification and measurement of risk are not value free. These activities are social processes that involve people's perceptions in order to frame the questions and determine the goals of risk evaluation (Beck 1992; Wynne 1989). Considering these insights, the analysis of risk is transformed from a singular focus on the probabilities of harm to also include the risk perceiver, and ultimately the different forms of social organization and underlying value systems (Bradbury 1989).

The subjectivist conceptualization of risk is particularly relevant in evaluating the viability and effectiveness of conservation/development projects that are designed to influence decision making and behavior. How one perceives the risks inherent in potential activities influences strategies for managing risk. Ultimately, the risk perceivers act in relation to the way concepts are framed and the constraints they face. Thus, understanding these concepts in context of the social, economic, ecological, and political framework of the risk perceiver explicitly reveals the value-embedded nature of the informant's knowledge of risk. If project implementers do not clearly interpret and address the concerns, values, and risk perceptions of the target project beneficiaries, the success and ultimate viability of the project activities can be substantially impaired.

Conservation and development programs need to be gauged by the values that a society defines for itself regarding issues of health and welfare. This type of reflective evaluation has often been a critical missing link in conservation and development efforts of the past (Castilleja et al. 1993). What a society, community, or individual values is reflected in how risks are perceived. The perception of various risks (social, economic, ecological) influences how one prioritizes and ultimately manages risks. Risk management, then, determines the boundaries of the resulting land-use decisions of an individual, community, or society. In order to influence and change land-use decisions of another agent, one needs to understand intimately how risks are perceived, prioritized, and managed in the target individual, community, or society.

WHAT IS THE AMISCONDE PROJECT?

I examine the structural makeup and functioning of a binational conservation initiative in Costa Rica and Panamá.[1] The McDonald's Corporation and its family of suppliers partnered with Conservation International (CI), academia (initially Clemson University and later Texas A&M University), and local nongovernmental organizations (NGOs) in Costa Rica and Panamá to help protect the La Amistad Biosphere Reserve (LABR) by working with local communities living near or in the buffer zone areas around the reserve. The emphasis of the AMISCONDE Initiative was to establish systems to alleviate the pressure on protected conservation areas by agricultural expansion into the buffer zones of LABR.

The project exclusively worked with small-scale farmers. These farmers produce for markets. However, they have limited access to direct markets and sell through cooperatives in Costa Rica and intermediaries (generally medium-size or large-scale farmers) in Panamá. Providing viable, long-term economic opportunities for people farming marginal lands that do not further degrade fragile ecosystems is critical to both the socioeconomic well-being of the country and to the people farming these lands. The AMISCONDE project serves as a potential model for addressing the socioeconomic needs of communities through focusing on the ecological sustainability of farming practices to improve long-term viability of agricultural activities on marginal lands.

Geographical Location and Biophysical Environment

The general area of focus in this study is the LABR of Costa Rica and Panamá (see figure 8.1). LABR extends over 1,000,000 hectares and comprises the largest functioning, binational conservation complex in Latin America. The core area of LABR is a 667,000-hectare binational conservation area linking Costa Rica and Panamá. La Amistad contains extensive undisturbed forest, including the largest tracts of cloud forest remaining in Central America (Conservation International 1998). Threats to the reserve include forest fires and encroachment of agriculture at the park's edges (Conservation International 1998).

The AMISCONDE Initiative selected two pilot watersheds and associated communities that represented typical conditions of LABR buffer zone communities, one in Costa Rica and one in Panamá (figure 8.1). Typical characteristics of buffer zone communities include accelerated degrada-

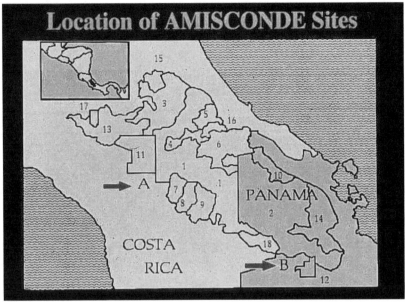

FIGURE 8.1
La Amistad Biosphere Reserve spans the border between Costa Rica and Panama. The numbered areas are the units of the Biosphere Reserve. The two larger units are the Costa Rican and Panamanian sides of La Amistad National Park, and the small parks are Chirripo in Costa Rica and Volcán Barú in Panama. The AMISCONDE project sites are indicated letters. The letter A stands for the San Jeronimo project site, and B stands for the Cerro Punta site. Modified from Lacher et al. (1995).

tion of land resources and susceptibility to agriculturally caused environmental problems such as soil erosion, agrochemical contamination, and forest fires (ANCON 1992; Calvo-Alvarado et al. 1992.

The Costa Rica communities are in the San Jeronimo-Zapotal area within the San Rafael River watershed, on the Pacific slopes of LABR's buffer zone in southern Costa Rica. The project area is about 6,000 hectares and is located 175 kilometers southwest of the capital city of San José. The estimated population of the project area is 2,500. The primary source of income in the area is agriculture. The cash crop is coffee, with some subsistence horticulture production. There is no mechanized production in the area, which was first settled in the 1930s. The average level of education is primary school. The average family size is five members. The average annual income is less than US$1,500. The community is not extremely

stratified in terms of landholdings or wealth. Few producers have legal title
to land, but the project has been working to correct this now that the community members are running the project. Average farm size is between
two and five hectares.

The Panamá communities are in the Cerro Punta area located on the
upper Rio Chiriquí watershed, within the buffer zone of the future LABR
in western Panamá. This region of Panamá is located near the intersection
of the borders of La Amistad International Park and Volcán Barú National
Park. Cerro Punta is the most important agricultural region in Panamá
(ANCON 1992). The Panamá AMISCONDE project area comprises
approximately 8,000 hectares and its population is estimated at 5,600 people. The primary source of income is agriculture. High agricultural production, primarily horticulture, produces 85 percent of the produce for
the nation (Lacher et al. 1995). Production is almost exclusively for market purposes and little is for personal consumption. The larger producers
in the area use mechanized production practices. History of land use and
settlement of the area is about fifty to sixty years. There is high incidence
of chemical pesticide, fertilizer, and herbicide use. The average level of
education is primary school. The average annual income varies, but for
project participants it is probably less than US$1,500. The community is
more stratified than the one in Costa Rica in terms of landholdings and
wealth. The majority of producers have legal title to their land. The average farm size of participating farmers during the five years was between
one-half and two hectares. This average reflects the mean for the small
producers in the region rather than a mean for landholdings in the region.

History of the Project

The inception of AMISCONDE transpired in early 1991, when CI coor-
dinated with a representative from the McDonald's Corporation to
develop a project to address forest fires, agrochemical use, soil erosion,
deforestation, and encroachment into the core area of La Amistad Reserve.
The principal goal of the initiative was to sponsor pilot projects in Costa
Rica and Panamá that would quantitatively demonstrate that degraded
areas could be rehabilitated and people's needs could be merged with conservation objectives. These projects would produce a positive change in
the lives of local peoples while guaranteeing the integrity of natural
resources. The unique partnership between CI and McDonald's Corpora-

tion was expanded to include academia to strengthen the research opportunities within the initiative. The project was funded by McDonald's Corporation and was implemented by CI and in-country NGOs [Centro Científico Tropical in Costa Rica and initially Asociación Nacional para la Conservación (ANCON) and later the Fundación para el Desarrollo Sostenible de Panamá in Panamá].

The proposed project outlined a plan for the conservation of watersheds and the provision of environmental education in the buffer zone of the reserve. At the project community sites, AMISCONDE established a revolving credit fund, started tree nurseries, attempted to diversify crops and establish market opportunities, introduced technologies to reduce soil erosion, provided technical training, enhanced reforestation, promoted environmental education in the communities, and attempted to strengthen the communities' abilities to manage their natural resources.

The time frame for technical and financial assistance was five years, 1992–1997. Technical assistance, financial support, and subsidies were considered the major inputs into the project. All subsidies and external/foreign technical expertise terminated in December 1997. The AMISCONDE project has completed the transition phase, and technical and financial responsibility for future endeavors is now under management of the beneficiary communities. Project documents and preliminary reports suggest that gains have been achieved with respect to the use of soil conservation techniques, and alternative corps, organic fertilizers, integrated pest management, and organic production processes have been adopted by some, but not all, farmers at both sites (Borel 1998; Kennedy et al. 1998). Both project sites are also providing some technical expertise and assisting in the transfer of the AMISCONDE approach to additional surrounding communities in La Amistad buffer zone.

METHODS

The use of an ethnographic face-to-face open interview process best allowed for the capture of the social construction of risk associated with the practice of agriculture from the perspective of the individuals associated with the AMISCONDE project. Eighty-two interviews were conducted during the course of the study (see table 8.1), including five initial informant (interviewee) categories; agriculturists (n = 29), technicians (n = 6), government (n = 5), teachers (n = 2), and executive (n = 5). Inter-

Table 8.1   Interview Data from Project Participants in Costa Rica and Panama, 1996–1998

Informant Category[a]	Costa Rica			Panama			Category TOTAL
	1996	1997	1998	1996	1997	1998	
Agriculturists	7	5	12	5	9	9	47
		(3)[b]	(1) ((3))[c]		(5)	(1) ((5))	[29 unique][d]
							(10) ((8))
Technicians	1	6	2	2	6	6	23
		(1)	(1) ((1))		(1)	(2) ((1))	[16 unique]
							(5) ((2))
Government	0	3	1	0	1	0	5
Teachers	0	1	0	0	0	1	2
Executive	—	—	—	—	—	—	5
Annual Total	8	15	15	7	16	16	*Grand*
		(4)	(2) ((4))		(6)	(3) ((6))	*TOTAL*
							82
							[57 unique]
							(15) ((10))

[a]Numbers are separated into informant categories of agriculturists from the project communities. (Agriculturists, includes project participants and nonparticipants), technicians employed by the project (Technicians), government employees with experience or knowledge of the project (Government), primary school teachers from participating community schools (Teachers), and the executive committee members (Executive).
[b]Number in parentheses represents the number of individuals interviewed from the previous period. In the final column, this signifies the number of informants who were interviewed twice during the course of the study.
[c]Number in double parentheses represents the number of individuals interviewed during each of the three field period.
[d]Number in brackets represents the number of unique individuals interviewed during the three field periods.

views with individuals in Costa Rica and Panamá were conducted in three phases: 31 May–21 June 1996; 22 October 1997–12 January 1998; 2 July–1 September 1998. Informants from the executive category were interviewed at convenient times during the course of the study.

The average time span for each interview was three hours (the range was from forty-five minutes to six and one-half hours). The interview process relied on key questions to guide the interview that encouraged informants to reveal their perceptions with a minimum of outside direction. Questions were framed so that informants discussed issues and risk perceptions at the present time and in reference to the current situation. Investigators deliberately did not constrain the concept of risk, to allow definitions of risk to be revealed from the informants' perspective. The goal of the interview was to make the informants' reality transparent so that it could clearly be communicated to someone outside the informants' culture in such a manner that the constraints and related perceptions of risk of the informant group could be understood. Interviews with the agriculturist category generally included a tour of the farm with the informants to gain insights on how the informants viewed the land and their related reasoning for the various farming practices used on the property.

All interviews were conducted with written consent of the informants and were conducted during times identified as convenient by the informants. Some interviews with key informants were conducted while the informant was working on his or her land. Whenever possible, interviews were audiotape-recorded (with written consent of the informant).

RESULTS

The primary risk-related concerns of the five informant categories appear to be substantially different. The concept of risk in these presented results is not constrained by any particular time frame and is an emic interpretation of the frustrations, problems, and concerns of the informant categories. First, a brief summary of perceptions is provided for each of the five informant categories. This is followed with a more detailed description of agriculturists' views and concerns.

Teachers

Local primary school teachers (n = 2) were exclusively concerned with the loss of traditional culture and the socioeconomic pressures families of the buffer zone face in trying to raise living standards. Both teachers discussed the lack of recreational, employment, and educational opportunities in the communities. These concerns were revealed in their discussions of a lack of opportunities for children to pursue education beyond primary school. Both project site teachers cited three reasons for this lack of opportunity: (1) the families needed child labor on farms, (2) families cannot pay for the books, clothes, transportation, and meals necessary to attend secondary school, and (3) applications for scholarships were difficult to complete, especially when the competition for such scholarships was high. This informant category sensed a change in community life during the past twenty years, mentioning increased vagrancy, alcohol and drug use, and the frequent emigration from the area for seasonal wage-labor opportunities. The teachers said that these factors weaken the family and community ties and transferred important labor and financial resources to areas outside of the communities.

Government Workers

Interviews from the government informant category (n = 5) indicated that they focus on a mixture of the ecological and social risks in the project communities. Legal concerns were primary. These informants expressed concerns about lack of knowledge of park boundaries, lack of understanding reasons for the park, and a general lack of environmental consciousness of communities in the buffer zone. Lack of technical expertise was a major concern, as was lack of physical infrastructural resources. Drug cultivation within the park boundaries in conjunction with drug and alcohol use in the communities were also relevant concerns of this informant category. Finally, many members of this group said that small agriculturists have no access to credit and that transition to some alternative cultivation practices can be financially difficult.

Executives

The executive informant category (n = 5) was primarily focused on the ecological risks in the buffer zone communities. A common concept discussed by these informants was the need to stabilize the farming frontier and establish stronger conservation measures. The focus of risk identification was on soil loss, agrochemical use, deforestation, and damage to LABR. Several socioeconomic issues (particularly lack of environmental education and physical and social infrastructure in the project communities) were also raised during the interviews, but not with the same frequency and duration as ecological concerns.

Technicians

The technician informant category (n = 6) demonstrated differences between the two countries. Overall, this category was more concerned with socioeconomic issues as they relate to ecological risks in the buffer zone communities. Technicians disagreed about what the critical ecological risk focus was at the two project sites, and there was a marked difference between the two sites as to what the socioeconomic factors contributing to various risks were. This is not necessarily unexpected because the two sites are culturally, politically, and biophysically distinct.

In Costa Rica, the focus was on alternative crops, fire control, and reforestation. Concerns of the technicians gravitated toward lack of socioeconomic means to carry out successfully the introduced cultivation alternatives and environmental protection techniques. These concerns included lack of leadership and unity within the communities, lack of access to financial credit or other financial resources, no land titles, poor roads, and a lack of technical expertise. In Panamá, the technicians were more focused on protection of the park as a distinct goal and were concerned with soil conservation and inappropriate agrochemical use. Many of the contributing socioeconomic factors were similar, including concerns regarding access to credit and land titles, transportation, and leadership. Issues that did not arise in Costa Rica, though, help demonstrate some of the cultural-political differences between the two sites. Some examples include volatility of the market for cultivated crops, lack of cooperation and planning to address market volatility, and an overall lack of financial and social stability in the communities.

Agriculturists

The concerns of the agriculturist informant category (n = 29) closely resembled those of the technician category, but with a slightly stronger emphasis on socioeconomic factors. This group of informants is, of course, primarily concerned with making a living and feeding their families through land use in the buffer zone. Their economic and social well-being is most critical to them. Their concerns, however, did not suggest that this informant group did not make the connections to the ecological ramifications of their land-use decisions.

In Costa Rica, where the primary crop is exclusively a cash crop or commodity and not a food crop (monoculture of coffee), many discussed a noticeable increase in fauna and flora with greater crop diversity and less agrochemical use. Recognition of these relationships was a source of motivation to do more conservation in some cases. Many Costa Ricans were also concerned about the state of the soil, although several farmers remained unwilling to invest the time and other necessary resources to cultivate using terraces or to install live barriers as soil conservation measures. In Panamá, many farmers would not allow their children to be in the fields or eat the cultivated crops in their households due to their knowledge of agrochemical contamination. Many Panamanian farmers commented on an overall lack of respect for the environment, but also felt relatively powerless to make the necessary changes in cultivation practices due to their resource constraints (financial, technical, and labor).

Differences between Two Project Sites

Although Costa Ricans stated that lack of community unity was a hazard contributing to ecological risks, the Costa Rican communities have a stronger history of cooperation and mutual support than Panamá. In Panamá, the flat, more fertile land was settled by immigrants of European descent during the 1940s; the individuals working the steep slope areas are more recent immigrants (1960s) and are of mestizo descent. In addition, a major labor force in Panamá is a group of indigenous Guaymí. The majority of Guaymí are transient and live in wooden structures provided by their employers, with no running water, electricity, or cooking facilities except a fire pit. The Guaymí are the most marginalized group in the project site communities. Land/class distinctions such as these contribute to an individualistic rather than cooperative approach to production in Panamá. For example, when the price of carrots is high, everyone plants carrots. This is individualistically rational, but as the increased supply of carrots causes market price to plummet, few small producers can break even, let alone profit because they already have difficulty merely getting their crops to market. Since there is no history of regional cooperation and planning in planting only the larger producers are able to absorb the new market volatility. As a result, the perceived risks of alternatives to traditional cultivation practices seem insurmountable to many small-scale agriculturists.

The project area historically produced over 80 percent of Panamá's produce for the nation. When Panamá liberalized its agricultural sector in 1994 to join the General Agreement on Tariffs and Trade and the World Trade Organization, farmers were accustomed to a protected market. This region is now struggling to compete in the global market, and many small producers can be considered insecure and ill prepared to make the transition. In many respects, a shift in cultivation techniques imposes grave, short-term economic risks to the small producers in Costa Rica and particularly in Panamá.

Summary of Economic Risks

This preliminary analysis suggests that agriculturists perceive that certain systems of land management introduced by the AMISCONDE project are more economically risky than some of the status-quo systems. The practice of using agrochemical in-puts (herbicides, pesticides, and fertilizers) can be interpreted as insurance in a risky world. Agriculturists who use excess fertilizers and agrochemicals are, in a sense, buying insurance. The objectives of the AMISCONDE project could thus be considered as attempting to develop alternative risk reducing instruments that would substitute for the application of an agrochemical in-put. Some of the alternatives focused on soil retention (cultivation on the contour, terracing, live barriers, and maintaining undergrowth), and others directly addressed agrochemical use (integrated pest management, crop diversification, organic fertilizers, and organic production practices).

Three kinds of economic risk can be interpreted from the concerns of the agriculturists about the use of agrochemicals and their alternatives. There is the risk of innovation, risk of expertise, and commercial risk. Innovation risk is encountered by the first person to try a new technique or set of technology. In this situation, there is no guarantee that it will work on the first agriculturist's land, even though it may have worked in a different region or country. Expertise risk is having insufficient information to know when and/or how effectively to apply agrochemicals or to use an alternative. It is hard to trust a technician with whom you have no history or method of evaluating his or her knowledge. If an agriculturist got results the previous year with a particular application method, why would they be willing to risk their harvest on the expert's knowledge? Finally, the commercial risk of some of the alternatives is a distinct possibility when agriculturists are relying on something as unpredictable as weather and insect population controls that they cannot directly control. Integrated pest management and organic production practices require a more intimate knowledge of fluctuations in natural systems than scheduled agrochemical applications. Accepting integrated pest management, and/or organic production methods removes some artificial controls from the production process, and leaves the agriculturists more economically vulnerable to natural hazards.

In addition, some of the alternative crops introduced at the project sites were not traditional. This created several marketing concerns. In Costa Rica, agriculturists rely on cooperatives to collect and sell their coffee. No such cooperatives exist for introduced citrus crops. A major concern of the project participants, who received loans to plant citrus, is whether they will be able to market their produce. Transportation of crops from the fields is primarily by people and horse. Without a cooperative to collect the crop from the *recibidores* (collection stations), there are few methods of getting the crop to market. Agriculturists rent vehicle use from the few who own trucks in the area, or they must transport the citrus by bus, both somewhat costly options. In Panamá, agriculturists are not familiar with introduced crop alternatives, a few of which are delicate commodities (endive and various types of berries). Packaging and transporting such fragile products can be substantial hindrances in commercialization of the crops, especially if markets are not local and available transportation options are not refrigerated. In some cases, agriculturists sought recipes and suggestions of how to eat and cook the introduced alternative crops. There was no history of using these crops in their diets, and some were unsure how to prepare them in their home meals, and/or how to suggest their use to potential customers.

Additional Technique to Determine Risks Associated with Cultivation in LABR Buffer Zone Communities

With the agriculturist informant category, a series of specific questions was developed for the third phase of interviews to help explore how this group classified and prioritized the risks of cultivation in LABR buffer zone. The questions were presented to the informant at an appropriate point in the interview process. Appropriate points were determined by a logical juncture where the informant had already brought up related issues in discussion of their daily activities on their farms or in relation to discussion of the AMISCONDE project. Four of those questions will be briefly discussed.

The first three questions were: (1) In your opinion, what are the risks to LABR? (2) What is your most important environmental concern? and (3) What is the most important concern you have in your daily life? The order and placement of these questions during the course of the interview were dependent on the informant and thus were not controlled from interview to interview. In general, however, these questions and similar types of questions were clustered in the middle of the interview process. Preliminary interpretations of each question are discussed separately.

Question 1: In Your Opinion, What Are the Risks to LABR?

Agriculturists from both project sites identified hunting and cultivation inside the park boundaries as risks to LABR. Costa Ricans also identified fire, economic pressure on the poor, removal of plants from the park, and the purchase of land by individuals from outside countries as additional risks. Additional risks presented by Panamanians included weak and/or corrupt law enforcement that allowed access to the park resources (e.g., trees and land for cultivation) by wealthy individuals. The project site area in Panamá has substantial tourism potential, and ownership of land in this area may potentially be quite lucrative in the near future. Where land ownership is not clear and legally documented, wealthy individuals who demonstrate a history of land use may contest areas of the park core.

Question 2: What Is Your Most Important Environmental Concern?

Informants from both sites brought forward water quality, soil conservation, deforestation, and agrochemical contamination (both of the soil and of people and wildlife) as their major environmental concerns. Costa Ricans also mentioned climate change and a loss of biological and ecological integrity as major concerns. One informant discussed at length how the forested areas of the tropics were the lungs of the planet that need to be protected and respected as a global resource.

Question 3: What Is the Most Important Concern You Have in Your Daily Life?

Informants from both project sites stated that their primary concerns were about economic sustainability, water quality and health, and the lack of opportunities for the youth in the communities. Costa Ricans also identified the loss of Tico culture, need for good roads, the recent vagrancy of the youth in the communities, lack of employment opportunities in the country, and a loss of spirit and drive in the individuals living in the project area. In Panamá, other issues discussed included the newly liberalized market, the poor economic situation of the agricultural sector as a whole due to the lack of dedication of the government to this sector, and the increasing incidence of alcoholism and the number of new taverns in the communities.

Prioritizing Concerns of the Agriculturists

The above three questions provide insight into how the agriculturists informant category separates, and to some degree, prioritizes social, economic, and ecological risks associated with living and cultivating crops in the buffer zone area of LABR. Another query technique used during the third phase of interviews allowed additional definition of how agriculturists prioritize their concerns. Using information from the previous two interview phases, a list of concerns was compiled and informants were asked to identify if the concern was either a very important, somewhat important, or not important concern in their daily lives. The distribution and frequency results for three selected concerns demonstrate the differences in perception both between and within the project sites with regard to their areas of concern.

Figure 8.2 represents the social variable "education of children." Prioritization for this variable differs between the two project sites. It appears to be somewhat less important in Panamá than in Costa Rica; although 50 percent from Panamá do consider education of children very important, 50 percent do not regard this as a high priority. In contrast, 72 percent from Costa Rica regarded it as very important. This differences between the two countries are representative of access to education opportunities. In Costa Rica, only primary education up to sixth grade is available in the

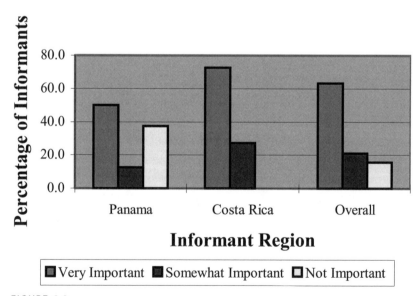

FIGURE 8.2
Frequency distribution for the prioritization of the social variable "education of children" by agriculturists in La Amistad Biosphere Reserve Bufferzone.

communities, and transportation costs are high to attend school outside the immediate communities. In Panamá, however, there is easier and cheaper access to transportation, and as a result, more children complete primary school and attend high school.

The next variable, "prices of seeds and other inputs," was considered an economic variable and is represented in figure 8.3. It was considered very important to all informants from Panamá, while the degree of importance varied in Costa Rica.

The last variable used to explore prioritization of concerns presented here is an ecological variable (figure 8.4), extinction of plants and animals. It represents markedly different prioritization for the two project sites. The majority of Panamanians (62 percent) did not consider this a very important concern in their daily lives, while the majority of Costa Ricans (53 percent) were very concerned about extinction of plants and animals.

CONCLUSION

The goal of this study was to explore the different risk perspectives of individuals associated with the AMISCONDE project. In summary, the above

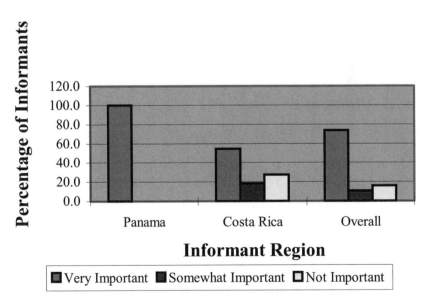

Informant Region

Very Important ■ Somewhat Important □ Not Important

FIGURE 8.3
Frequency distribution of the prioritization of the economic variable "prices of seeds and other inputs" by agriculturists living in La Amistad Biosphere Reserve Bufferzone.

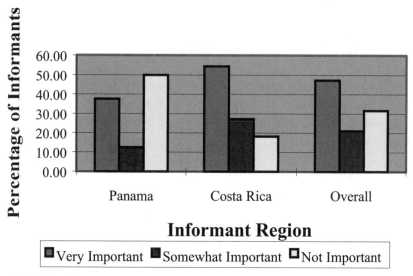

Informant Region

■Very Important ■Somewhat Important □Not Important

FIGURE 8.4
Frequency distribution for the prioritization of the ecological variable "extinction of plants and animals" by agriculturists living in La Amistad Biosphere Reserve Bufferzone.

preliminary analysis of risk perceptions indicates that for individuals associated with the project, there were substantial variations in values and how individuals defined the problems of communities practicing agriculture in the buffer zone of LABR.

In particular, teachers focused on social risks (lack of opportunities, emigration, vagrancy, alcohol/drugs, and a weakening family and community structure). The government focused on legal and economic risks (lack of knowledge and understanding of the park, drug cultivation, and limited credit opportunities of agriculturists living in the buffer zone). Ecological risks were the primary concern of the executive group (stabilization of the farming frontier, soil loss, chemical use, and deforestation). Technicians expressed socioeconomic and institutional concerns that were project specific (leadership, financial resources, lack of infrastructure and expertise). An important insight for the agriculturist group is that they were aware of ecological impacts of various agricultural practices, and that a failure to implement conservation strategies was not because of lack of education, but more strongly related to financial constraints the farmers faced. From the farmer's perspective, the cost-benefit analysis almost always indicated that the long-term benefits of many of the conservation practices, although they would improve long-term productivity and viability of the farm, were overwhelmed by the short-term costs the families faced (e.g., educating children, and increased labor costs). It also appears that there were important site-specific differences in risk perceptions for the two project sites. Agriculturists from the two project sites prioritized ecological, social, and economic variables differently.

The differences in problem definition or risk perception are determined within organizational groups and reflect values inherent to that particular group. These distinct differences in priorities imply critical boundaries of culture and identify perceptions that are largely shared within the groups. The distinctions between these groups' perceptions may create barriers to effective communication and trust between the groups. These distinctions between groups and the potential barriers they may constitute should be acknowledged. The difference between government and agriculturist concerns can impact the success and effectiveness of social, environmental, or economic programs implemented by government institutions. The effectiveness of educators in addressing the needs of communities is also potentially affected by the differences in risk perceptions. The site-specific differences suggest that similar strategies may not be equally effective at the two project sites.

The differences between the project implementers (executive and technician categories) and the agriculturists are most relevant in the evaluation of the AMISCONDE project. The obvious cross-cultural differences of U.S.-Panamá, U.S.–Costa Rica, or Costa Rica–Panamá were addressed by the project in the solicitation of community member input at the project inception and intermittently throughout the project, but the differences in risk perceptions may not have been made explicit. This lack of clearness would have made it difficult for project implementers and project recipients to know the true needs, desires, and objectives of the various stakeholders involved in the overall project execution.

Marsden and Oakley (1991) discuss frustrations in interpreting what is said and establishing trust between project planners and recipients during implementation. Commonly, project recipients, in order to receive project benefits, will say what they expect the donor wants to hear and understand. Project planners have similar self-seeking objectives and come to a project with distinct ideological and theoretical preconceptions. One of the roles of an interpretive evaluation such as this study is to explore the nature of these expectations and preconceptions and to present their possible impacts on the project's viability. Such insight may help us understand the complexities of the development/conservation process and better inform the process of constructing more appropriate strategies for intervention.

The distinctly different risk perceptions among the project implementers and recipients may help explain why only some of the community members at the project sites adopted the introduced conservation practices. Changes in practice are linked to personal perception of the degree of a problem, and risk management is directly related to that measure. If the project implementers (executive and technician categories) did not internalize and directly address the degree of concern held by the agriculturists regarding economic risk, it is conceivable that farmers' interest in the project was substantially diminished. The project implementers were specifically concerned with the ecological risks in the buffer zone communities and directed substantial resources to provide information and alternative land-use techniques that were more ecologically sound. The farmers also expressed ecological conditions as important, but were more concerned with making enough income to cover the needs of their families. The disparity in how farmers and technicians framed important risks suggests that the farmers may not have trusted that project implementers were addressing risk management needs of agriculturists in the participating communities. The agriculturists may have perceived an emphasis on priorities more related to first-world concerns (conservation), resulting in a rejection of the introduced conservation practices.

It is important, however, not to oversimplify the interpretation of perceived risks and their impacts on land-use decisions. An aversion to adopting introduced conservation practices may also be one of the economic survival strategies of the project community members. How a farmer acts to maintain economic viability has ecological implications, and the trade-offs between the two may have more to do with planning horizons than attitudes toward the environment or the AMISCONDE project.

Avoidance of economic risk can take more than one form. For example, one could be reluctant to sacrifice short-term returns for uncertain benefits of conservation practices, or one could accept conservation practices to avoid long-term risks of declining productivity. It is possible that other farmers will adopt some of the introduced conservation practices over time. This is most likely to occur if those agriculturists who adopted conservation practices (they have long-term planning horizons) are more economically successful over time than those who did not adopt the conservation practices (they have short-term planning horizons). A "follow the leader" process may ensue, and an evolutionary change may occur as more agriculturists adopt conservation strategies to become more economically and ecologically sound.

Further investigation and analysis of risk perceptions and land management decisions of agriculturists in the AMISCONDE project communities is necessary to understand more fully the reasons for adopting or not adopting conservation strategies. This study has highlighted some limited understanding of how social, economic, and ecological concerns may compel agriculturists' land-use decisions in the buffer zone communities of LABR. These preliminary findings indicate that economic risks appear to play a more important role than social or ecological risks in explaining agriculturists' land-use decisions. These findings may provide useful insights into how conservation and development projects can address these concerns better to achieve sustainable development objectives.

NOTES

I would like to acknowledge the valuable and constructive editorial comments of Thomas Lacher, Diana Burton, Jeff Cohen, Norbert Dannhaeuser, and Allen Gillespie, and the multiple insights into the social construction of risk provided by Susanna Hornig Priest. I likewise thank Jim Nations at Conservation International, Ray Cesca at McDonald's Corporation, and the AMISCONDE project community members for their time, support, and faith in this research endeavor.

1. The initiative is named AMISCONDE in reference to its objective (La AMIStad CONservation Development).

REFERENCES

Asociación Nacional para la Conservación (ANCON)
    1992 Strategy for the Institutional Development of the La Amistad Biosphere Reserve. Ministry of Natural Resources, Energy and Mines, Ministry of

National Planning and Economic Policy, Organization of American States, and Conservation International. Washington, DC: Conservation International.

Beck, Ulrich
1992 The Politics of Knowledge in the Risk Society. In Risk Society: Towards a New Modernity. U. Beck, ed. Pp. 51–84. London: Sage.

Borel, Roland
1998 Evaluación del período de transición del projecto AMISCONDE y proposiciones para acciones de continuidad. San José, Costa Rica: Conservation International.

Bradbury, Judith
1989 The Policy Implications of Differing Concepts of Risk. Science, Technology, & Human Values 14(4):380–399.

Calvo-Alvarado, Julio
1992 Master Plan: AMISCONDE Costa Rica Project. San José, Costa Rica: Tropical Science Center.

Castilleja, Guillermo, Peter Poole, and Charles Geisler
1993 The Social Challenge of Biodiversity Conservation. GEF Working Paper 1. Washington, DC: Global Environment Facility, United Nations Development Programme, United Nations Environment Programme, and World Bank.

Conservation International
1998 http://www.conservation.org/science/cptc/capbuild/unesco/default.htm. CI-UNESCO Biosphere Reserves Partnership.

Dake, Karl
1992 Myths of Nature: Culture and the Social Construction of Risk. Journal of Social Issues 48(4):21–27.

Economic Commission for Latin America and the Caribbean (ECLAC)
1991 Sustainable Development: Changing Production Patterns, Social Equity and the Environment. Santiago, Chile: United Nations.

Hornig, Susanna
1993 Reading Risk: Public Response to Print Media Accounts of Technological Risk. Public Understanding of Science 2(2):95–105.

Kennedy, Elizabeth, Thomas Lacher, Jr., and Diana Burton
1998 A Socio-Economic Analysis of the Development and Conservation Strategies within the Amistad Conservation and Development Initiative for La

Amistad Biosphere Reserve. Poster presented at the Texas A&M University Women's Faculty Network Conference, College Station, Texas, October.

Lacher, Jr., Thomas, Julio Calvo-Alvarado, Manuel Ramirez Umana, and Jeaneane Maldonado Dammert
1995 Incentivos economicos y de conservacion para el manejo de las zonas de amortiguamiento: La iniciativa AMISCONDE. *In* Abordagens interdiscipli-nares para a conservaco da biodiversidade e dinamica do uso da terra no Novo Mundo; Anais da conferencia international. G. A. B. da Fonseca, M. Schmink, L. P. S. Pinto, and F. Brito, eds. Pp. 315–334. Belo Horizonte, Brazil: Conservation International.

Marsden, David, and Peter Oakley
1991 Future Issues and Perspectives in the Evaluation of Social Development. Community Development Journal 26(4):315–328.

Miller, Kenton, and Steven Lanou
1995. National Biodiversity Planning: Guidelines Based on Early Experiences around the World. Washington, DC: World Resources Institute.

Slovic, P., B. Fischoff, and S. Lichtenstein [Elizabeth Kennedy]
1979 Rating the Risks. Environment 21(3):14–20, 36–39.

Wilson, Geoff A.
1996 Farmer Environmental Attitudes and ESA Participation. Geoforum 27(2):115–131.

Wynne, Brian
1989 Frameworks for Rationality in Risk Management: Towards the Testing of Naïve Sociology. *In* Environmental Threats: Perception, Analysis and Management. J. Brown, ed. Pp. 33–47 London: Belhaven.

9

The Women Left Behind: Potential Effects of Male Migrants' Return on Women's Fertility and Health in Bangladesh

Patricia Lyons Johnson

Bangladesh has been notable for the amounts of development funding donated to the country in an attempt to alleviate the overwhelming poverty and correlated misery that have characterized the nation since its inception in 1972. Most observers would agree that particular initiatives, such as fertility reduction through family planning and mortality reduction through better delivery of health care, particularly to women and children, have been highly successful.

Those same observers would also have to agree, however, that development programs designed to reform the Bangladeshi economy have not succeeded (Shand and Alauddin 1997:3). A major outcome of this failure is the continuing and increasing unemployment or underemployment of large segments of the labor force. One reaction to the economy's inability fully to employ the labor force has been a major movement of individuals through both rural to urban internal migration and international migration (Chaudhury 1978; Hossain and Roopnarine 1992; Mahbub 1985–86; Matin 1986; Osmani 1986). Much of this migration involves males whose wives remain at home. This paper deals with the potentially deleterious effects of these migrants' return on both the fertility and health of these wives who, because of cultural constraints, are unprepared to protect themselves against the possibilities of unwanted pregnancy and/or sexually transmitted diseases. I argue that both Bangladesh's peripheral position in a global economy and women's peripheral position within Bangladeshi society contribute to this problem.

MIGRATION

Migration is not a new phenomenon in Bangladesh. During the nineteenth century, while still part of India, East Bengal sent migrants to the west, particularly to the United Kingdom; the migrants came almost exclusively from the Sylhet area. While such migration continues even today, in the 1970s the major pattern of migration changed radically as Great Britain implemented stricter immigration legislation, while, at the same time, the oil-rich countries of the Middle East needed cheap and primarily low-skilled labor (Osmani 1986:24–26). Although Mahmood (1995:700) notes the presence of Bangladeshi migrants in South Korea, Japan, Taiwan, Hong Kong, Thailand, Malaysia, Singapore, Brunei, the United Kingdom, Germany, Sweden, Italy, the United States, and Canada, since 1971 labor migration has remained focused on the Middle East.

This migration has been characterized by short-term contracts of one or two years, with a much smaller number of three- or four-year contracts. These prosperous destination countries are interested in Bangladeshi migrants not as future citizens, but as temporary workers in low-wage jobs that require little in the way of training and skills. While it is extremely difficult to determine the current numbers of international migrants, the official number of Bangladeshis employed abroad in 1994 was a bit over 186,000; in 1998 it was almost 268,000, an increase over four years of about 44 percent (Bangladesh Bureau of Statistics 1999:179). These are official figures, which "significantly understate total labour outflows" (Athukorala and Wickramasekara 1996:555); they also do not include students, migrants who are not employed, and migrants who illegally reside in foreign countries. Between 1980 and 1990, almost 297,000 Bangladeshis were recorded as entering the Gulf States as migrants; by the early 1990s, the figure had risen to almost 508,000 (Massey et al. 1998:139).

Accurately assessing the number of Bangladeshi international migrants is extremely difficult, but it is even more problematic to determine the number of people who have migrated internally, since people move freely about the country. However, the magnitude of internal movement may be gauged by the effect on urban populations of rural-urban migration, the most important type of internal migration. In 1990, the population of Dhaka, the capital and a primary target area for rural migrants, was 6.2 million; the projected population by 2015 is 19.5 million (Consultative Group on International Agricultural Research 2000). While part of this increase will be due to the fertility of current residents, the "most important contributor to increased urban population has been rural-urban migration" (Mahmood 1995:710).

It is equally difficult to assess return flows of migrants, an important aspect of this paper, since records on returns are not kept either for internal or international migration. In some sense, it may not be reasonable to discuss return flows for internal migrants since in many cases, migrants return quite regularly as visitors to their home areas although they continue to live and work elsewhere. This oscillating or commuter migration is an aspect of return I will discuss below. With respect to international migrants, the brevity of labor contracts suggests a considerable return flow and Osmani (1986:34) has calculated, for a three-year period, return flows ranging between 43 and 69 percent.

I can provide some informal information from my own experience in Matlab, a rural area, where I conducted fieldwork for a year in 1998. Although my work had no direct connection with migration, one criterion for inclusion in my sample was that husband and wife be cohabiting. In the three largest villages of the six from which the research sample was to be drawn, there were 1,751 married women identified as potential members of the sample. However, 38 percent of these women had nonresident husbands who had migrated, either internally or internationally to pursue labor opportunities.

Once the sample was selected from those women who met all the criteria, including a resident husband, the situation became more complicated, but also more informative. Over the course of the project, a sizable number of women who had not been included in the sample subsequently asked to be included because their husbands had since returned. Conversely, many women who had been included in the sample had to be replaced because, between the drawing of the sample and the actual interview, their husbands had left. The lesson provided by this situation is that migration has become widespread and, even more important, that the status of "migrant" can be extremely fluid. It is precisely this fluidity, the unpredictability of male migrants' returning that bears on the questions this paper addresses: the fertility and health consequences for their wives when these men return.

FERTILITY

Bangladesh has experienced remarkable change in fertility over the past twenty-five years. In 1975, the country's total fertility rate (TFR) was 6.3 (Mitra et al. 1995:27). That meant that the average woman could expect to produce 6.3 children if she survived to age fifty, and current age-specific fertility rates continued. By 1994, TFR had declined to 3.4 (Mitra et al. 1995:27), and the international database of the U.S. Census Bureau estimates the 2000 TFR as 2.9 (U.S. Census Bureau 2000). This marked and rapid decline has been attributed to the success of family-planning programs and to the consequent increasing use of modern contraceptives. This is usually expressed in terms of increasing contraceptive prevalence rates (CPR). Those rates are calculated by dividing the number of women using contraception by the number of eligible women, and the number of eligible women is defined as the number of women exposed to the risk of conception because they are in marital unions. If 600 women are using contraception in a population of 1,000 eligible women, we talk about a 60 percent CPR.

Limiting "women at risk for conception" to married women often inspires skepticism. We know that women can be "at risk" and not married. But in Bangladesh, and possibly in many Muslim countries, that is probably a more realistic definition than in many other parts of the world, largely because of the effects of purdah, the seclusion of females that begins as they approach puberty. I focus on the concept of CPR because it is useful in trying to understand the ambiguity inherent in being the nonmigrant wife of a migrant husband.

In general in Bangladesh, entering into or exiting from marriage, through divorce or widowing, is relatively dramatic, and the probability of multiple marital transitions within short periods of time is small. For example, a woman might experience a sudden move from marriage to widowhood or divorce, but it is unlikely that over a short period of time she will move from marriage to widowhood to marriage to widowhood.

Unmarried women are also unlikely to move suddenly from the unmarried to the married state and become wives since marriage usually requires considerable negotiation and preparation. Most wives in Bangladesh are both officially and functionally married; their official status is "married woman" and they fulfill the functions, sexual and otherwise, of married women and are appropriately included in the number of women at risk for conception. Unmarried women, similarly, are officially and functionally unmarried; their official status is unmarried and they perform the functions of unmarried women, which means, among other things, that they are not sexually active and, consequently, not at risk for conception. In both these cases, official and functional statuses coincide.

The wives of migrants, however, occupy a position in which their official status and their functional status are not necessarily consistent at any one time. They are officially married, but functionally unmarried, because, like unmarried women, they are *culturally* not at risk for conception since they cannot properly engage in sexual intercourse because their husbands are not present. But what is probably more important is that, if husbands have migrated over short distances within Bangladesh they can return home regularly, and these women may change their functional married state every week, moving from "unmarried" to "married" in a matter of days. In the case of long-distance migration within Bangladesh or international migration, their functionally unmarried state is likely to be more long term, but their change back to a functionally married state may be equally unpredictable, in that a husband may return without forewarning. Either of these scenarios presents particular problems for these women in terms of family planning.

Using contraceptives implies the likelihood of sexual intercourse, since otherwise, there is no need to contracept. The most popular reversible contraceptives in Bangladesh are pills and injectibles, and both require advance planning if they are to be used effectively. This means that women who want to be protected against the risk of conception when their husbands return need to use these contraceptives during a period when their husbands are away, that is, when they do not have a resident legitimate sexual partner. The cultural assessment of women who use contraceptives when they have no resident legitimate sexual partner is highly negative, since this behavior can be interpreted as suggesting that they have or want to have illegitimate sexual partners. Not surprisingly, this interpretation does not encourage women to use contraceptives while their husbands are away, even if they want to limit family size. The result is that women who wish to avoid pregnancy and whose husbands return from migration are unlikely to be protected against the risk of conception at the time of the husband's return. What is needed in these cases is a contraceptive that can be used expediently and without prior preparation.

SEXUALLY TRANSMITTED DISEASES

A further consideration for these women and their families is becoming painfully clear as we learn more about the relationship between migration and sexually transmitted diseases (STDs). Recent research has brought to light a great deal of information about this relationship and the news is not good. "As people migrate, the rules of sexual behavior change, opening new avenues for sexual encounter, but also exposing the person to enhanced risk of HIV and STDs" (Herdt 1997:3). Caldwell et al. (1997), speaking of the African pandemic, emphasize the special connection: "AIDS probably has a closer relationship to migration than any other infectious disease . . . for migration is a primary cause of behaviour which facilitates the transmission from one person to another" (p. 51).

While any STD can have devastating effects, HIV/AIDS presents an especially serious prognosis and the almost certain mortality connected to this disease in impoverished nations makes efforts at prevention urgent.[1] Numerous studies have connected transmission of HIV to commercial sex (Caldwell et al. 1997; Carael 1997; Singhanetra-Renard 1997), a common behavior throughout the world for migrant men who are unaccompanied by their wives. It seems to me to be a special problem, however, in countries like Bangladesh and the Muslim countries of the Middle East, where families seclude their female members and virtually the only available extramarital heterosexual partners are sex workers. Data on commercial sex in Bangladesh are scanty, but a study done in a brothel in Tangail, about sixty miles north of Dhaka, provides some worrying figures: "Sex workers entertain an average of three clients per day. While 90 percent are aware of diseases like syphilis and gonorrhea, only 3 percent reported using condoms. Sixty percent reported having had an STD (20 percent have an active STD)" (AIDSfocus Newsletter 1997:1). In Bangladesh's major port, Chittagong, a study "found that nearly 42,000 men access sex workers every week . . . with each sex worker averaging between nine and

15 partners per week. . . . Chittagong sex workers rarely request condom use since condoms are known locally as useful only for family planning purposes" (MAP 1999:14). This same report goes on to say,

> In the Asia/Pacific region, sex workers are particularly vulnerable to HIV . . . and represent the most significant core group for transmission to the rest of the population through their clients. The critical factors influencing the rate of spread from sex workers include the number of clients per day and the proportion of men in a society who regularly visit sex workers. In nations with high levels of both of these factors and where sex is not protected by condoms, HIV epidemics spread very rapidly. [MAP 1999:16]

Clearly, when sex workers engage in unprotected intercourse with multiple partners, some of whom "live particularly high-risk lives" (Caldwell et al. 1997:51), the probability of contracting an STD increases both for them and for men who resort to commercial sex.

It seems relevant at this point to discuss what is known about the prevalence of HIV/AIDS in Bangladesh and in the Middle Eastern countries to which so many Bangladeshi migrants travel. Within Bangladesh, data are again few and pertain to small samples.[2] Officially, Bangladesh is listed as a country with low HIV prevalence and with projections over the next three to five years of a slow increase in prevalence. It is worth noting, however, that West Bengal, the contiguous Indian state with which there is considerable border crossing, has an adult HIV prevalence among high-risk populations of over 5 percent (MAP 1999: Annex 1, 13). Moreover, projections for India's future are dire: "With a population approaching one billion . . . three million to five million of its people are infected, and the number of new infections will double every 14 months" (Satcher 1999:1479). As in Bangladesh, figures from the World Health Organization on North Africa and the Middle East are low, with an adult prevalence rate in 1999 of 0.12 percent (World Health Organization 2000).[3] In both Bangladesh and the countries to which men predominantly migrate, it appears, on the basis of limited sampling, that there is not yet an HIV/AIDS epidemic. That means that in Bangladesh aggressive action taken at this point may be able to avert the effects of the predicted Asian pandemic. Indeed, a recent World Bank news release (2001:159/SAS) states "It is still possible for Bangladesh to avoid a nationwide AIDS epidemic [but] without strong, immediate action, Bangladesh runs the risk of experiencing . . . the full-blown epidemic seen in other countries."

We know that there are effective measures to limit the transmission of HIV/AIDS and that successful programs stress the importance of prevention, focusing on education and behavioral change. With respect to education, research concerning knowledge of HIV/AIDS in Bangladesh provides some depressing data. Only 19 percent of ever-married women and 33 percent of currently married men had ever heard of AIDS, and that knowledge is greatly skewed toward the educated and the urban in a country where most people have low levels of education and are rural. Of those who had heard of AIDS, 41 percent of the women and 27 percent of the men believed there was no way to avoid HIV infection.Of those who believed there was a way to avoid the disease, 69 percent of women and 51 percent of men have no idea of how that might be done (Mitra et al. 1995:181). In another survey of girls and boys aged fifteen to nineteen, approximately 95 percent of the girls and just under 90 percent of the boys did not know how to protect themselves against HIV (UNAIDS 2000:43).

Given the lack of knowledge about HIV/AIDS and its transmission and prevention, we now need to think about what the return of male migrants may mean for their wives, not only in terms of fertility, but also in terms of their health and, perhaps, their very lives and the lives of their children. For these women, contraceptives may be able to serve as both protection against unwanted pregnancy and protection against STDs. The ideal contraceptive method, then, for women whose husbands return from migration would be one that addresses both the problem of advance preparation already mentioned, and that also inhibits transmission of such diseases. As with any contraceptive, it would also be desirable that health side effects of its use be minimal or nonexistent. Low cost would also be an advantage. There is an obvious contraceptive method that fulfills all these requirements: condoms. They can be used expediently, they are low cost, their side effects are minimal, and they inhibit the communication of sexually transmitted diseases. In the words of a UNAIDS report, "All the scientific evidence points in the same direction: correct and consistent use of condoms of good quality vastly reduces the likelihood of HIV transmission" (UNAIDS 2000:59–60). The high rates of Bangladeshi male migration suggest that in areas characterized by such migration, development monies would be well used in programs that emphasize, promote, and encourage the use of condoms.

CONTRA-CONDOM ARGUMENTS

There are two major potential objections to policy measures that encourage condom use as an effective measure for the double protection of nonmigrant wives. The first is a practical objection based on the assumption that men will not use condoms. Indeed, based on past usage, this is not an irrational argument. Condom use has increased in Bangladesh, but condoms have never constituted a large percentage of total contraceptive methods, rising from 0.7 percent in 1975 to 3.9 percent in 1996–97 (Mitra et al. 1995:50).[4] This argument is clearly based on the assumption that because Bangladeshi men have not used condoms, they will not use condoms.

Perhaps the best counter to that argument is the history of family planning in Bangladesh. When family-planning programs began in the early 1950s in what was then East Pakistan, no one could have predicted their eventual success. It was assumed that, for a number of reasons, people would not use contraceptives to limit family size. Among those reasons were high infant and childhood mortality; a cultural preference for large families and especially for sons; the economic dependence of the elderly, especially women, on their children and, again, especially on sons; and the labor value of children. Nonetheless, as figure 9.1 shows, these programs enjoyed enormous success and a reasonable question concerns what created that success.

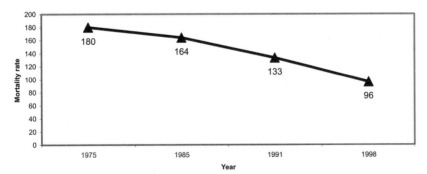

FIGURE 9.1
Decline in total fertility rate in Bangladesh, 1975–2000.

Some important supply-side factors influenced the course of family planning's success. In the early 1970s, the newly independent government of Bangladesh widened contraceptive options while simultaneously providing greater access through what has since been termed "doorstep delivery," in which contraceptives were delivered to women by health or family-planning workers. This delivery strategy was extremely important in a country in which purdah severely limits women's mobility.[5] But there have been important changes on the demand side as well. Infant and childhood mortality have declined dramatically (figure 9.2 and figure 9.3).

In 1979–83, there were 117 infant deaths per 1,000 live births. By 1989–93, that number had dropped to 87 (Mitra et al. 1995:14) and in 1998 to 72.8 (Development Data Group 2001). A similar decline has taken place in under-five mortality, from 180 deaths per 1,000 live births in 1979–83 (Mitra et al. 1995:14) to 96 in 1998 (Development Data Group 2001). What that means, of course, is that people can expect that a greater percentage of their offspring will survive; they no longer have to produce "excess" children in the expectation that some will be lost. The decline in mortality is, of course, welcome, but there are other factors contributing to lower fertility that are not such boons to Bangladesh.

Between 1960 and 1985, landlessness increased dramatically, from a total of 1.5 to 7.75 million landless households, and the percentage of families considered functionally landless (i.e., with 0.5 acres or less) increased from thirty-five in 1960 to fifty in 1978 (Hossain 1987:25). In 1998, 56 percent of all landholdings qualified as functionally landless (Bangladesh

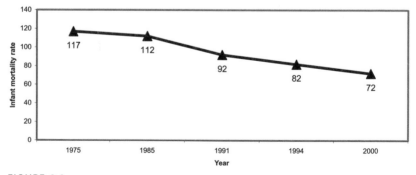

FIGURE 9.2
Decline in infant mortality rate in Bangladesh, 1975–2000.

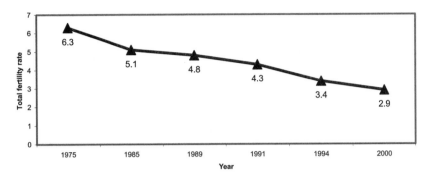

FIGURE 9.3
Decline in under-five mortality rate in Bangladesh, 1975–1998.

Bureau of Statistics 1999:196). Increasing landlessness has resulted from a combination of population growth, land loss through natural disaster, and land transfers that have sharply distinguished the landless poor from what have been termed "middle peasants" and large landholders (Hossain 1987:24) or what White (1992) has referred to as the distinction between *chotolok* (little people) and *borolok* (big people). The relative returns of agriculture and dealing in land (e.g., letting land to sharecroppers or tenants) make the latter a more profitable use of land. Because large landholders therefore opt to specialize in land dealing, even they do not provide agricultural opportunities for the landless poor. Consequently, the increase in landlessness has not been offset by increases in reliable agricultural employment, and landless farmers are forced into service or artisanal employment. At the same time, the decline in income from rural farming creates limited markets for goods and services, and people thus employed are seriously underemployed (Hossain 1987:22–24). Landless households cannot benefit from the labor of children on family farms, and the saturation of the agricultural labor market and the underemployment of nonagricultural workers in rural areas suggest that adults, not children, will benefit from the few employment opportunities available.

With respect to children's value as old-age support, telling evidence comes from Duza and Nag's (1993) research in Matlab. The authors discuss parents' views on "the notion that male children provide a form of old-age security" as elicited in focus group sessions (Duza and Nag 1993:73). Pointing to increasing scarcity of resources, including land, they summarize three reasons why parents now see sons as a less reliable source of support. One reason refers to perceived changes in marital relations such that sons are influenced more by wives than by parents. The other two refer directly to conditions of economic deterioration; adult children are seen as incapable of supporting themselves because of scarcity of land or employment and therefore incapable of supporting parents, either because of their limited income or their need to migrate for employment.

There are two points to be made here: Conditions change, and people have agency; when conditions change, people are capable of adapting to new situations with new behavior. This has certainly been the case with respect to the willingness to use certain contraceptive technologies. As people become more aware of the dangers of STDs, particularly of the potentially fatal danger of HIV and AIDS, practice can change as well. But motive, that demand element, will only follow education, and even the best motives will not be sufficient to effect the necessary change if programs do not emphasize the supply element and advocate the use of condoms.

The second objection to promotion of condom use is somewhat more complex and argues that such promotion ignores the underlying issues. Let me now address this objection that is sometimes referred to as a "band aid" argument—that is, as objecting to the use of temporary and expedient solutions instead of the radical solutions to underlying structural problems. There are two important and encompassing problems that need to be addressed: Bangladesh's peripheralization in a global economy and women's peripheralization in Bangladeshi society. I want to be clear here that I am using "peripheral" not as a synonym for unimportant, but rather in the sense associated with underdevelopment theorists, as simultaneously necessary for the continued operation of a system, and without power within the system (see Amarshi et al. 1979: xiv–xv).

Bangladesh has been peripheralized for a long time and with devastating effects. When the country was still East Bengal, the British consciously demolished the prosperous native textile industry in order to eliminate competition with British textiles and to provide a market for these British products. In destroying an industrial base, the policy also effected the relocation of urban textile workers and their greater direct reliance on an agricultural base, increasing the demands on rural resources. At the same time, British fiscal policy revised an existing prebendary system in ways that made it insensitive to fluctuations in production and increased the economic and political powers of the *zamindars* (tax collectors-landlords) in ways that still redound in village-level patron-client relationships.

East Bengal's agricultural production was also manipulated to meet British needs. When the Crimean War closed the Russian hemp trade to Britain, colonial policy encouraged production of jute and it became East Bengal's primary export. This cash crop became so important that land was removed from rice cultivation to meet the demand. But jute processing took place far from the local source. Factories were located in West Bengal as part of an overall process that assigned West Bengal, and especially Calcutta, to the position of internal core to East Bengal's periphery, a process that was to have further repercussions after Indian partition left Muslim East Bengal seriously lacking in industrial facilities and knowledge (Baxter 1997).

After partition assigned East and West Bengal to Pakistan and India, respectively, factories for jute processing were established in East Pakistan, but the capital for those factories came from West Pakistan, the richer, more politically powerful, and more technologically skilled province. Management also came from West Bengal and there was, consequently, little advancement or training in management for East Pakistanis. Moreover, Muslim Bihari refugees from northern India, Urdu speakers and consequently favored by West Pakistan,[6] were employed for skilled labor, further constraining opportunities for Bengalis in what was now their own country.

It is important to remember that Bangladesh is one of the most densely populated countries in the world, with a population of over 131 million in approximately 133,000 square kilometers. Almost 64 percent of the labor force is in the agricultural sector. Industrialization has increased in Bangladesh, but is still a minor element in terms of the number of people it employs. Independence has not changed Bangladesh's peripheral position in a global economy. What has changed is that, now, instead of exporting agricultural raw goods, Bangladesh is exporting people, a migrant labor force; so long as that labor force cannot be gainfully employed at home migration will continue and probably increase.

Just as Bangladesh and other developing countries are crucial to developed countries' prosperity, so are women in Bangladesh crucial to the continuation of patriarchy and the associated privilege of being male.

Hierarchy is a crucial concept in social relations in Bangladeshi society. An individual's access to power and material resources is largely determined by three attributes: class, age, and gender. Although there is room for individual variation, generally, rich supercedes poor, age supercedes youth, and male supercedes female. Kinship is based on patrilineal principles and postmarital residence is virilocal, with the result that wives produce members for, but are not themselves members of, the localized patrilineal group into which they marry.

Male children are preferred over female, and one of a woman's most important roles within the family is producing sons. The birth of sons, indeed, improves a woman's position within the kin group and sons provide her one of the few avenues through which she may be able to pursue her own interests. Sons are valued as perpetuators of the lineage, as repositories of social prestige, and as financial and political supports for their parents. Sons are especially important for women, since, in consolidating their position within the family, they provide their mothers some security against divorce. Sons are also expected to provide support for their mothers in the event of divorce or widowhood, the devastating effects of which arise from the institution that most seriously affects women's lives, their seclusion under the rules of purdah.

Purdah ("veil" or "curtain") enjoins the seclusion of women and the prohibition of their interaction with unrelated males. Girls become subject to rules of seclusion shortly before puberty. Although the degree to which women can be secluded varies, particularly by the wealth of a family, the ideal is for women to be confined to the *bari* (a homestead that encompasses a number of patrilineally related households) or to interconnecting homesteads, if they are joined by paths that enable women to travel without being seen by men. The degree to which a family is able to maintain its women in seclusion is an indicator of its respectability; a woman's chastity is directly associated with her family's honor.

Seclusion seriously curtails women's access to local knowledge, to formal education, and to economic opportunities beyond the household level. Purdah creates and reinforces women's dependence on men, especially their economic dependence. Indeed, the ideal of men's and women's roles within the family reflects this dependence: Men are responsible for supporting their families and can expect to receive in return deference and obedience from their wives. The division of the world into male public space and female private space, and the division of behavior into male initiative and female passivity both affect women's autonomy in ways that may influence women's sexuality. Women's economic dependence, a result of purdah, denies them power over most of Bangladeshi life, and, perhaps most poignantly, denies them power over their own bodies. It is difficult, if not impossible, under this system for women to define the conditions of sexual intercourse, to insist, for example, on the use of condoms.

Obviously, these internal and international inequities have to be addressed if Bangladesh's future is going to be better than its present. And, obviously, development funds can be used to address these problems, but the solutions that would create equity for Bangladesh in a world economy and for women in Bangladeshi society have not yet appeared. While I alluded earlier to the importance of agency, it is important to note that that agency was able to operate to change fertility patterns in Bangladesh only after the institutional commitment was made by the government and international funders to provide alternatives from which people could choose, a regime of natural fertility or reproductive control.

Changing Bangladesh's position in the world economy and women's position within Bangladeshi society are not matters of individual choice and will not be effectively addressed until there is the possibility that individual choices can be effective as part of larger movements. In the interim, my response to the "band aid" argument is perhaps best framed as an analogy. If you see people bleeding to death because they have been victims of a traffic accident, you don't ignore them while you focus on better traffic safety legislation. The developed nations have a responsibility to recognize the importance of advocating and supporting reform on the policy level that will work to overcome the current conditions that drive Bangladeshi men to choose to leave and that require Bangladeshi women to relinquish control over the conditions of their own sexuality. But we cannot abdicate the responsibility to work for expedient measures until such reforms are enacted. Something has to be done in the meantime for the people whose lives are in danger, and I argue that advocating as simple a change as condom use, in this case, is not a band aid but rather a tourniquet that may, in fact, save the lives of many men, women, and children while they wait for the better day.

NOTES

1. To describe HIV/AIDS as a sexually transmitted disease is, of course, to isolate and focus on one of several modes of transmission. However, preliminary data from Bangladesh indicate that sexual transmission is, at this point, the most common mode of infection in that country.

2. It is worth noting that the government of Bangladesh, despite limited resources, began testing of high-risk groups in 1998. The samples, however, are necessarily small.

3. The World Health Organization groups North Africa and the Middle East in the reporting of these statistics, and it is not possible to separate the two regions. Some Bangladeshis do migrate to North Africa, particularly to Libya, but that migration is quite minor when compared to the Middle East. For this grouped region, the main modes of transmission are intravenous drug use and heterosexual intercourse; it is not possible to determine from WHO data which mode is more important in each area.

4. Interestingly, husbands report a higher rate of use, 5.7 percent, than do their wives, 3.9 percent. The discrepancy may reflect "contraceptive use with nonmarital partners, which is presumably higher among men than women" (Mitra et al. 1997:56).

5. The government has recently moved toward more centralized delivery, a change that will test whether the demand for contraceptives can overcome the limits that purdah sets on women's ability to move freely.

6. One of the most deeply resented of the many onerous policies that West Pakistan attempted to impose on the eastern state was the establishment of Urdu, spoken in West Pakistan, as the official language of the entire country. Bengalis are fiercely proud of their language, Bangla or Bengali, which has a long and glorious literary tradition. Bangladeshis will often point out to foreigners that they speak "the language of Rabindranath," referring to the Nobel laureate, Tagore. Despite a number of substantive and justifiable complaints about West Pakistan's political and economic oppression, it was the question of language that provided the popular spark to the War of Independence that resulted in the establishment of Bangladesh as a separate and sovereign nation.

REFERENCES

AIDSfocus Newsletter
    1997 CARE-Bangladesh: The Peers. Electronic document. http://www.care.-org/publications/aidsfocus/nov97/focus1.html/

Amarshi, Azeem, Kenneth Good, and Rex Mortimer
1979 Development and Dependency. The Political Economy of Papua New Guinea. Melbourne: Oxford University Press.

Athukorala, Prema-Chandra, and Piyasiri Wickramasekara
1996 Internal Labour Migration Statistics in Asia: An Appraisal. International Migration XXXIV 4:539–565.

Bangladesh Bureau of Statistics
1999 Statistical Pocketbook of Bangladesh 1998. Dhaka: Bangladesh Bureau of Statistics.

Baxter, Craig
1997 Bangladesh: From a Nation to a State. Boulder, CO: Westview Press.

Caldwell, John C., John K. Anarfi, and Pat Caldwell
1997 Mobility, Migration, Sex, STDs, and AIDS: An Essay on Sub-Saharan Africa with Other Parallels. In Sexual Cultures and Migration in the Era of Aids: Anthropological and Demographic Perspectives. Gilbert Herdt, ed. Pp. 41–54. New York: Oxford University Press.

Carael, Michel
1997 Urban-Rural Differentials in HIV/STDs and Sexual Behavior. In Sexual Cultures and Migration in the Era of Aids: Anthropological and Demographic Perspectives. Gilbert Herdt, ed. Pp. 107–126. New York: Oxford University Press.

Chaudhury, Rafiqul Huda
1978 Determinants and Consequences of Rural Out-Migration: Evidence from Some Villages in Bangladesh. In Economic and Demographic Change: Issues for the 1980s, vol. 2, Proceedings of the Conference, Helsinki, Finland. Pp. 213–228. Liege, Belgium: IUSSP.

Consultative Group on International Agricultural Research
2000 Asia Goes Urban. Electronic Document. http://www.cgiar/IRRI/Hunger/Urban.htm

Development Data Group
2001 World Development Indicators. Electronic document. http//devdata.worldbank.org/epidemicupdate/

Duza, M. B., and M. Nag
1993 High Contraceptive Prevalence in Matlab, Bangladesh: Underlying Process and Implications. In The Revolution in Asian Fertility: Dimensions,

Causes and Implications. Richard Leete and Iqbal, eds. Oxford: Clarendon Press.

Herdt, Gilbert
1997 Sexual Cultures and Population Movement: Implications for AIDS/ STDs. *In* Sexual Cultures and Migration in the Era of Aids: Anthropological and Demographic Perspectives. Gilbert Herdt, ed. Pp. 3–22. New York: Oxford University Press.

Hossain, Mosharaff
1987 The Assault That Failed: A Profile of Absolute Poverty in Six Villages of Bangladesh. Geneva: U.N. Research Institute for Social Development.

Hossain, Ziarat, and Jaipaul L. Roopnarine
1992 On the Fringes: Urban Living among Squatters of Sarajganjtown in Bangladesh. Urban Anthropology 21(1):45–65.

Mahbub, A. Q. M.
1985–86 Mobility Patterns of Working People from Rural Areas in Bangladesh. Oriental Geographer 29–30:73–91.

Mahmood, Raisul Awal
1995 Emigration Dynamics in Bangladesh. International Migration 33 (3–4):699–728.

MAP (Monitoring the Aids Pandemic) Network
1999 The Status and Trends of the HIV/AIDS/STD Epidemics in Asia and the Pacific. Electronic document. Family Health International: http://www.fhi.org.

Massey, Douglas S., Joaquín Arango, Graeme Hugo, Ali Kouaouci, Adela Pellegrino, and J. Edward Taylor
1998 Worlds in Motion. Understanding International Migration at the End of the Millennium. New York: Oxford University Press.

Matin, Khan A.
1986 Residence Background and Fertility Change in Chittagong, Bangladesh. Genus 42 (1–2):141–151.

Mitra, S. N., A. A. Sabir, A. R. Cross, and K. Jamil
1995 Bangladesh Demographic and Health Survey, 1993–94. Dahaka and Calverton, MD: NIPORT.

Osmani, S. R.
1986 Bangladesh. *In* Migration of Asian Workers to the Arab World. Godfrey Gunatilleke, ed. Pp. 23–65. Tokyo: The United Nations University.

Satcher, David
    1999 The Global HIV/AIDS Epidemic. Journal of the American Medical Association 281:1479.

Shand, Ric, and Mohammad Alauddin
    1997 Economic Profiles in South Asia: Bangladesh. Canberra: Australia South Asia Research Centre, Research School of Pacific and Asian Studies, Australian National University.

Singhanetra-Renard, Anchalee
    1997 Population Movement and the Aids Epidemic in Thailand. *In* Sexual Cultures and Migration in the Era of Aids: Anthropological and Demographic Perspectives. Gilbert Herdt, ed. Pp. 70–86. New York: Oxford University Press.

UNAIDS
    2000 Report on the Global HIV/AIDS Epidemic.

U.S. Census Bureau International Data Base
    2000 Electronic document. http://www.census.gov/ipc/www/idbsum.htm/.

White, Sarah C.
    1992 Arguing with the Crocodile. Gender and Class in Bangladesh. Dhaka: University Press.

World Bank Group
    2001 News release 2001/159/SAS. Electronic document. http://www.worldbank.org

World Health Organization
    2000 Report on Global Surveillance of Epidemic-Prone Infectious Diseases. Electronic document. http://www.who.int.

III

LOCATING DEVELOPMENT AND NEW AVENUES FOR RESEARCH

10

Gifts, Bribes, and Development in Post-Soviet Kazakstan

Cynthia Ann Werner

Employing self-interested bureaucrats, disregarding cultural and gender differences, straining local environments, and planning projects without local participation have all been touted as explanations for failed development projects (Brain 1996; Cernea 1991; Ferguson 1990; Hill 1986). In response to these critiques, development planners have made concerted efforts to develop culturally compatible projects, to think about sustainability issues, and to put people first. Although these changes have certainly improved development projects in the past two decades, they have not provided a magical cure for alleviating global inequality. In 1990, after forty-five years of development efforts, there were over one billion people living in absolute poverty, with annual incomes of less than $370 (World Bank 1990). This poor track record has prompted donor nations and their constituents to question whether development aid is a worthwhile expenditure. From 1991 to 1997, official development assistance has declined by one-third in real terms, from approximately $73 to $44 billion (World Bank 1998a). What can the development industry do to preserve its resources and reputation? In recent years, development experts have increasingly placed the blame on a familiar but forgotten culprit—corruption (Elliott 1997; Kaufmann and Siegelbaum 1997; Tanzi 1998).

Bribery, pilferage, and patronage are just a few of the more common forms of corruption that have been around for centuries. For a long time, these practices were regarded with some ambivalence. Bribery, after all, can be useful for "greasing the machine's wheel" or for speeding things up. In the 1960s, a number of scholars argued that corruption might have some beneficial effects on economic and political stability in developing countries (Bayley 1966; Leff 1964). Similar yet stronger arguments have been made in the case of socialist countries (Ericson 1984; Grossman 1984; Kramer 1977). Accepting these realities, industrialized countries, with the exception of the United States, have generally permitted bribes outside of their borders as tax-deductible business expenses.[1] The emergence of a global anticorruption campaign in the mid-1990s, however, has led to a reconsideration of these practices. No longer viewed as a benign tumor, corruption has been rediagnosed as the leading threat to economic and political stability in developing and transition economies around the world.[2]

As the global anticorruption campaign gets under way, experts are trying to come up with ways to define and measure corrupt practices. One of the many problems involved with measuring and comparing corruption is that the forms of corruption vary widely from one society to the next, for both historical and cultural reasons. In fact, the boundaries between "corrupt" behavior and "cultural" behavior are not always clear. This is especially the case when it comes to the distinction between "bribes" and "gifts." Where does one draw the line?

In an International Monetary Fund (IMF) report on corruption, Vito Tanzi, a leader of the anticorruption campaign, acknowledges that it is difficult yet important to make this distinction. The way he distinguishes the two, however, should raise an eyebrow or two among economic anthropologists. He states: "In many instances, bribes can be disguised as gifts. A bribe implies reciprocity while a gift should not." In a footnote, he elaborates further: "In practice, those who give gifts may expect some form of payment for them. For example, we expect love or good behavior from our children when we give them gifts; but the recipients of the gifts do not have an obligation to reciprocate" (1998:9). Clearly, Tanzi has not read Marcel Mauss's (1925) classic treatise on gift exchange. Further, by using the obligation to reciprocate as the primary criterion for distinguishing bribes from gifts, he has mistakenly linked reciprocity to immorality.

With this conceptual maneuvering, the global anticorruption campaign has rolled right into anthropological territory. For decades, anthropologists have argued that most forms of gift exchange involve an obligation to reciprocate, although reciprocity may come in the form of goods, services, or values. In many cases, gift exchange helps to create webs of relationships based on mutual obligations. These informal networks, moreover, function as safety nets for people with few economic resources, insufficient state welfare benefits and/or limited access to goods and services. (Halperin 1991; Ledeneva 1998; Sharma 1986; Stack 1973; Werbner 1990; Werner 1998; Yan 1996; Yang 1994). In the current atmosphere, development experts would probably define some of the gifts exchanged within these networks as bribes, especially when the recipients are employees of the state.

At this point, should anthropologists unite to defend the practical aspects of gift exchange against attacks from the anticorruption campaign? Or, should this be viewed as a conceptual misunderstanding that should *not* prevent anthropologists from also jumping on the anticorruption bandwagon that allegedly stands for economic and social justice? This chapter addresses these questions by exploring the relationship between development and corruption and the distinction between gifts and bribes in post-Soviet Kazakstan.

There are at least two reasons why Kazakstan provides an ideal setting for studying these issues. First, foreign and local development planners are convinced that the future of Kazakstan, which is in the midst of a difficult economic and political transition, hinges on the current efforts to curb widespread corruption. Even though corruption is not new to Kazakstan, it is viewed as a serious threat to economic and political stability during this very important historical moment. Second, the case of Kazakstan is interesting because gifts and bribes both have a conspicuous presence, yet the boundary between the two is blurred. On the one hand, gift exchange is a defining aspect of Kazak culture. Kazaks regularly exchange gifts and they explain their preoccupation with gift exchange in terms of generosity and hospitality, two important values in Kazak culture. In the Kazak language, there is no single, generic term like the English word "gift." Instead, the language contains several different terms for specific categories of gifts and other ritual payments (as indicated in table 10.1). On the other hand, some of these gifts function in part as bribes, thus blurring the boundary between the two forms of exchange.

Table 10.1   Categories of Gifts and Ritual Payments, South Kazakstan Province, 1990s

Name	Context	Content
Syilyq	Refers to feast gifts and "large" gifts; used interchangeably for *shashu;* also refers to a contest prize (*priz*)	Varies
Suynshy	Small gift presented to bearer of good news, like a new birth	Cloth, clothing, money
Baighazy	Gift to congratulate kin/friend for something new	Clothing; money
Korimdik	Small gift presented to a family for showing something new, like a new baby, a bride or prepared *kiit*	Usually money
Shashu	Feast gift from guest to host (especially for a wedding feast)	Usually money
Priz	Counter-gift from host to guest given during a feast (also referred to as a *syilyq*)	Varies (clothing, toys)
Qalyng-mal	Bridewealth payment from groom's family to bride's family	Livestock; money
Zhasau	Dowry payment from bride's family to bride (sometimes referred to as *tosek-oryn*, literally "bedding")	Clothing; household goods
Kiit	Gifts to in-laws (*quda*) broadly defined	Cloth; clothing
Minit	Gifts to in-laws (*quda*) broadly defined (sometimes referred to as *kiit*)	Livestock; money

DEVELOPMENT IN POST-SOVIET KAZAKSTAN

Before examining the problem of corruption in contemporary Kazakstan, it is important to consider the post-Soviet transition. The origins of the transition can be traced back to the late 1980s, when Mikhail Gorbachev introduced economic and political reforms, under the rubric of perestroika (restructuring) and glasnost (openness). The perestroika campaign sought to improve economic efficiency by creating new incentives for state-controlled production, while the glasnost campaign permitted open criticism of public policy and increased access to information. The glasnost campaign also involved the last of many historical efforts to rid the Communist Party of political and economic corruption (Clark 1993).

In December 1991, four months after the failed military coup in Moscow, Kazakstan somewhat reluctantly achieved independence, with neither struggle nor celebration. Shortly afterward, the pace of economic and political change intensified. Following the lead of Russia, the government of Kazakstan, headed by President Nursultan Nazarbaev, launched the dual transition from a socialist, planned economy to a capitalist, market economy and from a one-party authoritarian system to a multiparty democratic system. In 1993, Kazakstan introduced its own currency (the tenge) and initiated a comprehensive structural reform program. As elsewhere, these structural reforms include the liberalization of prices for consumer goods; the reduction of state subsidies for transportation, housing, and other services; the privatization of some state-owned enterprises; and the downsizing of other state-owned enterprises.

In 1997, in an effort to regain lost support for economic change and to remind citizens that market economies do not develop overnight, President Nazarbaev repackaged the structural reforms as the "Kazakstan 2030" program. According to this plan, the country should be on par with advanced industrial nations by the year 2030. In Nazarbaev's opinion, the development of the Central Asian republics in some ways will parallel the development of the "Asian Tigers" (South Korea, Taiwan, Hong Kong, and Singapore). However, the Central Asian path will be distinctive because these countries already have a highly educated population and some established industries. Thus, Nazarbaev has declared that Kazakstan will soon become the leader of the "Central Asian Snow Leopards."

Throughout the 1990s, Kazakstan's new position within the post-Soviet global economy has influenced the transition process. With the waning of subsidies from Russia, Kazakstan has increasingly relied on the international community for investment capital, development aid, and technical advice. Of the five Central Asian republics, Kazakstan has received the most attention from foreign investors. This is in part due to economic policies that encourage foreign investment and in part due to the fact that the country contains vast supplies of valuable petroleum and mineral resources (including gold, iron ore, coal, and copper). Between 1992 and 1996, foreign investments in Kazakstan reached $2 billion (USAID 1996).

In addition to these investments, the country has received multilateral and bilateral aid packages and assistance programs from a variety of sources, including the World Bank, the IMF, and the U.S. government. Kazakstan joined both the World Bank and the IMF in July 1992. Since then, the World Bank has approved nearly $1.2 billion for fourteen different projects in Kazakstan (World Bank 1998b) and the IMF has provided Kazakstan with $386 million in credit (IMF 1995). Meanwhile, the U.S. government has sponsored a variety of programs for economic, political, and social development through the U.S. Agency for International Development, the U.S. Information Agency, the U.S. Department of Commerce, and the U.S. Department of Agriculture. These aid programs will probably continue in the future, as long as Kazakstan continues to follow a number of undisclosed conditions for restructuring economic and political institutions, which most likely include anticorruption measures.

The transition from a socialist, planned economy to a capitalist, market economy has not been easy for the people of Kazakstan. While a small percentage of the population has benefited from the transition, the average standard of living has declined sharply throughout the 1990s due to increased unemployment, delayed salaries, and high inflation. Although the official unemployment rate is only 2 percent, the World Bank estimates that this figure would be closer to 12 percent if involuntary leaves and part-time furloughs were included (World Bank 1998b). Employment in and of itself does not guarantee economic security in post-Soviet Kazakstan. In the mid-1990s, state salaries for many occupations were delayed for months. High inflation has also been difficult for everyone. In 1994, several months after food prices were liberalized and the new currency was introduced, the annual inflation rate in Kazakstan reached an all-time high of 1,160 percent. The annual inflation rate dropped to 60 percent in 1995 and 12 percent in 1997 (World Bank 1998b), but the cost of living remained high for the average family since state salaries and pensions did not increase enough to compensate for the new economic situation.

In the post-Soviet period, employed and unemployed adults have sought alternative ways to make ends meet, or "to see the sun" (kun koru), as Kazaks say. In addition to becoming more subsistence oriented, rural families have sold and slaughtered private herds of livestock for cash and food. More conspicuous, perhaps, is the growth of small-scale trade in urban and rural areas. In the post-Soviet period, people have flocked to the bazaars to buy and sell imported and domestic consumer goods. These activities can put considerable strains on households since some family members may spend days or weeks in other towns while trading. For successful merchants, economic profits may outweigh the social costs, but not all merchants are successful.

Social stratification is an unmistakable consequence of the post-Soviet transition. Some Kazaks are purchasing Mercedes Benzes and traveling abroad, while others are selling their last sheep to buy flour and eggs. It is difficult to determine the numbers, but it is clear that a minority of the population is benefiting from the transition, while the majority is not. Not surprisingly, perceptions of the transition process tend to reflect these differences. Those who are doing well generally support market reforms and blame the poor for being lazy, whiny, and inflexible. Meanwhile, those who are not faring so well resent the pace and extent of reforms and lament the end of an egalitarian ideology. As they search for explanations, many are finding scapegoats in the form of wealthy "biznezmen," "Mafia" leaders, and "corrupt" officials who allegedly have little concern for the welfare of others.[3]

LOCAL AND GLOBAL CAMPAIGNS AGAINST CORRUPTION

Public attitudes toward corruption have been heavily influenced by the local media, which regularly carries stories on crime and corruption. In the 1990s, the emergence of an independent media, combined with the loosening of controls on the state media, has led to a new style of reporting that corresponds to the overall transition toward democracy. When it comes to certain taboo subjects, such as the president's family ties and the political role of tribal lineages, the Kazakstani media has remained relatively self-censored.[4] However, when it comes to corruption, the media has truly tested the limits of this new democracy. Through opinion pieces and investigative reporting, a number of journalists, especially those employed by independent newspapers, have been leading the local anti-corruption movement in Kazakstan. Their articles frequently include practical discussions and popular surveys on what should be done to eliminate or reduce corruption.

In addition to criticizing corruption on a general level, some journalists have gone a step further by writing exposés on specific cases of corruption, including cases where officials abused their positions of power, accepted bribes, and stole public property during privatization. In at least one case, the accused responded in a different independent newspaper, claiming that the original accounts were slanderous. Such counterdefamations are just one of the perils faced by these journalists. According to one Kazak journalist, officials who are guilty of corruption sometimes try to offer preemptive bribes to journalists in exchange for their cooperation, while officials who are accused of corruption sometimes threaten and physically harm the journalists who expose them.

Although media reports of corruption were not uncommon in the

Soviet era, the nature of reporting has changed dramatically in the past few years. During the Soviet period, the state controlled the media and thus manipulated the reporting of corrupt activities to its own advantage. Reports on corruption, for example, increased during the early 1960s, after Khrushchev initiated a massive attack on criminal and corrupt practices. Later, during the Brezhnev years (1964–82), a number of illegal activities, such as report padding and supply hoarding, were largely ignored by the legal system and the media, in part because government officials realized these activities were beneficial to the state economy. Media accounts of corruption, moreover, often increased after a change in political leadership, when high-profile officials associated with the old guard were accused of embezzlement, bribery, report padding, and other crimes (Clark 1993:71–99).

Whereas the articles on corruption in the Khrushchev and Brezhnev years tend to serve the interests of the state, the articles in the late Soviet and post-Soviet years tend to serve the interests of the public. As the articles themselves point out, many corrupt practices, such as bribery and pilferage, benefit the elite at the expense of the common people. Not only do these articles push the state to take further action, they also arm the public with new knowledge. In the region where I worked, the public voraciously reads and heatedly discusses newspaper accounts of local corruption. Although a few people discount these articles as mere slander, many believe these articles confirm their worst suspicions of local leaders. For better or worse, these negative portrayals of greedy officials shape the way they understand their own situation.

These local attacks on corruption coincide with the global anticorruption movement. While local struggles against corruption are nothing new, the fight against corruption has taken on global dimensions in the 1990s.

First, anticorruption movements have appeared almost simultaneously in a significant number of countries across the globe. Beginning with Italy in 1992, the "corruption eruption" has spilled into France, Japan, South Korea, India, Mexico, Columbia, Brazil, South Africa, and other countries (Glynn et al. 1997:7).[5]

Second, local corruption has been reconceptualized as a problem that adversely affects the global economy. As economists note, the integration of the global economy makes it more difficult to contain local corruption and more ridiculous to permit transnational bribery (Glynn et al. 1997:15–24).

Third, after decades of complacency, all of the relevant international organizations have condemned corruption and introduced measures to fight it. The legality of transnational bribery has been a big issue. In 1977, the United States became the first country to have a law specifying that the payment of a bribe in a foreign country is illegal. In 1996, the Organization for Economic Cooperation and Development (OECD) finally recommended that its twenty-six member-states should also implement laws to end the tax deductibility of foreign bribes and to criminalize transnational bribery (Pieth 1997:119).[6] In the late 1990s, similar efforts to make transnational bribery illegal and to coordinate anticorruption law enforcement have been made by the United Nations, the European Union, the World Trade Organization, the World Customs Organization, and the Organization of American States (Elliot 1997:2–3).

Another important issue has been the misuse of international development aid. In June 1996, the World Bank responded to this problem by revising its guidelines in a way that emphasizes "governance issues" in lending policies and ensures greater transparency and accountability in bank-sponsored projects (World Bank 1998c). Through these measures, the expansion of the global anticorruption campaign is influencing local anticorruption campaigns throughout the world, including Kazakstan.

In the past few years, the "corruption eruption" has also received considerable attention from scholars, especially in the fields of economics and political science. In this paper, I would like to consider the potential contribution that anthropologists could make to the study of and the struggle against corruption. Corruption, like poverty, is a global problem that negatively affects many of the people that anthropologists study. At the same time, the global campaign against corruption, like the fight against poverty, is something that deserves a critical assessment. In particular, anthropologists could play an important role by comparing the way local people define corruption with the way it is defined by powerful global organizations. In so doing, anthropologists could make recommendations for devising culturally appropriate development programs for fighting corruption. In the remainder of this chapter, I will make a limited effort to do this by describing local practices of gift exchange and bribery, as well as local attitudes toward these practices.

GIFTS AND BRIBES IN KAZAKSTAN

Any anthropologist who wants to do research and write about bribery or corruption must be prepared to deal with a number of ethical, methodological, and conceptual problems. These dilemmas may help to explain why there are so few anthropological studies of bribery and corruption, even though anthropologists frequently conduct research in countries with very high levels of corruption.

Due to the nature of anthropological fieldwork, it is impossible to conduct research on bribery and corruption without encountering some ethical problems. Is it possible for anthropologists to write about these practices without putting their informants and friends in serious jeopardy? Can the benefits of writing about corruption outweigh the potential costs? I believe it is possible for anthropologists to write about corruption and bribery in a responsible way. I also believe such writings may have some positive impact on the implementation of local and global anticorruption campaigns.

To protect those who may be associated directly or indirectly with my research, I have intentionally withheld any information that could be traced back to any particular individual, whether informant or alleged bribe receiver. Identifying people who shared these stories with me would be much like finding a needle in a haystack. Few of the accounts mentioned here have any connection with people living in "my" town. Many of the accounts are based on conversations I had while living in the former capital Almaty or while traveling on trains from Almaty to Shymkent.[7] Without underestimating the potential risks, I would like to add that the information I gathered is relatively harmless. I never directly observed any bribe giving or bribe receiving, and all of the secondhand accounts that I did manage to collect are limited to relatively small forms of corruption. Through careful selection and presentation of materials, the potential benefits of writing this article should outweigh any costs that I was not able to foresee. In terms of benefits, writing about bribery can lead to new theoretical perspectives for understanding exchange and the informal economy and to new practical insights for developing culturally appropriate methods for fighting corruption in Kazakstan.

In studying bribery, as soon as the ethical hurdles are cleared, the methodological hurdles approach. How will interview questions about bribery and corruption shape the process of building and maintaining trusting relationships with informants? Who is going to admit bribe giving or bribe receiving in a context where both practices are considered illegal and, in some contexts, immoral? If somebody does describe an incident that involves other participants, how can any version of the story be confirmed? These three problems make it difficult to study bribery, and unfortunately there are no easy solutions.

I will briefly sketch how I have dealt with these problems. It was probably to my advantage that I did not intend to study bribery and corruption. Since I set out to study gift exchange and market exchange, most of my interview questions centered on these less-sensitive issues. Only in the process of doing this research did I become interested in bribery. As my research moved in this direction, I started to ask people hypothetical questions about bribery. Since corruption is a frequent topic in the news and in daily discourse, this was not perceived as an unreasonable request. People who claimed they did not have any personal experiences with bribery had learned quite a bit about the subject through rumors and gossip, and they did not mind sharing this information.

During some of these conversations, I felt comfortable enough to ask somebody to talk about situations where they had actually given bribes (*para*), but I never felt it was appropriate to ask someone to disclose whether or not they had accepted bribes. Although the morality of bribery is widely contested today, Kazaks generally regard bribe receiving to be much more offensive than bribe giving.

In the former Soviet Union, as elsewhere, the penalties for accepting or extorting bribes were much higher than the penalties for offering a bribe (Clark 1993:79–85). Although the criminal laws have changed in the post-Soviet period, this general rule has remained true. Correspondingly, people were more willing to admit incidents where they presented a bribe to someone else. Sometimes, this information was even volunteered, when I was asked questions about household expenses. In contrast, only a few drunken braggarts divulged the fact that they received bribes. Given the ethical complications, I never tried to substantiate any specific accounts of bribery. While my approach to studying bribery is somewhat haphazard, I did manage to acquire considerable information about the contexts in which bribes are most frequently presented, the cash value placed on bribes for various services, and the proper etiquette for presenting bribes.

Ethical and methodological problems aside, the study of corruption also presents a conceptual challenge. It is no easy task to define corruption or any one of its constituent forms. It appears in a wide variety of forms—including bribery, fraud, embezzlement, nepotism, and patronage—with varying degrees of malfeasance. The generally accepted definition of corruption is the "abuse of public power for private gain." Scholars, however, have noted that each of the three elements in this definition can be problematic. First, corruption is not limited to the public sector, although private-sector corruption is not a major concern from the development perspective. Second, regarding private gain, corrupt acts sometimes benefit somebody or something other than the public official who commits an illegal act. And, most importantly, what constitutes abuse will vary depending on legal and cultural standards (Johnston 1997:62; Tanzi 1998:8–10). I would add that the informal procedures for successfully engaging in corrupt activities are also embedded in the local culture.

One form of corruption, bribery, is particularly difficult to define in cultural settings, where it takes on the guise of gift exchange. This is the case in China, where the exchange of wedding gifts often creates social debts that may be reciprocated in part through the abuse of public power (Kipnis 1997; Yang 1994). Comparable forms of gift exchange take place in Kazakstan. Anthropologists, in a rather extensive body of literature on gift exchange, have critically examined the boundary between gifts and commodities (Gregory 1982; Hunt 2002; Levi-Strauss 1969; Mauss 1925). There are relatively few studies, however, that explicitly address the boundary between gifts and other forms of noncommodity exchange, such as barter exchange and bribery (Bloch and Parry 1989; Humphrey and Hugh-Jones 1992; Ledeneva 1998; Smart 1993). Although some of the established criteria for distinguishing gifts and commodities can be useful for teasing out the distinctions between gifts and bribes, it is necessary to examine the gift-bribe boundary in its own right. This is not just a question of semantics. In fact, I believe that it is impossible and imprudent to draw a firm boundary between the two forms of exchange. This is especially true for Kazak society, where the category of gift is clearly an imported construct, as there is no single, generic concept that applies to all categories of gifts and ritual payments.

Why, then, am I even interested in looking at what can only be an artificial boundary between gifts and bribes? First, the search for this nonexistent boundary reveals the very limitations of anthropological categories such as gifts and commodities. Second, this investigation sheds some light on the contested ways in which Kazaks perceive corruption and morality and the ways in which these perceptions are changing in the post-Soviet period. These insights, in turn, might be useful for developing local programs for fighting corruption.

In table 10.2, I have listed several possible criteria for distinguishing gifts and bribes. These criteria are based on the ways in which gifts and bribes, as well as gifts and commodities, are typically distinguished in the social science literature. Since my central argument is that there is no clear boundary between gifts and bribes, this table should be regarded as a heuristic tool, not a perfect typology. Before going further, I should mention that many gifts exchanged in Kazakstan have nothing to do with bribery, just as many incidents of bribery bear little resemblance to gift exchange. In order to define the blurred boundary between the two forms of exchange, I will first discuss gift exchange and bribe exchange in Kazakstan as if there were no conceptual quandary. Then, I will turn to a few examples that suggest that some types of exchange fall somewhere between a gift and a bribe.

Gift exchange has a very conspicuous presence in Kazakstan. The families I surveyed believe they spend over half of their household income on gifts and ritual payments, especially during the feasting season, which runs from late summer to late fall. It is difficult to calculate the amount of resources spent on gift exchange because some, but not all, of the goods exchanged are recycled.

The various Kazak terms that can be translated as gift in English are not synonyms. As table 10.1 indicates, different situations call for different categories of gifts. For example, whenever the family receives some exceptionally good news, they give the bearer of good news a small gift of cloth or money, called a *suynshy*. For example, after learning that her twenty-year-old daughter had safely delivered a baby boy, the mother of my host family gave a suynshy gift to the person who first informed her of this news. While the suynshy recognizes the bearer of good news, the recipient of good news may also become the recipient of another type of gift, the *baighazy*, if the good news relates to the acquisition of a new object. For example, one day somebody presented me with a small amount of money as a baighazy to congratulate me on the fact that somebody else had just given me a sheep.

Table 10.2   Possible Criteria for Distinguishing Gifts from Bribes

Criteria	Gift	Bribe
Content of exchange	Not cash	Cash
Quality of relationship between giver and recipient	Personal (long-term)	Impersonal (short-term)
Location of exchange	Not at work	At work
Employment status of recipient	Irrelevant	Official
Obligation to reciprocate	Understood, but when and how not stated	Explicitly stated
Time before exchange is reciprocated	Delayed	Immediate
Number of exchanges	Multiple	Single
Motive for exchange	To maintain relationship; to return a gift; etc.	To get something done quickly; to avoid a hassle
Cultural definition of exchange	Traditional	Immoral
Context of exchange	Gift-giving occasion	Not a gift-giving occasion
Transparency of exchange	Transparent	Discreet
Legal definition of exchange	Legal	Illegal

A large assortment of gifts and ritual payments are exchanged in connection with weddings and other life-cycle events. To begin, close friends and relatives congratulate each other on the birth of a new child or the arrival of a new bride by presenting a *korimdik*. The word korimdik comes from the root word *kor*, to see, and refers to a small gift of money offered in exchange for viewing something new for the first time. In addition, a different type of gift, a *syilyq* or *shashu*, is presented when a family sponsors a large feast (*toi*) to commemorate a new birth, a new marriage, male circumcision, or a birthday. On these occasions, each of the families invited to the feast presents the host household with a gift. Anywhere from one hundred to eight hundred guests may attend the large wedding and circumcision feasts.

The term syilyq most often refers to nonmonetary gifts, such as rugs, livestock, and electronic goods, while the term shashu generally refers to monetary gifts. The value of either varies depending on the context and the relationship between guest and host households. Finally, during the course of a feast, the host household gives most of the guests a smaller countergift, or *priz*. The countergifts are usually presented by the feast master of ceremonies, who also ensures that all of the guests are invited to the front area, in small groups, where they have the opportunity to give a short toast to the host household. After each set of toasts and a musical interlude, the master of ceremonies gives each of the toast givers a countergift, such as a woman's headscarf, a man's dress shirt, a child's toy, or perhaps a shot of vodka.[8]

Finally, for a new marriage, the two principal families present each other with several additional categories of goods. This includes the bridewealth (*qalyng-mal*), a ritual payment from the groom's family to the bride's family, and the dowry (*zhasau* or *tosek-oryn*), a ritual payment from the bride's family to the bride herself. In addition, an expensive array of gifts, including both clothing (*kiit*) and livestock (*minit*), are exchanged between the two sets of new in-laws (*quda*).

Though less conspicuous than gifts and ritual payments, bribes are also exchanged in Kazakstan on a frequent basis for a variety of occasions. I will never forget the first time I got off a plane in Kazakstan. I was anxiously dreading the long and infamous process through passport control, customs, and baggage claim, when I jealously noticed a fellow traveler, a well-dressed Kazak, go no more than ten steps from the bottom of the jet's stairway, across the tarmac, and into a foreign, chauffeur-driven automobile. Assuming that this man must be somebody important in order to get around airport security and customs procedures, I asked the European businessman who sat next to me on the flight if he had any idea who this man might be. He had already spent several months in Kazakstan, and in his opinion, the man was probably not an important political figure. Most likely, his driver had simply bribed the guards in exchange for easy tarmac access, as Kazakstan was a place where "nothing is allowed, but everything is possible."

I heard numerous accounts of bribery including accounts of traffic police and customs officials who take bribes for real and imagined offenses; judges who receive bribes for favorable sentences; employers who secure bribes in exchange for available positions; and university officials who accept bribes for admission. The Kazak word for bribe, para, is consistently used in reference to these illegal exchanges with various authority figures. Alternatively, the word syilyq may be used, especially if the bribe comes in the form of an object, such as a watch or suit that is given to a doctor in exchange for a more thorough examination.

Bribery is by no means peculiar to Kazakstan. Throughout the world, bribery frequently occurs in situations where public officials who are underpaid are given the exclusive power to regulate a number of activities. In other words, bureaucrats who control the flow of documents, such as building permits and passports, or the observance of regulations, such as traffic laws and legal procedures, have the potential to abuse their authority by extracting bribes. Officials who choose to cross this line generally provide a quick service or a limited privilege to individuals who offer or pay bribes. Meanwhile, they use several arbitrary explanations to stall, refuse, or harass individuals who don't pay a bribe. Given the structure of the system, there are personal incentives for both the bribe giver and the bribe recipient to partake in the system.

The fact that something is legally and culturally regarded as a bribe does not mean that it is equal to all other bribes—the monetary value of a bribe may be either a nominal amount or a large sum, and the nature of exchange may be either voluntary or forced (Elliot 1997:188–193). For example, in Kazakstan, a traffic policeman may extort a relatively small amount of money, the local equivalent of a few dollars, from an innocent driver. In a different context, a young man who needs a job might voluntarily pay a bribe of $500 to $1,500 to a military official, who in return will forge a document specifying that the young man was exempt from military service for health reasons ($500) or a document specifying that the young man actually did complete military service ($1,500).

In Kazakstan, everybody realizes that para exchanges are illegal, but people take different positions when it comes to the morality of such exchanges, which further varies depending on the context. In popular discourse, views on the morality of bribery are context-specific in that people factor in the content of the bribe, the official's personality and generosity, his or her regular salary, the estimated amount of income received from bribery, how this income compares to other officials in the same position, and whether or not the bribes are voluntarily presented. Needless to say, these factors are not the same factors that international development experts mention when they talk about the problem of corruption.

The examples of bribery I have presented suggest that perhaps "everything is possible" in Kazakstan. But, this is only true if you know the rules and have the right connections. Similar to gift exchange, there are culturally informed etiquette procedures for presenting bribes. Individuals who want to give a bribe must know who is willing to accept a bribe, how much and what they need to give, when and where they can safely give the bribe, and what they need to say or do when they make the presentation. In many respects, bribery is an acquired skill. For this reason, older men who have lots of experience, as well as lots of connections, handle the most important bribes for a family. This includes the large bribes that are presented for university admission and employment acquisition.

The etiquette associated with bribery varies greatly depending on the nature of the bribe. For example, bribes for university admissions or employment require personal connections, bribes for traffic tickets or small documents do not. Bribes for certain documents, such as the forged military documents, are based on a fixed scale, while bribes for other services, such as a high grade in a university class are based on a sliding scale that may take into account the student's parents' income. Bribes for most documents must be in the form of cash, while bribes for certain services, such as grades and medical care, may be presented in the form of material goods. The value of a bribe for a traffic infraction is explicitly demanded, while the value of bribes for documents and services must be acquired through informal research.

Although bribery practices depend on the context, there are a few general rules. For example, bribes should be presented in a discreet manner. In most offices in Kazakstan, the supervisor has a private office, while his subordinates do not. A cash bribe given to a subordinate who shares an office with others should be concealed in a folder with other documents pertaining to the case. When the bribe is presented, the bribe giver might signal that he or she has placed a bribe in the folder by saying something like "This is for your children" or "This is for you to have some tea," implying that the giver understands that times are hard and the amount is of little consequence.

As these examples demonstrate, most of the criteria listed on table 10.2 to distinguish bribes from gifts do not apply in all situations. Thus, sometimes it is impossible to distinguish gifts from bribes by examining the content of the exchange. Simply put, some gifts come in the form of cash and some bribes come in noncash forms. It is also impossible sometimes to distinguish a gift from a bribe by determining the quality of the relationship between bribe giver and bribe recipient. Since bribery is illegal, bribes of a significant value often entail some kind of personal relationship between the giver and the receiver. Bribe receivers are less likely to accept bribes from somebody they do not know personally and therefore cannot trust. In Kazakstan, people who do not have the necessary connections themselves may rely on an intermediary who can vouch for them or actually present a bribe on their behalf. Personal connections are also invaluable when the bribe is presented in exchange for a limited commodity, such as a job.

The very fact that bribes sometimes involve personal relationships makes it even more difficult to use other criteria to distinguish bribes from gifts. For example, if the giver and the recipient are friends or relatives, the site where the exchange takes place is irrelevant. In other words, just as a gift can be presented at work, a bribe can be presented at somebody's home. Similarly, the employment status of the bribe recipient is a bad criterion for distinguishing bribes from gifts, because there is no valid reason why a friend or relative cannot give a culturally appropriate gift to a government official. The issue of reciprocity is also complicated when it comes to exchanges between friends and relatives. At this point, the form of corruption often changes from bribery to nepotism. In these cases, a bribe payment may be waived altogether, especially if there is an equivalent exchange of favors which may or may not also involve the official abuse of power.

Certainly, the motivation behind an exchange is an important criterion for distinguishing bribes from gifts. But, what happens when the motivations behind gift giving are complex? In Kazakstan, this is especially the case when it comes to certain types of gifts which sometimes function in part as bribes. Here I would put more emphasis on feast gifts (syilyq and shashu) and in-law gifts (kiit and minit) than on the other categories of gifts. The "sometimes" refers to occasions where a government official is sponsoring a feast (toi) or taking part in an in-law party (qudalyq), and thus in a culturally appropriate position to receive expensive gifts from relatives and friends, and in the case of the in-law parties, from previous strangers.

In-law parties are particularly interesting when it comes to the dynamics of household networking, because they provide a chance for each party to a new marriage to introduce their inner circle of friends and relatives to the other side. When the bride's parents or the groom's parents attend an in-law party, they strategically think about who they should invite to go with them to their new in-laws' home where they are showered with hospitality and gifts. A number of factors go into the selection of the seven or eight "in-laws." One factor that is usually considered is the fact that the presence of a government official conveys the important social message that the family is well connected. Persons of authority, therefore, are frequently invited to participate in an in-law party delegation. As part of the delegation, they receive an assortment of gifts from the hosts, who may have been virtual strangers before, but in the course of a single day, are transformed into kin.

So, when government officials are involved as the recipients of these categories of gifts, I suggest that these gifts, despite the fact that they are presented in a transparent manner during a culturally appropriate moment, function in part as bribes. This does not mean that Kazaks conceive of these gifts as bribes. On the contrary, these gifts are viewed as traditional forms of exchange, which express hospitality and generosity. However, the motives for presenting these types of gifts are complicated. On the one hand, feast gifts and in-law gifts are exchanged as a way to maintain and create new social relationships, to avoid the shame of not giving a gift, and to convey messages about social status. But, on the other hand, there may also be a more strategic element to these forms of gift giving. People know that persons of authority can grant them favors and they know that personal connections are helpful in obtaining favors that involve the abuse of an official office. In this way, personal connections, which are maintained and extended through gift exchange, serve to reduce or nullify the cost of a bribe.

Perhaps the only criterion left to distinguish gifts from bribes is the legality of the exchange. But this criterion does not help to explain why some forms of exchange are acceptable in the first place, while others are not. Although the legal definition of bribery would include the motivation, the obligation, and the content of the exchange, as well as the bribe recipient's employment status, this article demonstrates that the boundary between gifts and bribes is much more difficult to determine.

CONCLUSION

Corruption hinders development efforts in post-Soviet Kazakstan. Stirred by the global campaign against corruption that emerged in the 1990s, local journalists and politicians are initiating local anticorruption movements in post-Soviet Kazakstan. If legal efforts are necessary to fight corruption, should Kazakstan simply adopt the anticorruption legislation promoted by powerful global organizations? Among other things, these laws prevent government officials from accepting gifts from other individuals, thus reducing the temptation to show favoritism toward those who provide gifts.

From an anthropological perspective, the adoption of such legislation is problematic on many levels. First, it is important to take a critical look at why global organizations are strongly promoting anticorruption measures. Are these organizations primarily interested in fighting the social injustices resulting from corruption? Or, are they primarily interested in protecting the investments of Western-dominated transnational corporations? The latter seems to be the case, since powerful countries, such as the United States, are taking relatively small steps toward eliminating their own culturally accepted forms of corruption, such as campaign donations (Bell and Avenarius 1999). However, by encouraging anticorruption legislation in developing countries such as Kazakstan, global organizations make it easier for international businessmen to avoid the hassle of learning unfamiliar business practices.

Second, before implementing new anticorruption laws, it is important to consider the possible unintended consequences. In Kazakstan, gift exchange is viewed as an important part of Kazak culture. Although some gifts function in part as bribes, the exchange of gifts is not perceived to be immoral behavior. To be effective, anticorruption legislation must develop measures to limit the exchange of gifts that function in part as bribes. These measures, however, would probably be viewed as an unwelcome attack on Kazak culture. In addition to being perceived as an attack on Kazak culture, anticorruption laws may have the unintended consequence of targeting the wrong individuals. As Soviet history demonstrates, the introduction of anticorruption campaigns often opens the door for practices akin to witch-hunting. Individuals who would ideally be targeted by these efforts tend to possess both the connections and the skills necessary to avoid being caught. At the same time, the most corrupt individuals often use these campaigns to root out their enemies.

Finally, it is important to consider whether the anticorruption legislation promoted by powerful global organizations is appropriate for a local setting where gift exchange is an integral part of the culture. As this article demonstrates, global organizations and local actors do not necessarily share the same understandings of what constitutes corrupt behavior. This is particularly the case when it comes to the distinction between gifts and bribes. Although there are no easy solutions in the fight against corruption, developing countries such as Kazakstan should develop anticorruption legislation that takes local perceptions of morality into account. On a practical level, it would be much easier to gain support for an anticorruption campaign that is initially targeted against those forms of exchange already perceived to be immoral. At the same time, the government could introduce educational programs that link the anticorruption movement to notions of nationalism, patriotism, and social justice.

NOTES

I am indebted to a number of people who have influenced my ideas in various ways. I owe the most to my Kazak friends and acquaintances who shared their lives and experiences with me. I am also grateful to the following individuals who gave me advice, inspiration, language assistance and/or published materials: Nazif Shahrani, Richard Wilk, William Fierman, Gregory Gleason, Duran Bell, Robert Hunt, Norbert Dannhaeuser, Jeffrey Cohen, Tom Ilgen, Elizabeth Constantine, Derek Johnson, Douglas Northrup, Michelle McClellan, William Reising, Alan Schrift, Kelly McIntyre, Zhanna Torebaeva, Taribye Orazbekova, Tlanat Mawkhanuli, and Maira Dzharyl-Gafarovna. I also thank *Human Organization* for permitting this paper to be reprinted here. The original paper was published in 2000, Volume 59, Number 1, pp. 11–22. The following organizations have funded various stages of my research: the International Research and Exchange Board, with funds provided by the U.S. Department of State, Title VIII program, and the National Endowment of the Humanities; the Joint Committee on the Soviet Union and Its Successor States of the Social Science Research Council and the American Council of Learned Societies, also with funds provided by the U.S. Department of State, Title VIII; the Wenner Gren Foundation for Anthropological Research; Pitzer College; the Department of Anthropology at Indiana University; and the Center for Global Change and World Peace at Indiana University. And, for institutional affiliation, I thank the Akhmed-Yasawi Kazak-Turkik International University in Turkestan and the Kazakstan Academy of Sciences.

1. This was also true for the United States until 1977 when the Foreign Corrupt Practices Act (FCPA) made it illegal for U.S. businessmen to pay bribes to foreign government officials. This law was prompted by the Watergate scandal, which included money laundering through foreign banks, and the Lockheed Corporation case, which involved $25 million dollars of bribes to Japanese officials and the subsequent criminal conviction of the Japanese prime minister. Many U.S.

businessmen have argued that the FCPA gives them an unfair disadvantage in international markets which has cost them tens of billions of dollars in contracts (Glynn et al. 1997:17–19).

2. Economists and political scientists today unanimously agree that bribery is bad for the economy and society as a whole. Among other things, bribery diverts resources, exacerbates income inequities, deters foreign investments, facilitates organized crime, and undermines political legitimacy (Elliot 1997:1–5; Rose-Ackerman 1997:31–34; Tanzi 1998:22–29).

3. These groups are neither mutually exclusive, nor perceived to be such.

4. The independent press is theoretically a "free press," but there are still a number of challenges. According to a *New York Times* article (10 October 1998), "Many journalists accuse the government of making it difficult for a new press to register a new publication and putting quiet pressure on editors to stick to the official line." After a few years of increased freedoms, these pressures intensified in the second half of 1998 as the January presidential election approached.

5. Moises Naim coined the term "corruption eruption." Possible explanations for this corruption eruption include advances in technology, which have brought increased access to information, and the end of the Cold War, which had long provided an external enemy (Glynn et al. 1997:7–15; Tanzi 1998:4–8).

6. The OECD Convention on Combating Bribery of Foreign Officials entered into effect on 18 February 1999. Twenty-nine member-states (now expanded to include Poland, Czech Republic, and Hungary) and five nonmember-states (Argentina, Brazil, Bulgaria, Chile, and the Slovak Republic) have committed themselves to ensuring that their national parliaments will approve the convention and make the necessary legal changes (OECD 1999).

7. From 1992 to 1998, I have spent a total of eight months in Almaty. I have made the journey from Almaty to Shymkent on numerous occasions, often alone, where I have had lengthy conversations with other travelers.

8. The quality of the countergifts, like the quality and the quantity of the food and drinks, is one way people measure and evaluate the household's social standing relative to other households. On a few limited occasions, I attended a feast with the family and we all came home empty-handed. People pointed out that this was not particularly unusual, especially if the guests were simply acquaintances of the host household, but it was somewhat inappropriate.

REFERENCES

Bayley, David H.
1966 The Effects of Corruption in a Developing Nation. Western Political Quarterly 19:719–732.

Bell, Duran, and Christine Avenarius
1999 *Guanxi*, Bribery and Ideological Hegemony. Paper presented at the 98th Annual Meeting of the American Anthropological Association. Chicago, 17–21 November.

Bloch, Maurice, and Jonathan Parry, eds.
1989 Money and the Morality of Exchange. Cambridge: Cambridge University Press.

Brain, James L.
1996 The Ugly American Revisited. *In* Talking about People: Readings in Contemporary Cultural Anthropology. 2nd. ed. William Haviland and Robert Gordon, eds. Pp. 230–233. Mountain View, CA: Mayfield Publishing Company.

Cernea, Michael M., ed.
1991 Putting People First: Sociological Variables in Rural Development. 2nd ed. Oxford: Oxford University Press.

Clark, William A.
1993 Crime and Punishment in Soviet Officialdom: Combating Corruption in the Political Elite, 1965–1990. Armonk, NY: M. E. Sharpe.

Elliott, Kimberly Ann, ed.
1997 Corruption and the Global Economy. Washington, DC: Institute for International Economics.

Ericson, Richard
1984 The "Second" Economy and Resource Allocation under Central Planning. Journal of Comparative Economics 8(1):1–24.

Ferguson, James
1990 The Anti-Politics Machine: "Development," Depoliticization, and Bureaucratic Power in Lesotho. Cambridge: Cambridge University Press.

Glynn, Patrick, Stephen Kobrin, and Moises Naim
1997 The Globalization of Corruption. *In* Corruption and the Global Economy. Kimberly Elliot, ed. Pp. 7–27. Washington, DC: Institute of International Economics.

Gregory, Chris
1982 Gifts and Commodities. New York: Academic Press.

Grossman, Gregory
1984 Studies in the Second Economy of Communist Countries. Berkeley: University of California Press.

Halperin, Rhoda
1991 The Livelihood of Kin: Making Ends Meet the Kentucky Way. Austin: University of Texas Press.

Hill, Polly
1986 Development Economics on Trial. Cambridge: Cambridge University Press.

Humphrey, Caroline, and Stephen Hugh-Jones, eds.
1992 Barter, Exchange and Value: An Anthropological Approach. Cambridge: Cambridge University Press.

Hunt, Robert C.
2002 Economic Transfers and Exchanges: Concepts for Describing Allocations. In Theory in Economic Anthropology. Jean Ensminger, ed. Pp. 105–118. Walnut Creek, CA: AltaMira Press.

International Monetary Fund (IMF)
1995 IMF Approves Stand-By Credit for Kazakhstan. 5 June. Online. The IMF. Available: http://www.imf.org/external/np/sec/pr/1995/pr9534.htm. Access date: 19 March 1999.

Johnston, Michael
1997 Public Officials, Private Interests, and Sustainable Democracy: When Politics and Corruption Meet. In Corruption and the Global Economy. Kimberly Elliot, ed. Pp. 61–82. Washington, DC: Institute for International Economics.

Kaufmann, Daniel, and Paul Siegelbaum
1997 Privatization and Corruption in Transition Economies. Journal of International Affairs 50(2):419–458.

Kipnis, Andrew
1997 Producing Guanxi: Sentiment, Self and Subculture in a North China Village. Durham, NC: Duke University Press.

Kramer, John M.
1977 Political Corruption in the USSR. Western Political Quarterly 30(2):213–224.

Ledeneva, Alena V.
1998 Russia's Economy of Favours: Blat, Networking and Informal Exchange. Cambridge: Cambridge University Press.

Leff, Nathaniel H.
1964 Economic Development through Bureaucratic Corruption. American Behavioral Scientist 8(3):8–15.

Levi-Strauss, Claude
1969 [1949] The Elementary Structures of Kinship. New York: Beacon Press.

Mauss, Marcel
1925 [1990] The Gift: The Form and Reason for Exchange in Archaic Societies. W. D. Halls, trans. New York: W. W. Norton and Company.

OECD (Organization for Economic Development)
1999 OECD Anti-Corruption Unit: Combating Bribery and Corruption in International Business Transactions. 15 February. p://www.oecd.org/dof/ uocorruption. Access date: 24 May 1999.

Pieth, Mark
1997 International Cooperation to Combat Corruption. In Corruption and the Global Economy. Kimberly Elliot, ed. Pp 119–131. Washington, DC: Institute for International Economics.

Rose-Ackerman, Susan
1997 The Political Economy of Corruption. In Corruption and the Global Economy. Kimberly Elliot, ed. Pp. 31–60. Washington, DC: Institute for International Economics.

Sharma, Ursula
1986 Women's Work, Class and the Urban Household: A Study of Shimla, India. New York: Viking Penguin.

Smart, Alan
1993 Gifts, Bribes and Guanxi: A Reconsideration of Bourdieu's Social Capital. Cultural Anthropology 8(3):388–408.

Stack, Carol
1973 All Our Kin. New York: Basic Books.

Tanzi, Vito
1998 Corruption around the World: Causes, Consequences, Scope and Cures. IMF Working Paper. Washington, DC: International Monetary Fund.

United States Agency for International Development (USAID)

1996 USAID Country Profile: Kazakhstan. October [last update]. Online. Available: http://www.info.usaid.gov/countries/kz/kaz.htm. Access date: 14 March 1999.

Werbner, Pnina

1990 The Migration Process: Capital, Gifts and Offerings among British Pakistanis. London: Berg.

Werner, Cynthia

1998 Household Networks and the Security of Mutual Indebtedness in Rural Kazakstan. Central Asian Survey 17(4):597–612.

World Bank

1990 World Development Report: Poverty. Washington, DC: World Bank.

1998a Assessing Aid: What Works, What Doesn't and Why. Washington, DC: World Bank.

1998b Kazakhstan: Country Overview. January 1998 [last update]. Online. World Bank. Available: http://www.worldbank.org/html/extdr/offrep/eca/kazcb. htm. Access date: 14 March 1999.

1998c Preventing Corruption in Bank Projects and Keeping Our Own House in Order. July 1998. Online. World Bank. Available: http://www.worldbank. org/html/extdr/anticorruption/preventing.htm. Access date: 15 March 1999.

Yan, Yunxiang

1996 The Flow of Gifts: Reciprocity and Social Networks in a Chinese Village. Palo Alto, CA: Stanford University Press.

Yang, Mayfair

1994 Gifts, Favors and Banquets: The Art of Social Relationships in China. Ithaca, NY: Cornell University Press.

11

Globalization, Privatization, and Public Space in the Provincial Philippines

Ty Matejowsky

INTRODUCTION

Possibly the most distinctive and broadly acknowledged architectural manifestation of Spanish colonial urbanism in the Philippines is the uniform design of the towns and cities found throughout the Hispanicized areas of the archipelago. This settlement pattern—known as the plaza complex—maintains a standardized arrangement of streets modeled on a grid scheme as well as a nuclear core of structures around which local life is organized. With the conspicuous commercialization of town centers in numerous localities around the country, important questions arise regarding how this historical urban form will be affected by the encroachment of large-scale trade facilities.

ISSUES

Over two decades ago, Reed (1978) stated that the basic design of Philippine municipalities instituted during the sixteenth century would still be recognizable despite the "predictable modifications" caused by "the relentless processes of modernization and urbanization" experienced in the last century (p. 67). Although his assertion is accurate in that the essential layout of settlements has remained intact, it did not anticipate the profound impact subsequent urban development would have on the built environment. Due in part to the substantial inroads made by forces of globalization, many communities in the Philippines are currently undergoing a considerable transformation in their structural morphologies (Filio 1997; Harper 1996; Maulana 1997).

The globalizing trend this chapter is primarily concerned with is privatization that entails a shift in the regulation of public assets from state agencies to private organizations. Typically, industries involved with utilities, banking, health care, transportation, and communication are most affected by this process, although publicly held real estate is increasingly subject to private management (Romano 1996). Privatization emerged in the 1970s as a viable solution for governments of the industrial West looking to reduce budgetary pressures and foster competitiveness among national firms (Beesley 1992; Chutterback et al. 1991). As the nations of Eastern Europe and the Third World assumed more market-oriented policies in the last two decades—due in large part to the guidelines established by aid agencies like the World Bank and international financial institutions like the International Monetary Fund—privatization became a strategy integral to vitalizing stagnant economies as well as ameliorating prevailing social conditions (Adam et al. 1992; Baldassari et al. 1993; Hanice 1987). Although the move to privatize public holdings in developing societies like the Philippines has done much to streamline basic services, this chapter will show that such measures have not occurred without certain trade-offs.

This study will add to the literature in two distinct areas. First, the transnational phenomenon of retail trade concentration (Dannhaeuser 1996b:245–258), which, among other things, involves a proliferation of large Western-style commercial enterprises like fast-food restaurants, department stores, warehouse clubs, 24-hour convenience stores, and shopping malls, has advanced to such a degree in the Philippines that properties heretofore designated as public are now being developed as commercial real estate. Subsequently, the previous balance maintained between private land and communal space on the municipal level is being significantly disrupted. Second, contrary to earlier work that showed that advocacy for the preservation of town centers was not a primary concern of those living in provincial Philippine communities (Dannhaeuser 1996a), I present cases demonstrating local inhabitants' active interest in maintaining and protecting historical sites.

To support these assertions, I look at three municipalities that have sustained a comparable erosion of public space in their urban centers in recent years. Specifically, this work will investigate Dagupan City, Urdaneta City, and Bayambang, all of which are located in one of the country's most populated provinces—Pangasinan. After providing a brief overview of Spanish colonial urbanism in the Philippines, I examine the significance of the plaza complex and the socioeconomic characteristics of Dagupan, Urdaneta, and Bayambang. Furthermore, I document their respective experiences involving a transformation of the historical urban core. Additionally, I describe how individuals in each community have acted to resist or facilitate this phenomenon. In conclusion, I synthesize the comparison of the three localities.

THE PLAZA COMPLEX

The standardized organization of urban landscapes in the Philippines is a product of Spain's colonial experience in Latin America. Although other European powers founded settlements primarily as trading posts to coordinate the extraction of natural resources, Spain intended to bring about a physical and social change to their overseas holdings. On 13 July 1573, King Philip II of Spain formally issued a comprehensive body of statutes known as the Laws of the Indies. The codes specified that the layout of towns and cities should conform to a grid design whereby the primary components of the plaza complex are erected in a fixed relationship to one another and adhere to established dimensions.

The Philippine plaza complex consists of three principal components: (1) an open square known as the plaza proper, (2) the *municipio* or municipal government building, and (3) the stone cathedral and adjunct buildings maintained by the Catholic Church. This organizational assemblage is situated within a municipality's *poblacíon* (urban center) and is usually surrounded by a school and marketplace along with several large elite residences and trade establishments. This group of structures typically serves as the focal point around which urban development occurs.

Although the church and government buildings are commonly viewed as physical manifestations of authority, the plaza proper, due to its accessibility to all sectors of society, is seen as the architectural embodiment of the community (Hart 1955:8). Recognized as the primary sanctuary of greenery and open space downtown, the archetypal Philippine plaza of today contains a number of built features. Spread across the center is a rectangular slab of concrete containing a stage or kiosk as well as permanent seating and rest rooms. On either side of this middle section are recreational facilities such as children's playgrounds, athletic courts, and monuments honoring both national revolutionary heroes and prominent politicians.

Traditionally, the plaza functions as the principal arena for local civic, cultural, and religious events (Malcolm 1939:27). It serves as the location for many of the ceremonies associated with Holy Week and as the main site where citizens can legally gather for political demonstrations. Perhaps more significantly, the public plaza is where all segments of the community congregate during annual fiesta celebrations. For several weeks of the year, customarily between December and May, plazas across the Philippines are transformed into sites for a variety of activities including musical performances, beauty contests, political speeches, and fireworks displays.

The public plaza is also integral to municipal rehabilitation. Following a catastrophe, the square can be utilized as a temporary refuge for displaced citizens and as an area where itinerant vendors can establish a makeshift marketplace. Yet, because the plaza is viewed as public domain, it has, in virtually all instances, been inaccessible to private commercial development on a permanent basis. Indeed, since 1909, the country's high courts have handed down several decisions in cases pertaining to the legality of establishing permanent trade structures on local plazas. Overwhelmingly, these rulings have upheld the concept of the plaza as community property and, therefore, "beyond the commerce of man" (Official Gazette 1948; Philippine Reports 1909, 1915, 1935, 1958).

COMPARISONS

Dagupan City, Urdaneta City, and Bayambang are all located within two hundred kilometers of Metro-Manila in the north-central province of Pangasinan. The two former cities, in most instances, demonstrate more similarities than when contrasted with the latter municipality. Dagupan and Urdaneta are classified by the national government as medium-range provincial cities, while Bayambang is designated as a rural municipality.

Even though the respective populations for Dagupan, Urdaneta, and Bayambang are not dissimilar (128,000 Dagupenos, 106,000 Urdanetans, and 85,000 Bayambangans), the population densities for each municipality reveal the urban character of the two larger communities. Dagupan has about 2,900 persons for every one square kilometer, followed by approximately 830 inhabitants per square kilometer in Urdaneta, and roughly 450 residents per square kilometer in Bayambang. Urdaneta and Dagupan have higher degrees of urban development than Bayambang. Both contain a thriving poblacíon, composed of multilevel structures and bisected by a network of paved streets. Bayambang's built environment, by contrast, remains less developed, with only a few low-rise edifices lining the town's main street.

The retail structures of the three communities also exhibit a closer parallel between Dagupan and Urdaneta in relation to Bayambang. There were almost 3,200 registered commercial firms in Dagupan, about 2,300 in Urdaneta, and nearly 420 in Bayambang as of 1996. The commercial morphology of each municipality is best represented by the dichotomous formal/informal economic model. However, compared to Dagupan and Urdaneta, the trade structure of Bayambang has, up until now, been less receptive to the encroachment of formal sector enterprises. There are many Western-style supermarkets, chain fast-food restaurants, department stores, and warehouse clubs in Dagupan and Urdaneta; Bayambang contains no such enterprises of a similar magnitude.

Correspondingly, the social compositions of Dagupan and Urdaneta's trade communities are more similar to one another than to Bayambang. The merchant populations of both cities are multicultural, while Bayambang's is virtually homogenous in terms of ethnic affiliation. In addition to the numerous Filipinos working as marketplace and independent street-store operators, there is also a small number of ethnic Chinese[1] in Dagupan and Urdaneta who have dominated local commerce for generations. Even though they are less than 5 percent of the aggregate population in both Dagupan and Urdaneta, Chinese-Filipinos control almost all of the wholesale enterprises, supermarkets, warehouse clubs, appliance stores, hardware firms, and other large-scale retail facilities in each city. In comparison, Bayambang's more modest merchant community has remained almost exclusively Filipino.

DAGUPAN CITY

Similar to municipalities throughout the Philippines, Dagupan is organized around a plaza proper, municipio, and cathedral complex. The city hall and public square are situated next to one another along the downtown's primary thoroughfare, while the church compound stands directly in back (see figure 11.1). Since Dagupan was formally recognized as a municipality by the Spanish in 1643, the three institutions have maintained this fixed arrangement. Yet, in the last three decades, the community's architectural core has shown signs of fragmentation. Instances involving the alteration of historical structures and the encroachment of private enterprises on public land have contributed significantly to this transformation.

Local Plaza Complex

The most conspicuous cases of local architectural revision have occurred within Dagupan's plaza complex. Incremental changes to the original design of the municipal hall and cathedral compound in the 1970s, coupled with the degeneration of the plaza proper into an area where squatting, drug dealing, and prostitution were common in the 1980s, preceded more radical modifications to the city's institutional cen-

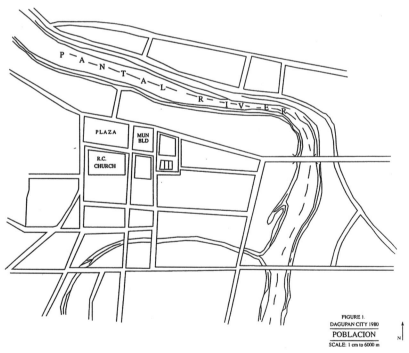

FIGURE 11.1
Urban center of Dagupan City, Philippines, 1980.

ter following a major earthquake in 1990. The erosion of Dagupan's nuclear core was also preceded by several events involving the privatization of community space. Even though all construction within the city must conform with a comprehensive zoning ordinance, over the years exceptions have been granted to this general land-use strategy.

Beginning in the late 1960s, local administrators approved the privatization of communally held real estate adjacent to the city's plaza complex. Of significance was the conversion of a public park across from the municipio to a site where small-scale traders could legally establish a marketplace. By the mid-1980s, this vendor site was developed by a Manila-based ethnic Chinese firm into a two-story shopping complex of Western-style retail outlets. Similarly, in 1986 a vendor facility regulated by city hall was converted into a private market despite the protest of affected merchants. Located behind the municipal building and across from the cathedral compound, this property was franchised to Magic Inc., owned by local ethnic Chinese entrepreneur Benjamin Lim.[2]

Public property in Dagupan was further diminished following a massive earthquake in 1990. Beside destruction of numerous buildings, roads, and bridges, the city's principal site for small-scale trading—the Old Public Market (OPM)—was damaged extensively. With the loss of this structure, hundreds of stall holders were displaced and subsequently relocated by the municipal government to the adjacent public plaza. Rather than redevelop the collapsed OPM as a public concern, however, the city entered into a build-operate-transfer agreement with a local ethnic Chinese enterprise, City Supermarket Inc. (CSI). This lease contract stipulated that CSI would construct and manage a private commercial complex on the site for the next fifty years before it reversed back to municipal proprietorship.

The franchise awarded to CSI was called into question by most of the itinerant vendors on the plaza who had formed a cooperative and, likewise, prepared a bid for the project (as did Magic Inc.). The crux of their complaint was that, under the law, cooperatives enjoy a favorable position when it comes to the management of public market facilities. For unspecified reasons, local officials ignored this privileged status and did not accept the vendors' development plan. The cooperative filed a lawsuit against the city that was later dismissed by the Philippine Supreme Court in 1993.

The high court's decision coincided with the opening of the CSI Market Square Mall, the largest commercial facility north of Metro-Manila.

Plaza Privatization

In the six years following the earthquake, most of Dagupan's small-scale vendors occupied a temporary marketplace on the public plaza. Although some were eventually accommodated with spaces in one of four market sheds erected behind the CSI mall, most continued to endure an austere existence on the plaza. Not only did their makeshift marketplace represent a fire hazard and an endangerment to public health, their extended occupancy of the square also necessitated the transfer of the city fiesta and other traditional community events to adjacent sites—the most notable being the parking area fronting the CSI mall.

In April 1996, the municipal government announced its intentions to clear the temporary stalls from the plaza and begin its P3.7 million rehabilitation ($1 = P26). The city's redevelopment project outlined changes that would radically alter the plaza's conventional morphology. Less controversial improvements included leveling the plaza surface, establishing a local museum, and installing brick walkways and tree lanterns. What generated opposition from many in the community was the proposed transfer of the monument commemorating Dr. José Rizal (the national hero of the Philippines) from the eastern third of the plaza to its original site in the southwest corner to make way for a three-story shopping mall. The private retail facility would reduce the total area of the plaza site from 12,375 square meters to 8,250 square meters.

The Save-the-Plaza-Coalition-for-Pro-People-Development

Preliminary rehabilitation work for the entire plaza began in August 1996. Although the demolition of the temporary vendor market was greeted positively by the community as a whole, this upgrade was soon overshadowed by the prospect of a truncated plaza proper occupied by a permanent commercial mall on its eastern third. Public opposition to the city's plan began to crystallize rapidly. By September 1996, a consortium of over forty student, religious, environmental, and architectural preservation organizations had united to form the Save-the-Plaza-Coalition-for-Pro-People-Development (SPCPD). The alliance's core membership was composed primarily of local professionals including university professors, lawyers, journalists, and community activists. In addition to this central group, several Metro-Manila residents with ties to Dagupan were also involved in the association. Some city officials dismissed the SPCPD's opposition as the product of a "colonial mentality" whereby the city hall, church, and plaza must exist in a cohesive assemblage, but the coalition's stance on the matter soon became too powerful to ignore. The administration scheduled an open assembly to assess the sentiment of the community at large on the issue.

First Public Hearing on Plaza Privatization (October 1996)

The public hearing was held in the city's session hall on the morning of 18 October 1996. Hundreds of the SPCPD rank and file arrived in identical yellow t-shirts and plastered the meeting room's walls with "Save D Plaza" posters. The City Development and Planning officer presented the outline of the municipal government's restoration plan. The city claimed the multilevel shopping mall facility on the public plaza was necessary to house those displaced vendors who were evicted from the square but not selected for stalls in the recently completed market building. Moreover, it was the administration's position that the unconfined space inherent to Philippine public plazas would be retained since the proposed trade center would, in actuality, be an "atrium mall" and, hence, constructed around an open courtyard.

By and large, coalition proponents expressed unequivocal support for local commercial expansion, not to mention most of the upgrades outlined in the municipality's plaza restoration plan. Yet, they strongly disagreed with city planners on the issue of allowing a sizable parcel of the public square to be developed and maintained by a private firm. They noted that the conversion of a significant portion of the plaza was not only incongruous with the local zoning ordinance, it was also inconsistent with the development recommendations in the comprehensive community rehabilitation plan officially adopted by the municipal government after the 1990 earthquake. Correspondingly, they felt citizens stood to benefit far more with the plaza as a noncommercial zone rather than housing a private trade structure.

The SPCPD indicated that within close proximity to the plaza were already located large-scale shopping facilities owned by Magic, Inc. and CSI. The construction of another multitiered retail enterprise in this immediate vicinity would exacerbate an already-tenuous parking and traffic situation and, as a corollary, compound environmental concerns about downtown's air quality. Likewise, the SPCPD argued that no section of the plaza should be commercialized since there were already properties both publicly and privately maintained just outside the poblacíon that could better accommodate the three-story trade structure. Finally, the group had serious reservations over the plight of the displaced vendors in whose name the atrium mall was being established. They maintained that most of these small-scale merchants could not afford rent in the proposed atrium mall.

Repercussions of First Public Hearing

While the SPCPD's strong showing did not persuade city officials to terminate the project, it did convince them that selling the idea of an atrium mall to the community-at-large would take more effort. Thus, another hearing on the issue was scheduled for February 1997. In the weeks preceding the meeting, the local government began to use its influence to garner public support. The city began to court favor with groups with whom they had previously maintained an antagonistic relationship. In particular, administrators enlisted the support of the local market vendors' association. As potential benefactors of the project, the small-scale trade community became outspoken advocates for the atrium mall.

As the second meeting approached, an erosion of the SPCPD's membership base began. Many in the coalition withdrew their support when it was learned that Magic, Inc. CEO Benjamin Lim was to be the prime developer of the proposed atrium mall on the plaza. Several more pulled out after attacks from municipal officials began to appear in Dagupan's media. These reports scrutinized connections between politicians unseated in the last round of local elections (1992) and several coalition leaders. Incumbent officeholders contended that the antiatrium mall movement was essentially a vehicle for local partisan politics.

The SPCPD approached leaders in the national government for assistance in response to the escalating conflict. An appeal to the National Historical Institute resulted in a ruling that stated that the proposed transferal of the Rizal monument from the eastern third of the plaza to its original location in the southwest corner to make way for the three-story commercial center was against the law. Moreover, the SPCPD held a People's

Forum in December 1996, where a former Philippine senator looking to reclaim his legislative position in the 1998 national elections, Aquilino Pimentel, was the primary speaker. As author of the Local Government Code of 1991 that, among other things, dictates the procedure city governments are to follow when converting public land to private property, Pimentel noted that the project had, thus far, circumvented this established process.

Second Public Hearing on Plaza Privatization (February 1997)

Like the public assembly in October 1996, the second meeting was heavily attended by both proponents and opponents of the atrium mall project. The SPCPD elected to present its case in a nontraditional manner (choreographed dance numbers and local school children's poetry), anticipating that the event would be a biased one favoring the city. However innovative, this novel approach did little to change the minds of the public officials who needed only to draft an ordinance for the project to commence. The meeting was the last time the subject was publicly addressed by the municipal government. Since the city failed to generate widespread community support for the atrium mall and, moreover, because local elections were just over a year away, an implicit moratorium on the issue took place.

Plaza Redevelopment

For the next eighteen months, improvements to the central and western sectors of Dagupan's public plaza continued. Several monuments honoring national figures were erected on the western third. More substantial, however, was the opening of the two-story Landmark and Tourism Center at the front of the plaza in the latter half of 1998. During this same period, important community events, including the fiftith anniversary of Dagupan's city charter, were celebrated on the restored sections of the public property.

As municipal and national elections approached in May 1998, support for the SPCPD's cause began to fade from the local consciousness. Even though the organization's leadership contended that the city would in all probability pass an ordinance finalizing construction of the atrium mall sometime after election day, they could not mobilize their members to make the plaza a campaign issue. Punctuating this loss of momentum was

Benjamin Lim's successful bid for Congress. Given his growing political influence, not to mention the financial backing of numerous moneyed investors, the privatization of the public plaza's eastern third now appeared imminent. In fact, the city administration initiated steps following Lim's taking office to transfer the local municipio and adjunct police station to a less central location in the poblacíon. This move was approved by officials so that Lim could consolidate his downtown commercial holdings. The completion of such developments would, for all intents and purposes, signify the end to the historical arrangement of Dagupan's architectural core.

URDANETA CITY

Due to historical circumstances, the formation of Urdaneta's built environment followed a different path than either Dagupan or Bayambang. Consisting mainly of low- and mid-rise buildings, the city's central business district is intersected by two major highways. The city hall and public plaza are diagonally across from one another and separated by an east-west thoroughfare. Partially isolated from these structures and insulated by two market sheds directly behind the plaza stands the cathedral compound (see figure 11.2).

Local Plaza Complex

The establishment of Urdaneta in 1858 represented a significant departure from the customary procedure whereby new towns were chartered. Atypically, the initiative for instituting the municipality was not imposed by the provincial administration. Instead, local officials representing three neighboring towns petitioned the regional administration for the consolidation of their adjacent precincts to form a new urban center. Approval for the establishment of Urdaneta as a township partially hinged on the community's ability sufficiently to fund basic operations. Subsequently, the provincial government authorized the charter by specifying that a large parcel of municipal property be designated as public agricultural land. This area was not to be sold, since its produce would provide the financial support for the local government. Notwithstanding the novel method by which Urdaneta was founded, the municipality's fundamental morphol-

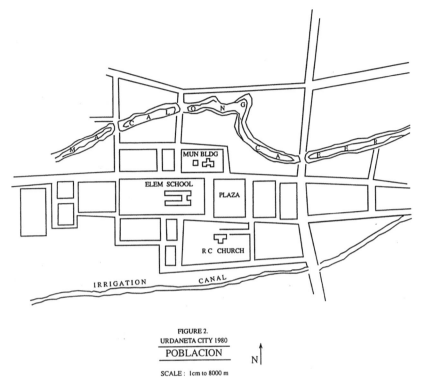

FIGURE 2.
URDANETA CITY 1980
POBLACION   N↑

SCALE : 1cm to 8000 m

FIGURE 11.2
Urban center of Urdaneta City, Philippines, 1980.

ogy conformed to the standardized design for towns and cities initiated by Spanish colonial planners.

Urdaneta remained organized around a poblacíon where local institutions were constructed of nondurable materials such as nipa, wood, and bamboo for the next quarter century. The cityscape assumed a more permanent character in 1884, when a prominent local family donated substantial acreage to the municipality so that a brick cathedral compound could be erected. The contributed land also contained sites for a new public plaza and city hall. The translocation of the plaza complex was completed around the turn of century, when Urdaneta constructed the first municipio in the province with stone masonry, galvanized metal roofing, and a contemporary colonial facade adjacent to the plaza proper (Cortes

1990). The architectural components of Urdaneta's nuclear core have maintained this basic configuration for close to a century.

Urdaneta Commercial Complex

Although it ran somewhat counter to municipal zoning ordinances, administrators sanctioned the occupation of Urdaneta's public plaza by local vendors in the early 1980s. As hundreds of makeshift stalls were erected over the next few years, the plaza became known as the Urdaneta Commercial Complex (UCC) and emerged as one of the primary venues for small-scale trading in the community. Curiously, general opposition to the transformation of the plaza proper from an accessible public square to an assemblage of semipermanent market sheds was virtually nonexistent. Subsequently, community events had to be transferred to an adjacent schoolyard.

By the mid-1980s, after hundreds of vendor stalls were destroyed by fire, the entire UCC facility was officially condemned. Local administrators faced the equally expensive options of either rebuilding a more permanent commercial complex at the site or restoring the plaza to a semblance of its historical character. Ultimately, the city government endorsed the former alternative because rehabilitation funding would be provided exclusively by the Urdaneta Market Vendors Association (UMVA) and the new marketplace would remain under municipal control. This arrangement clearly benefited the city more than the vendors.

In the years that followed, Urdaneta emerged as one of the most economically progressive communities in Pangasinan. Though the community had become increasingly attractive to various national and multinational firms wanting to locate commercial outlets in the provincial areas of the country, it was the 1990 earthquake that considerably augmented the city's status as a regional trading center. Many displaced merchants from Dagupan and other affected municipalities relocated to Urdaneta after the trade structures of their respective communities collapsed. Of consequence were several large-scale retail enterprises owned and operated by Chinese-Filipino entrepreneurs out of Dagupan including CSI and Magic, Inc.

Plaza Privatization

In July 1996, local retailers were surprised when the municipal government issued a press release outlining a build-operate-transfer lease of the

UCC site to a private concern for the erection of a Western-style shopping mall. This project, which was to be the largest commercial center ever undertaken in the greater Urdaneta area, entailed the construction of a P450 million, four-story commercial complex with adjunct parking facilities that would encompass approximately 11,600 square meters of the original plaza and would stand between the Urdaneta City Hall and local cathedral compound. According to the administration, the city stood to gain about P17 million each year from the leasing of this property. Moreover, the proclamation named Urdaneta Builders and Realty Corporation (UBRC), a subsidiary company of Dagupan City's Benjamin Lim, as the mall developer. Although municipal officials did not adhere to the procedure mandated by the local government code of holding a public hearing prior to the conversion of public space into private land, the resolution was approved.

While the city's resolution brought about little, if no, response from the community-at-large, it did create a panic among the hundreds of UCC marketplace traders. Not only was their primary source of income threatened, they stood to lose the substantial sums that they had invested in the reconstruction of the site over a decade earlier Their apprehension was exacerbated by the refusal of many wholesalers—fearing they would not be remunerated for credited merchandise—to allow the affected traders to purchase stock on a consignment basis. Likewise, rumors began to spread that individuals in the administration would benefit from the construction of the UBRC project. As the anxiety heightened, so too did the pressure on the municipal government to address the concerns of the UMVA.

Public Hearing on Plaza Privatization (October 1996)

Thus, on the morning of 18 October 1996, more than one hundred UCC stallholders crowded the municipal session hall for a meeting with the city on the proposed shopping mall. Because representatives of the UMVA were not permitted to speak, the hearing was a summarization of the corresponding rental rates for the various mall spaces by local officials. Administrators assured UMVA members that their worries were largely unfounded because they would be given first priority to present bids for stalls in the complex. However favorable this concession appeared, it was largely an empty gesture since the goodwill fee for the smallest commercial stall in the facility was an inflationary P75,000.

Political Repercussions of Public Hearing

In the weeks following the hearing, the UMVA leadership began exploring legal remedies to prevent their removal from the former public plaza. Upon hearing of similar cases in neighboring communities, the organization hired former Senator Pimentel as their attorney. He advised them to file suit against the city, not only for disregarding their preferential position as market stallholders and approving a resolution that favored a private concern at their expense, but also for ignoring the Local Government code of 1991. The group submitted their petition to the regional trial court in December 1996.

In order to consider the merits of the case, the provincial magistrate issued a temporary restraining order against the city from pursuing the UBRC project. Despite this injunction, local administrators continued to follow through with their intentions. Notice was served to the stallholders that their licenses to conduct business in the UCC would no longer be valid within ten days of 31 December 1996. Citing a presidential decree that gives government enterprises designed to promote general welfare a top priority, the city claimed the UCC should be demolished. This announcement precipitated a defection by some in the UMVA who began publicly to support mall construction in an apparent effort to secure prime spaces at the new facility.

Vendor Ejection from Urdaneta Commercial Complex

On 10 January 1997, the regional trial court dismissed a petition filed by the UMVA to extend the injunction prohibiting any work on the UBRC project. The plaintiff's attorneys promptly submitted an appeal against the ruling that was forwarded to the Court of Appeals. Not waiting for another legal impasse to further delay the project's construction, the municipality acted decisively. Within hours of the judgment, the UCC's water, electricity, and telephone lines were cut off as approximately one hundred city workers converged on the marketplace. In less than an hour, over one hundred stallholders and their employees had been evicted and the area was completely enclosed by a metal fence. Armed men were posted along the UCC's perimeter to prevent vendors from retrieving their belongings. For the next month, vendors awaited the higher court's ruling as their stalls were systematically dismantled. Although the lower court's motion was eventually overturned by the appellate court so that the case could be judiciously reviewed, the adjudication arrived weeks after the vendors' stalls had been demolished.

Plaza Redevelopment

The UMVA's case against the city remained under deliberation by the Court of Appeals for well into the next year. Because the litigation progressed at such a gradual pace, many local residents became convinced the construction of the UBRC project was inevitable. The fact that a large billboard advertising the commercial facility was erected outside the disputed area only served to confirm this sentiment. This general acceptance of the shopping mall's establishment seemed, likewise, to exhaust whatever support the UMVA had thus far engendered from the community at large. In fact, only a handful of those displaced from the UCC continued actively to pursue the case. By the spring of 1998, most vendors had decided to drop the case in exchange for monetary compensation.

The UMVA's limited pool of financial resources and apparent lack of local political clout, coupled with the general indifference of most Urdaneta citizens, did little to elevate the matter as a 1998 campaign issue. Even though no major structural work had been completed by election time, the mall's construction appeared certain with Benjamin Lim's successful congressional bid. His election represented not only the transition of ethnic Chinese from hegemony in local retail trade into national politics; it, likewise, precipitated an unprecedented reorganization of Urdaneta's historical urban core.

BAYAMBANG

The political and social development of Bayambang began early in the sixteenth century when the community emerged as an indigenous settlement in Pangasinan's south-central frontier. Although the locality was formally recognized by the Spanish provincial government in 1792, the local population had been organized into a clerical estate administered by the Dominican Order for almost two hundred years. By the beginning of the nineteenth century, the primary components of Bayambang's contemporary plaza complex were already instituted in congruence with the Laws of the Indies. In 1741, a stone cathedral and adjunct church facilities were erected in the municipality's center. Later, a wooden municipio building was established in an adjacent lot, while, the public plaza, set somewhat apart, occupied a tract of land near the Agno River.

Local Plaza Complex

The town's architectural core maintained this traditional configuration for almost two hundred years. The parcel of vacant land separating the cathedral compound from the plaza proper was divided by a stretch of national highway in 1918. The unoccupied acreage was eventually contributed to the municipality by a distinguished local family in the years preceding World War II. Since Bayambang's original public square had become overrun with permanent trade stalls, the donated plot was converted into the current public plaza. This relocation involved transferring the Dr. José Rizal memorial from its original site to a more visible location at the new plaza. Directly behind the statue, a kiosk for local fiesta activities was erected. Likewise, the city built a monument dedicated to President Ramón Magsaysay on the plaza's southeast corner in the early 1960s. The structural morphology of Bayambang's nuclear core has remained basically unchanged since the community became Hispanicized (see figure 11.3).

Plaza Privatization

In the summer of 1995, a fire gutted several commercial sheds of the local market compound in downtown Bayambang. The town government condemned the entire facility with a pledge to renovate the site by 1998. Those traders displaced by the conflagration were moved to the public plaza's south side. As clusters of market stalls began to pervade the area, municipal officials initiated several measures that departed significantly from the town's zoning ordinance.

In October 1995, the administration secretly adopted a resolution approving the commercial development of the plaza's 4,000-square-meter eastern edge. They discreetly entered into a build-operate-transfer scheme with a local financial institution. This agreement permitted Homeowner's Savings & Loan Association, Inc. (HOSLA) to erect and maintain a two-story bank building on a lot within the plaza's newly designated commercial zone. Although these declarations involved the conversion of community land into private holdings, they were ratified by Bayambang's civic government without adherence to the local government code.

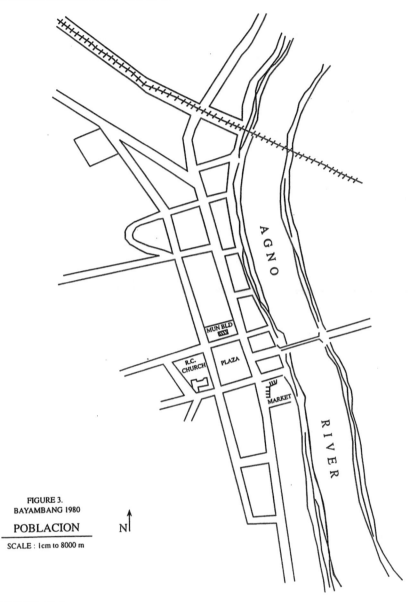

FIGURE 3.
BAYAMBANG 1980

POBLACION   N↑

SCALE : 1cm to 8000 m

FIGURE 11.3
Urban center of Bayambang, Philippines, 1980.

Public Resistance to Plaza Privatization

Many in the community were confounded when the area was fenced off and construction on the HOSLA edifice commenced in July 1996. As groundwork on the site progressed, speculation that elected officials had a vested interest in the completion of the enterprise began to grow. A group of local professionals concerned about the plaza's integrity began making inquiries to determine what involvement the Bayambang government had in the new bank building. These citizens retained former Senator Aquilino Pimentel as their pro bono legal counsel. Through Pimentel's efforts, they learned that the push for plaza privatization by town officials went well beyond the HOSLA. The municipality intended to enter into an agreement with an unnamed developer to construct and manage a multilevel shopping mall and adjunct parking facilities on the plaza's eastern edge. Like the plaza malls in Dagupan and Urdaneta, this commercial complex would be composed almost exclusively of formal sector enterprises as well as include comparable consumer amenities.

Pimentel submitted a complaint against the municipality on this group's behalf in regional trial court. Although their lawsuit was filed specifically to stop construction work on the HOSLA building, an intended aim of the litigation was to prevent any other private structure from going up on the public plaza (i.e., the much larger shopping mall). They questioned the legality of both projects, since town administrators did not follow the established procedure for converting a public property into a private concern. The court ordered the temporary suspension of all building activities related to the savings and loan structure so that the facts of the litigation could be properly considered.

In an effort to generate community support, the municipal government made known their intentions regarding the public square through the local media. Officials argued that the temporary stalls operating within the plaza's southern third had effectively compromised the aesthetics of downtown Bayambang. To improve the poblacíon's image as well as facilitate economic expansion, administrators authorized the commercial development of the plaza's eastern edge. This move would not only significantly reduce the aggregate sum of public space in the plaza, it would also necessitate the transfer of the Rizal and Magsaysay monuments to a less accessible site that, according to city hall, was endorsed by the National Historical Institute. The government contended that the site would retain its traditional character since most of the property would not be privatized. Finally, and perhaps most importantly, local officials revealed that, from a legal standpoint, no public plaza has ever existed within Bayambang's poblacíon. The disputed area was never formally recognized by the municipality as a plaza, therefore any restrictions prohibiting the construction of permanent structures on the site were not applicable in this instance.

The Save the Bayambang Town Plaza Movement

With a preliminary hearing on the HOSLA case scheduled for late November 1996, popular opposition to the plaza privatization continued to gain momentum. In addition to the small group of individuals suing the municipality, several civic, educational, and religious groups united to form the Save the Bayambang Town Plaza Movement (SBTPM). Composed chiefly of local professionals as well as some former Bayambang residents now living in Metro-Manila, the consortium maintained a loose membership of several hundred pro-plaza activists. Although the original litigants and the SBTPM equally opposed the administration's stance regarding plaza privatization, the former party declined the SBTPM's invitation to join their coalition. The SBTPM, thus, submitted its own suit against the municipality. Whereas the coalition relied predominantly on more demonstrative tactics, the original litigants adopted a less overt approach on the matter. Because local officials possessed the political leverage to generate thousands of support signatures, the initial group of opponents involved a minimal number of persons in their case. On the contrary, the SBTPM engaged in a contest of numbers with the town government by sponsoring a petition drive as well as staging numerous protest rallies in front of municipal hall. Questions about the effectiveness of either methodology became moot, however, when the court consolidated both claims into one lawsuit a week before the hearing.

Legal Developments

Despite a restraining order that suspended all work on the HOSLA edifice, city hall permitted construction to continue. As a way of legitimizing the project, administrators enlisted the support of a descendant of the family that donated the plaza's current location. Insisting that the absence of a written contract entitled him to reclaim the lot, he vowed not to seize the property as long as both the bank building and commercial mall complex were erected. Such attempts at legitimization were undermined considerably by a letter from the National Historical Institute that contradicted the municipality's prior claim that the organization endorsed the plaza's conversion.

Within hours of convening on 21 November 1996, the regional magistrate handed down his decision on the suit. The judge sided with the plaintiffs and ordered both the municipality and HOSLA to cease and desist from all construction. The defendants promptly filed a petition to the high court. In an apparent effort to delay the appeals process so that exterior work on the bank could proceed, the defendants filed numerous motions that postponed the preliminary case review for months. By February 1997, work had been completed so that the savings and loan facility had become inhabitable. Soon after, office equipment was covertly moved into the building. Alarmed, opposition members asked that the court levy a severe penalty against town and bank officials to prevent the financial institution's opening. Not only was their request granted, the judge also ordered the municipality to submit its memorandum for appeal by March 1997.

A little over a year after the administration entered into the agreement with HOSLA in 1996, the Court of Appeals struck down their application seeking an overruling in the initial suit. On the grounds that the judges in both cases were biased, however, the local government was able to submit their case for reconsideration to the Supreme Court of the Philippines. This unusual development not only meant that the opening of the bank was still very much a possibility, it also kept alive the prospect of a Western-style commercial mall on the town plaza's eastern edge.

Political Repercussions

A growing feeling of indifference concerning the privatization of the plaza among Bayambang residents was quickly reversed by the campaigns of those candidates looking to unseat incumbent officials in the elections of May 1998. The Rizal monument became their main focus. By this time, both the HOSLA edifice and clusters of marketplace stalls had obscured the statue from public view. Since preparations for the celebration of the Philippine Centennial coincided with the elections, candidates attacked officials' neglect of the site as an affront to the nation's history.

Despite the plaza's return as a public issue, however, nearly all citizens believed the dispute had only reached a temporary impasse that the city would eventually overcome. Unfavorable legal decisions to the contrary, a two-story savings and loan building had been erected within the public square. It seemed unlikely to most local inhabitants, therefore, that the government would ever actually yield to the will of the court and permit the demolition of this multitiered structure. Similarly, many residents began to anticipate that construction work on the proposed shopping mall would soon commence since banking operations on the plaza now appeared imminent. Whatever the dispute's outcome, it was not lost on most locals that the historical morphology of Bayambang's plaza complex had already been significantly altered by the financial institution's construction.

DISCUSSION

Towns and cities in the Philippines are becoming increasingly globalized (Pertierra 1995). Globalization involves the emergence of corresponding structural conditions that can give rise to similar reactions on the municipal level (Featherstone 1990; Friedman 1994). As the cases of Dagupan, Urdaneta, and Bayambang affirm, privatization and retail trade concentration have become important transnational forces shaping community life in provincial Philippine localities. Given the geographical proximity and prevailing socioeconomic conditions of all three communities, it is not surprising that the three plaza disputes have progressed along similar lines.

On the surface, events in Dagupan, Urdaneta, and Bayambang resemble one another in several fundamental ways with regard to the commercialization of the respective plazas. In all three communities, the move to privatize was preceded by events going back several decades. Of significance was the facilitative role of disasters in accelerating the processes of privatization and retail trade concentration on the municipal level. Likewise, the public squares experienced a comparable devitalization in their architectural composition and traditional character since they were being used as makeshift market sites for displaced traders. In 1996, the three town governments instituted site renewals involving the construction of privately maintained shopping malls inside the plazas. None of the municipalities adhered to the legal guidelines for establishing such plans. All of the plaza schemes impacted local trade structures, especially the vendor communities, and altered the historical urban form instituted by the Spanish. Also, the projects created divisions between those favoring plaza commercialization and those against it. Finally, mall projects in each community were initiated by the municipal governments but were either never completed or were significantly delayed due to the actions of organized oppositionists.

Although the preceding examples demonstrate certain similarities, they are by no means identical. Differences include disparity in the duration of vendor occupations on the plaza sites, discrepancies in the types of structural upgrades outlined in each renewal plan, dissimilar levels of public concern for the preservation of the municipal squares, contrasts in the degree the individual cases became 1998 campaign issues, and the pursuit of litigation by oppositionists in Urdaneta and Bayambang, but not in Dagupan. Of more notable consequence is the involvement of ethnic Chinese entrepreneurs in the developments of Dagupan and Urdaneta. Considering the pivotal role played by Benjamin Lim, both cases can actually be regarded as local manifestations of the same phenomenon.

Contrasts are also apparent when the general position of the contending parties in each dispute is analyzed in terms of social hierarchy. Those against plaza privatization in Dagupan and Bayambang (professionals and Metro-Manila residents with ties to their respective communities) maintain a close socioeconomic proximity to those implementing the mall projects (government officials and commercial developers) in the overall class structure of each municipality. In comparison, a considerably wider gap separates the social rank of Urdaneta's mall oppositionists (small-scale market vendors) from those instituting the commercialization of the city's public square (high-ranking municipal administrators and influential local retailers).

The conflicts in Dagupan and Bayambang can perhaps best be grasped as political disputes between rival segments of the same social strata (the local elite). The plaza struggle in Urdaneta, although definitely not without some degree of partisanship, seems better understood as a case of class antagonism. Here, those with greater political clout and access to financial resources are able to forward their agenda more effectively than those with only modest influence. Notwithstanding such differences in detail, however, the overall effect engendered by the plaza projects in all three communities remains unaltered: namely, the usurpation of public space by private concerns with a subsequent erosion of the traditional urban form instituted by the Spanish over four hundred years ago.

The equivalent timing of the plaza projects in Dagupan, Urdaneta, and Bayambang appears to be more than coincidental. In the last twenty years, the Philippines, in general, and the three localities, more specifically, have experienced conditions facilitating economic growth. This market expansion has been driven largely by the privatization of basic service industries and state-owned properties. Concurrently, urban development has progressed to such an extent that the market for downtown properties, especially those that can accommodate multitiered shopping centers, has turned very competitive.

The limited availability of sizable commercial space within the communities' poblacíones has compelled some developers to move into outlying districts where acreage is substantial and relatively inexpensive. Yet, constructing a retail facility just beyond the urban periphery presents a significant risk considering consumer flows are already concentrated within the established business core. Moreover, the recent push for trade liberalization on the national agenda—which would, among other things, authorize up to 100 percent foreign ownership of retail outlets in the Philippines—has pressed many local firms to acquire primary lots before the country's economic terrain is substantially transformed.[3] Given the premium placed on inner-city real estate, alternative sites previously deemed off-limits to permanent retail development are now being recognized for their commercial viability. Since public plazas encompass large areas of minimally occupied space as well as maintain the most centralized locations within the built environment, they are more vulnerable than ever to privatization. With the inherent advantages of the build-operate-transfer scheme—specifically, the opportunity to inherit a building without having to bear construction and maintenance costs as well as the lease and tax revenues such operations generate—local administrations have increasingly viewed such ventures as smart investments.

Although the threat facing public plazas and other significant landmarks within Philippine communities has recently intensified (Harper 1996), it has not gone unchecked. As the mobilizations of citizens in the preceding cases demonstrate, many provincial residents are beginning to take an active interest in the preservation of vernacular architecture.

Though still a primary concern of those living in major metropolitan centers (Navarro 1996), the recent move by some provincial inhabitants
toward the protection of culturally valued structures has emerged after
numerous historical sites have endured years of neglect and poor maintenance by respective administrations. Coinciding with this upsurge in
structural conservation have been the preparations leading up to the Philippine centennial celebration in June 1998. Since a primary objective of
the government's National Centennial Commission has been public education concerning the architectural heritage of the Philippines, more than
half of the organization's operating budget has gone toward the renova-
tion of historical structures throughout the country (Bordadora 1997).

Yet, this newfound interest concerning landmark preservation in localities all over the Philippines is not without political dimensions. As the
conflicts in Dagupan, Urdaneta, and Bayambang illustrate, individuals on
both sides of the issue have co-opted the recent popularity of this social
cause to varying degrees of success. Government administrators have
asserted that respective commercial projects will not significantly compromise the conventional character of their urban centers but instead
improve the downtowns' aesthetic appearance and, more importantly,
facilitate local economic expansion.

On the contrary, many architectural conservationists, often belonging
to political parties opposing incumbent officeholders, are nothing if not
nostalgic in their portrayal of the disputed sites. Often, these activists fail
to acknowledge the dynamic role the Philippine plaza complex plays on
the municipal level. For generations, this institutional core has traditionally functioned as the epicenter of local cultural change.

Likewise, the plans to commercialize certain sections of historical properties, in many instances, are only components of much more comprehensive schemes aimed at structurally upgrading public holdings that have
deteriorated considerably over the years. Whatever the socioeconomic
costs and benefits of erecting permanent trade facilities within sites of cultural significance, the concept of architectural conservation continues to
be a principal concern of local elites. Since the advantages of maintaining
such structures are relatively intangible compared to the many consumer
amenities provided by large-scale retail enterprises, it remains improbable
that the preservation movement in the Philippines will move very far
beyond this upper echelon of society.

CONCLUSION

How does mall development affect the quality of municipal life in the examined localities? The conspicuous presence of a state-of-the-art shopping mall inside the confines of the public squares would profoundly redefine both the utilitarian and traditional roles that plazas serve in contemporary Philippine towns and cities. Not only would the sum total of communal space be diminished by the construction of such a large-scale trade facility, a reduction in the number of residents able to participate in community activities would likewise result. Furthermore, limiting public accessibility to the plazas would alter the character of the various civic, religious, and cultural gatherings that would be held on the sites. Due to their proximity to events, the occupying retail structures would be associated, for better or worse, with subsequent public occasions. Of particular consequence would be the effect private commercial enterprises would have on the public's right to congregate for political demonstrations. Given that the plazas serve as the principal venues for peaceable assembly, a decrease in their ground areas would deny occupancy to numbers of protesters and, in a sense, would constrain free speech among the citizenry. What is more, the plaza's role as the primary refuge for open space and greenery within the urban context would be reshaped by the daily operation of a shopping mall complex and adjunct parking facilities within its perimeter.

Although the plaza developments have important implications for the status of local life in all three municipalities, such ramifications will be more strongly felt in Dagupan and Bayambang as compared to Urdaneta. While the plazas in the former localities continue to be utilized by their communities-at-large, the nearly two-decade vendor occupation of Urdaneta's public square has devitalized local sentiment regarding the site's condition.

Yet, this indifference toward architectural preservation by Urdaneta's general population may prove beneficial for the city's long-term economic future. Local officials, recognizing that Urdaneta is starting to rival Dagupan as the principal site for commerce in Pangasinan, have begun to act more decisively in matters related to the city's commercial development. Even when retail enterprises threaten to alter irreparably the traditional morphology of Urdaneta's built environment, this assertive approach has met a modicum of community resistance. Since Dagupan is already established as the trade capital of the region, government administrators there have the option of acting prudently when it comes to balancing economic considerations with historical preservation. Similarly, given the fact that provincial towns such as Bayambang are unlikely to reach a level of commercial activity comparable to Dagupan or Urdaneta any time soon, the latter city faces an opportune moment to augment significantly its status as a regional trading power.

What about the future? Taking into account the past experiences of local administrations in Pangasinan converting public property into private retail space, it is likely that mall enterprises will eventually be allowed to inhabit the public plazas in Dagupan, Urdaneta, and Bayambang. Yet, the commercial occupation of the sites will, in all probability, not occur for some time. This anticipated delay is due not so much to the efforts of those advocating architectural conservation but has more to do with the recent economic recession affecting the Philippines and other Southeast Asian countries. Since the downturn in the regional market began in the summer of 1997, many major retail projects in Pangasinan have been significantly postponed or abandoned altogether. In most cases, mall developers no longer possess the monetary resources to erect such facilities, much less the consumer base to sustain them once operations begin. Correspondingly, the number of state-of-the-art shopping centers within the province may soon outstrip all demand for these types of ventures.

Aside from the malls to be established on the plazas, six other large-scale trade complexes, most of which are financed by Chinese-Filipinos, are slated for construction in Dagupan, Urdaneta, and other localities within Pangasinan sometime in the next few years. Considering that several Western-style commercial structures are presently operational and that the majority of provincial residents continue to rely on the informal trade sector to meet basic consumption needs, such additions would very likely saturate the provincial retail market. Based on these conditions, it seems most probable that the examined plazas will, at least for the immediate future, remain conspicuously undeveloped.

At the outset of this chapter I referred to the statement by Reed (1978:67) concerning the plight of the urban settlement pattern instituted by Spanish colonial planners in localities throughout the Philippines. The author noted that modifications in the original architectural design would be anticipated because of modernization and urbanization. In the last twenty years, however, a far more radical erosion of this traditional morphology has occurred. In fact, as the cases of Dagupan, Urdaneta, and Bayambang illustrate, this trend has recently intensified. Public plazas and other historical structures, previously culturally venerated sites, are now subject to an unprecedented degree of permanent commercial development. Subsequently, the equilibrium maintained between public and private space on the municipal level has, for better or worse, been upset in favor of the latter. Considering that the processes currently transforming several major municipalities in Pangasinan are also operative in other Philippine provinces, albeit to varying degrees, the devitalization of plaza complexes within the examined localities holds important implications for the historical urban cores of communities throughout the archipelago.

NOTES

The material presented in the chapter was collected in the Philippines between 1997 and 1998. Part of the research was supported by a fellowship from the Leland T. and Jessie W. Jordan Institute for International Awareness, Texas A&M University. I also did research while I was a visiting research associate of the Institute of Philippine Culture, Ateneo de Manila University, Quezon City.

1. The majority of those citizens with a Chinese heritage in Dagupan, Urdaneta, and elsewhere now identify more closely with Filipino culture than did their immediate ancestors (Lim 1997). Given this ever-increasing assimilation into mainstream society, one can no longer accurately distinguish the culture of the Filipino majority from that of the ethnic Chinese minority. Notwithstanding this significant degree of cultural absorption, divisions between the Chinese-Filipino community and the more general Filipino population still persist in the eyes of many area residents. While the criterion for distinguishing ethnic Chinese from Filipinos is, then, quite admittedly arbitrary, for the purposes of this chapter, I intend for the term "ethnic Chinese" or "Chinese-Filipino" to be understood in the same manner that locals use when they differentiate ethnic Chinese-Filipinos from native Filipinos.

2. Three years earlier (1989), in the neighboring community of Lingayen, Lim was involved in a similar dispute. This time, portions of a public park were leased to one of his subsidiary companies by the municipal government for the establishment of a private market facility. In this case, local vendors displaced by the construction of the firm's new market building sued all parties involved in the con-

tract. Despite much public support for the plaintiffs, the regional trial court ruled the agreement between the administration and Lim was legal and binding.

3. This current package of legislation would effectively dismantle those barriers established by the Retail Trade Nationalization Act (passed in 1954 and implemented in the early 1960s), which attempted to wrest control of the country's retail sector away from the hegemony of ethnic Chinese. Despite the initial blow to their elevated position in national commerce, the ethnic Chinese merchant population was soon able to reassert its dominance in local trade since the majority of affected retailers opted for Filipino citizenship. Recently, the next generation of naturalized Chinese-Filipino merchants has emerged as among the most vocal proponents for retaining the protectionist trade policies that were instituted, ironically, to exclude their immediate ancestors from retailing.

REFERENCES

Adam, Christopher, William Cavendish, and Percy S. Mistry
  1992 Adjusting Privatization, Case Studies from Developing Countries. Portsmouth, NH: Heinemann.

Baldassari, Mario, Luigi Paganetto, and Edmund S. Phelps
  1993 Privatization Process in Eastern Europe, Theoretical Foundation and Empirical Results, Certain Issues in Contemporary Economic Theory and Policy. London: Routledge.

Beesley, M. E.
  1992 Privatization, Regulation and Deregulation. London: Routledge.

Bordadora, Norman
  1997 Apathy Bugs Centennial Organizers. Manila: Philippine Daily Inquirer.

Chutterback, David, Susan Kernaghan, and Deborah Snow
  1991 On-Going Private Privatization around the World. Chutterback and Associates.

Cortes, Rosario Mendoza
  1990 Pangasinan 1901–1986. A Political, Socioeconomic and Cultural History. Quezon City, Philippines: New Day Publishers.

Dannhaeuser, Norbert
  1996a Trade Concentration in Hassfurt (Germany) and Dagupan City (Philippines) Globalization or Localization? Journal of Developing Societies 12:175–190.

1996b Two Towns in Germany: Commerce and the Urban Transformation. Westport, CT: Bergin and Garvey.

Featherstone, Mike
1990 Global Culture: An Introduction. *In* Global Culture: Nationalism, Globalization and Modernity. M. Featherstone, ed. Pp. 1–14. London: Sage.

Filio, Candido P.
1997 Where Have All the Downtowns Gone? Manila: Philippine Daily Inquirer.

Friedman, Jonathan
1994 Cultural Identity and Global Process. London: Sage.

Hanice, Steve A.
1987 Privatization and Development. Sacramento, CA: International Center for Economic Growth.

Harper, Bambi L.
1996 Will They Ever Learn? Manila: Philippine Daily Inquirer.

Hart, Donn V.
1955 The Philippine Plaza Complex. A Focal Point in Cultural Change. Yale University Southeast Asia Studies. Cultural Report Series No. 3. New Haven, CT: Yale University Press.

Lim, Benito
1997 The Dagupan Chinese. Chinese Studies Journal 7:16–36.

Malcolm, George A.
1939 The Commonwealth of the Philippines. New York: D. Appleton-Century Company.

Maulana, Nash B.
1997 FVR 'Misled.' Mall to Occupy School Ground. Manila: Philippine Daily Inquirer.

Navarro, Nelson
1996 Fighting the Barbarians. Manila: Manila Standard.

Official Gazette
1948 Capistrano et al. vs. Mayor of Manila et al. 44(8):2798–2806.

Pertierra, Raul
1995 Philippine Localities and Global Perspectives. Essays on Society and Culture. Quezon City, Philippines: Ateneo de Manila University Press.

Philippine Reports
1909 Harty vs. Municipality of Victoria. 13:152–157.
1915 Municipality of Cavite vs. Rojas. 310:602–609.
1935 Director of Lands vs. Roman Catholic Bishop of Zamboanga. 61:644–654.
1958 Espiritu et al. vs. Municipal Council, Pozorrubio, Pangasinan et al. 102:867–870.

Reed, Robert R.
1978 Colonial Manila. The Context of Hispanic Urbanism and Process of Morphogenesis. Berkeley, CA: University of California Press.

Romano, Genielle B.
1996 Philippine Public Enterprise and Privatization. Mandaluyong City, Philippines: Fiscal Administration Foundation, Inc.

12

Looking into the Future: Anthropology and Financial Markets

Monica Lindh de Montoya

Societies throughout the world are becoming increasingly integrated into national and global markets through the goods they produce and consume. This article discusses another kind of integration—the increasing involvement of people worldwide in financial markets through investment in stocks or funds. There has been extensive study of economic integration in anthropology; early studies of exchange in nonmarket economies soon broadened to include trade in developing areas where markets began to penetrate, often coexisting with other forms of exchange. Anthropologists have shown how integration into the larger economy has led to the disappearance of indigenous models of trade and how modern and traditional, Western and non-Western economic practices and discourses articulate (Parry and Bloch 1989; Taussig 1980).

Recent years have seen the emergence of new directions in economic anthropology, with more focus on the modern marketplace. Studies such as those of Abolafia (1996), Carrier (1997), Dannhaeuser (1989, 1996), Dilley (1992), Friedland and Robertson (1990), and Hertz (1998) are a handful of recent works that have focused on the modern market, using anthropological analyses to decipher the meanings and consequences of the activities carried out there.

Most anthropological studies of the economic lives of communities have focused on production and circulation, and more recently, on consumption. Less-detailed analyses exist of processes of negotiation and the complicated issues of risk and trust, particularly in Western economies. However, there has been almost no attention to peoples' activities within modern financial markets, national or international, although the world of finance is rapidly gaining territory in all peoples' life-worlds as noncapitalist alternatives disappear and states relinquish an increasing portion of their responsibilities to the free market.[1] In view of the desire within anthropology to direct the discipline's analytical eye toward Western cultures and to encourage a cultural critique (Marcus and Fischer 1986), attention to this area of economic life is overdue.

How might anthropologists study this immense and complex field of human activity? Certain suggestions come to mind. One is to consider how financial markets can be defined within earlier anthropological frameworks of economies. How do they fit within economies? Are they best described as a form of production? Economists might say so; stock markets, for example, can provide the capital necessary for industry. But the active trading and liquidity of financial markets also make them exemplary of the field of circulation, while individuals' activities within them can also be likened to a form of consumption. Perhaps one might conceive of the financial world as a sphere that floats above more concrete, day-to-day transactions? Although the world of finance can be analyzed fruitfully from several frequently used perspectives, most fascinating, perhaps, is the challenge of unraveling how these markets—so much in the ether—are linked to concrete human endeavors, and the meaning people create as they act within them.

Different levels of study are necessary. There are the nuts-and-bolts studies of human interaction within markets, which can focus on traders, investors, gatekeepers, and the information and meaning that flows between them. How do different markets operate? This would focus on the market as a network of social relationships, and such a view could pay attention, for example, to how access to markets and financial products are regulated and to peoples' potential for changing social orders through negotiating the terms of market transactions.

Another perspective might consider the complex array of "financial instruments"[2]—including stocks, bonds, funds, options, and derivatives—as ingenious human inventions, our relationships with which reveal something about our societies and values. Earlier studies of markets have described them as "mirrors"[3] of societies (Cook and Diskin 1976; Eder 1976; Mintz 1976), reflections of the social system and ecology in which they are embedded. The goods traded, the paths they follow, and descriptions of actors and transactions are all assumed to provide an image through which relationships within the larger society can be deciphered and understood.

If this metaphor has been relevant in studies of non-Western trade and in discussing processes of integration, what relevance might it hold for studies of the current financial arena? Concepts such as Bourdieu's of capital (1986), and Baudrillard's sign (1981) may be useful in analyzing the use and significance of financial innovations. Certainly, various forms of capital—not only economic, but social and cultural—are deployed by actors in the world of finance, and a diversity of signs circulate in these markets-charts, prognoses, and assessments of risk. And in this day and age, when we hear that industry no longer drives financial markets, but that financial markets drive industry, might we not turn the mirror metaphor around and consider in what ways these markets insinuate their logic into our lives, transforming our way of looking at daily economic processes and responsibilities?

Sassen (1998b) has noted that globalization studies should pinpoint the spots in communities where the global impinges on the local and should concretely document how this change takes place in order to make possible a clearer understanding of the mechanisms at work. The activities within financial markets in the process of penetrating into different societies seem, to me, to exemplify such social nodes, which can illustrate how history, innovation, and power shape possibilities and opportunities.

Although little research has been carried out on peoples' reasoning about and behavior within financial markets,[4] there are recent research issues that do offer valuable new directions for such studies. Within economic sociology, Granovetter's (1985) work on the concept of embeddedness, comes to mind, as does that of Swedberg (1994) and other sociologists who point out that the analysis of values, ideas, and culture add a necessary dimension to sociological studies of the modern market. The recent work on globalization and increased cultural complexity (Hannerz 1992, 1996; Lash and Urry 1994; Robertson 1992; Sassen 1996, 1998a) and on the issues of risk and trust (Beck 1992; Giddens 1991) are also of obvious interest because of the new concepts and perspectives that they have introduced into the study of modern society.

MARKETS AND MODELS

The last decade has seen a series of events that have made financial markets more prominent in peoples' minds than ever. The demise of the Soviet Union brought predictions of a future of worldwide unhindered capitalism. In Europe, the economic downturn of the early 1990s and consequent cuts in social services, privatizations, and the demands and benefits of the European Union transformed nations' economies considerably. Worldwide, we see constellations of nations that both aim at the liberalization of trade and that group themselves together into trade blocks.

The enormous flow of capital around the globe and the decade-long rise in stock markets during the 1990s—clouded at the end of the century by turbulence in the emerging markets—have put economic matters on a par with political concerns. The economy is spoken of as being global, and the power of transnational corporations, loss of local industries, spread of consumer goods throughout the world, and investment power of large funds are frequently explained in terms of global financial processes. The market is blamed for countries' apparent loss of control over their national economies, but is simultaneously held up as a means of providing for innumerable public needs. In a number of European countries, some of these needs, from health care to pension plans, were formerly the responsibility of the state. How do these transformations influence peoples' ideas about the relationship between the interests of economic actors and those of society?

Bernstein (1992) has documented the evolution of financial theories with the development of computing power and the application of academic models in stock market investment. The world's capital markets in stocks, bonds, and cash has grown from two trillion dollars in 1969 to over twenty-two trillion dollars at the end of the 1990s; just under half of this is traded in the United States, and the other half in the rest of the world (Bernstein 1992:4). The diversification in ways of investing and the expansion in the amounts of capital available has led to the participation of increasing numbers of people in the financial sphere. In a recent article, Lindqvist (1999) has suggested that these new choices and practices of investment in abstract forms are transforming attitudes and values, and are part of a change from modernism to postmodernism.

Large-scale, planned economies have proved untenable in practice, yet they have left a legacy,[5] and, I suggest, drew much of their original force from moral tensions inherent in economic life: those between the individual and the community and between the desire to realize one's potential and the need to recognize socially legitimated boundaries. How do people reevaluate their own position as paradigms change? In what ways do knowledge and habits shift—how do people learn, as Bourdieu (1990) suggests, to want that which is possible? At some point in life, we all have to come to terms with our place in the market and make our peace with it; and in so doing, we model it.

Anthropologist Stephen Gudeman (1986) contends that non-Western cultures have their own, local models of how the economy works—or should work—that are specific and grounded in particular economic relationships. Peoples' economic models in Western societies, formulated with the aid of abstract logic and mathematical equations, are conceived of as universal and applicable to all economies. But Gudeman argues that even these universal models can be seen as being local, in that they have been formulated to explain particular economic phenomena bounded in time and space.

The mental connections people make, and the relationships they see, shape their models and their ideas about savings and consumption. Grounded in the individual's upbringing and personal experiences, schooling, and productive life, such models are also loaded with emotion and moral assumptions. They are shaped by family histories, by the economic history of the nation, and by political forces—the different incentives that governments bring to bear in their attempts to steer peoples' economic choices. The role of public opinion and debate, and evaluations of the economic life of the nation as reported through the media and as experienced in the face-to-face encounters of daily life, should not be underestimated. Models are created from the materials of daily life, which is lived out in continuously changing circumstances that provide fresh tools for modeling (Lindh de Montoya 1996; Swidler 1986). People find new metaphors, and long-used ideas fall into disfavor as the flow of events eddy around them, changing fields of power and making certain ways of looking at things more resonant, and more useful, than others.

This chapter explores the mental conceptions, ideas, or models of the financial market held by individual investors in Sweden.[6] I am interested in how personal models are related to investment behavior, and to what degree one might be able to speak of a general model shared by many; or of several more or less commonly held conceptions of the market. My data have been gathered through open-ended, volunteered interviews with twenty-five shareholders, most of whom participated in investment education courses organized by Aktiespararna, a Swedish shareholders' association. The findings presented here are of a preliminary nature, as the research is in progress, and will eventually include one hundred interviews with investors. Information available through banks, financial analysts, popular financial publications, and advertising is also of interest. I am concerned with the overlap and interplay between the ways the market is modeled by the government and its agencies, those images created by the market itself via information and advertising, that image projected by the media, and small investors' own conceptions of the financial arena.

INVESTORS IN SWEDEN AND AKTIESPARARNA— A SHAREHOLDERS' ORGANIZATION

Sweden is a country in which an exceptionally high percentage of the population has savings in stocks, either through investments in mutual funds or through direct placement. In a poll of 1,500 people between the ages of fifteen and seventy-five carried out by *Temo* in 1997, 51 percent owned stocks of some kind, but the majority owned stock in a mutual fund.[7]

Yet a survey of stockholders registered at Värdepapperscentralen, the national agency that tracks stock ownership, shows that of those investing in individual stocks, 72 percent did not carry out any transactions in 1997, and 14 percent carried out only one transaction. Nor do small investors tend to spread their risks: 61 percent owned only one stock, and 16 percent owned two.[8] At the same time, investment in mutual funds is increasing, and the rise in value of stock market shares throughout the 1990s undoubtedly encouraged new ways of participating in the financial market worldwide. One of these new ways is investing in particular funds designed to support social goals, such as those focusing on ethical investments or the development of new technology or those contributing part of their earnings to charitable causes.

Today, Sweden has Europe's most rapidly growing market for mutual funds, and international companies such as Fidelity and Templeton have established offices in Stockholm.[9] Also, the current implementation of a new national pension system has increased savings in mutual funds, as employees save toward their pensions by investing part of their government pension savings in funds.[10]

Nonetheless, when pointing out that just over half of the population is active in the stock market, one has to remember that just under half avoid stocks, and if they save, they choose different strategies. Richard Wahlund of Handelshögskolan (Stockholm Business School) discusses people who save in short spurts and keep their money in the bank, paying off loans on their homes, for example, when a certain amount has accumulated.[11] Leif Vindevåg, research director at the Stockholm Stock Exchange (Stockholmsbörsen) feels, however, that Swedish households should be encouraged to save in stocks over time, since individual shareholders reduce the volatility of the stock market, balancing the large-volume, more short-term trades of institutional investors.[12]

Swedish investors have an important resource in their dynamic shareholders' association, Aktiespararna. Formed in 1966 and now made up of over 124,000 members and 140 local branches all over the country, this organization plays an active role in encouraging individual investment. Its goal is to create the best possible environment for stock investors, and it emphasizes education, in the belief that people should know enough about the market to be able to make their own informed decisions. To this end, the organization publishes a much-appreciated monthly magazine discussing investment and the significance of the major events occurring within the Swedish marketplace, sponsors meetings for its members with company managers, and offers a series of courses to the public. There are classes for beginners that explain how the stock market operates, how to buy and sell, and the basic tenets of the association, called the shareholders' golden rules: Choose stocks depending on your goals, plan to hold your investments over a long term, invest regularly, spread your risks, be very careful about investing borrowed money, and know what you are buying.

As can be deduced from its "golden rules," the association encourages fundamental investment,[13] and one might say that on the whole, its ideal investor is one who regularly invests savings in successful and well-established Swedish companies. The process of financial globalization and the growth of the Internet, with subsequent developments such as online brokerages, popular software programs for technical analysis, and new financial products have, however, changed the nature of the marketplace and the interests of investors, leading the association to add courses in options, on-line investing, and technical analysis. The association has also opened its own Web site and a digital investment service.

Beside education, a major aim of the association is improving the national environment for small investors and protecting their interests. An important part of this is working to eliminate double taxation, and working to reduce taxes on profits made in the financial market. But another aspect is exerting pressure on important Swedish companies on the part of individual investors: Aktiespararna was instrumental in stopping Volvo deals twice; once in 1978–79 when 40 percent of the company was almost sold to the Norwegian state, and in 1993, when it blocked the Volvo-Renault merger.[14] Aktiespararna also opposed the Astra-Zeneca merger in 1999, on the grounds that it was not advantageous for Astra shareholders, was far too risky, and did not solve Astra's basic problem—the need for new patents.

The association is critical of the fact that in recent years a number of important Swedish companies have either moved their headquarters from Sweden or were sold to foreign interests. These companies include Pharmacia, Volvo, ABB, Enator, and Nordbanken, a major Swedish bank that merged with Finnish Merita. Mergers and company relocations are a consequence of the realignment of trade within the European Union. Since Sweden is a small country (demographically speaking) with an unattractive taxation system and is located in the periphery of the union, it can be tempting for Swedish companies that merge with companies in other countries to resettle in major business centers such as London.

Companies weigh a series of factors when deciding whether to relocate, among them production costs, taxation for employees and for the company itself, the possibility of recruiting qualified personnel, visibility in the marketplace, goodwill, and competition with other companies; it is both a strategic move and a financial decision. Swedes fear, however, that the relocation of major companies translates into a loss of local jobs and of cutting-edge research and development facilities; they also regret the fact that foreign interests have the power to make decisions in Sweden's major companies. They believe that, in the long run, this trend will hinder the development of new Swedish companies, weakening the country's future economic prospects.

Although many investors complain about the high taxes in Sweden—not only on market profits, but on income in general—in other ways, Sweden's public welfare policies probably aid in fomenting investment and making wide participation in the financial market possible. Since the state, via taxation, provides for much of its citizens' needs, people do not need to save extensively for emergencies and for the family's future. Swedes receive monthly state subsidies for their children, pay modest fees for day care, pay little for medical care and medicines, and education, including college education, is free. State services are of good quality, making alternatives few and generally unnecessary. Unemployment insurance is generous, and retirement pensions are guaranteed. Such protection enables Swedes to tie up savings in long-term investments since they do not need substantial liquid funds for emergency medical care or in the eventuality of unemployment, for example. Some, citing the recent popularity of emerging market funds, suggest that their confidence in state social benefits make Swedes willing to take greater risks with their capital than investors in other countries.

With these rudimentary words to set the scene, I would like to discuss some of the findings of my initial fieldwork. Through Aktiespararna's investment courses, I have begun to contact and interview individual investors. Preliminary results from interviews indicate that investors approach the stock market in a wide variety of ways, from different life situations and needs, something that Gyllenram (1998) makes abundantly clear in his book on the psychology of the stock market. Obviously, the people I have interviewed are a special segment of the group of investors as a whole—those who are motivated enough in their investment to seek out and attend a relatively expensive evening course. Among those I met, there are both mutual fund investors, who invest indirectly and seldom change their holdings, and very active traders, who concentrate on specific stocks, buying and selling with market fluctuations. Of the spectrum of investors, three main groups are apparent, so far: young investors, who are very absorbed in and knowledgeable about the market, and trade actively to build up capital; a broad, diverse middle-aged group (about thirty to fifty-five years of age) that invests primarily for retirement needs; and finally, older investors, many of them retired, who have bought stocks for years but now have more time to dedicate to their portfolios.

YOUNG INVESTORS

Between twenty and thirty years old, the young investors (three men) are by far the most enthusiastic about the possibilities of the stock market. Stock prices have been rising since they were teenagers, so they have no direct experience of a considerable stock market slump. The volatility of markets in 1998, when these interviews were carried out, gave them some anxiety, but also provided them with opportunities to use their skills in buying and selling in the Swedish market.

They come from varied backgrounds. Magnus, for example, works as a painter; Jonas has just started his own firm; and Bengt holds an entry-level job in an insurance company. Not infrequently, they are the only ones in their families particularly interested in stocks, although a business background in the family is common. They are all well versed in computers and the Internet, do their investing on-line in particular stocks, and obtain a considerable amount of the information they act on via the Web. None invested in or were interested in mutual funds.

Interestingly, all told me that their enthusiasm for stocks awoke when as teenagers, they invested savings—not large amounts—in stocks, and were successful with one stock, but not others. The realization that it was possible to make substantial gains in the market with the right stock encouraged them to learn more about investing, and some became members of Unga Aktiespararna, the youth organization of the shareholders' association. All are interested in technical analysis and in options and hope to use these to increase earnings and decrease risk. "You can't invest by just looking at fundamentals," said Bengt. "I like to see that a company is doing well—I never buy one that isn't making money—but it's just as important to look at the charts."

They had taken losses, but gamely said that this was part of being in the market, and the point was to learn from one's mistakes. In general, they studied particular stocks to get to know their behavior well, and traded in these particular choices, buying and selling with swings in the market. Risks were minimized in their conversations, and opportunities maximized. Bengt explained,

> I used to think the stock market was risky, but after trading for a couple of years I don't think there is such big risk involved, any more. You have to watch your stocks every day, but if you do, you'll be OK. Technical analysis

helps. I used to make money with half the stocks I bought before, but now I do well about 70 percent of the time. When I lose money, I figure out what I did wrong, and I've made a list of rules I try to follow. When things don't go my way, it's usually because I broke one of my own rules.

"I earn 500 crowns a day, after tax, as a painter," says Magnus. "But some days I come home and see that while I was working, my stocks earned, say, 3,000 crowns. Because of the tax system, investing is the only way you can get ahead in this country."

The aim of these young men is financial independence, and they believe that they can attain it before too long: "I'm only twenty-one now, and if I continue to do as well as I have up until now, I'll have a million by the time I'm twenty-five," says Bengt. "And when I retire, I'm not going to need a government pension." All work regular jobs and look forward to a day when they will be able to live off their investments, something that they feel would leave them plenty of time for other activities. With a note-book computer and access to the Internet, Magnus noted, it would be easy to keep up with one's investments while traveling the world—something that he was eager to do.

Their interest in stocks has made these young men avid newspaper readers: "I never used to worry about whether Boris Yeltsin would have a heart attack or not," said Jonas. "But when I started with stocks, I began to pay attention." All invest in technology or telecommunications stocks, some heavily so, and find it a challenge to figure out what new product will be the one to take off in the future. "I talk to a lot of people about innovations, and sit around with my friends trying to figure out what the next hot product is going to be," said Magnus. "The next super-compa-nies are out there already." In this way, investing makes them very aware of what's happening in the world, and they try to reason through to the consequences of ongoing social, political, and technological changes.

Two of these young investors were the offspring of immigrants (Asian and Eastern European) and found in the stock market a level playing field, where they could compete unhindered by language or prejudice. The same applies to the shy, socially unskilled, and those who never did well in school; in the marketplace, social and academic barriers fall, and the pun-ishments and rewards are immediate, concrete, and unambiguous.

Young investors experience the market as a challenge and an adventure.

Still unmarried, they have time on their side and can take risks without the same qualms as investors with family responsibilities. Talking to them, one senses that they are in the stock market for the exhilaration of testing their judgment, as much as for profits; investing is fun. Magnus spoke also of the virtual portfolios that he kept up with on-line in order to learn from them. These youths are knowledgeable and eager to experiment and spend a substantial amount of time tending their stock portfolios. Although a very interesting group, they are hardly representative of the mass of investors active in Sweden today.

ADULTS

As the statistics above demonstrate, most Swedes who invest seldom buy and sell, but hold their stocks or funds over long periods. The main group of investors I interviewed, who fall between the ages of thirty and fifty-five (nine men and six women), is very diverse and I will only note a few of their concerns. This group is more uneasy with the stock market and has less confidence in it, perhaps because they are less active and informed. All but two of the women I conversed with fell into this group; I did not encounter women among the very active young investors in the courses at Aktiespararna, and the two among the older investors saved in funds. However, my sample is quite small so far, and it is likely that women will turn up in these categories in future interviews.

Most of these middle-aged investors are saving for the future, for their children, and for their retirement. Although a few invest via the Internet or brokerages, the majority use the services of a bank. In addition to individual stocks, banks offer a variety of mutual funds with different degrees of risk: Some mix stocks and bonds, some trade aggressively, and others invest in emerging markets, either of particular countries (such as Russia) or regions (Asia, Latin America, or eastern Europe). Generally, people commented that banks were eager to sell them their particular funds, and that they had to "shop around" with different banks, until they found what they felt would suit their own needs.

An important concern for a couple of investors in this group was that the stocks in the funds they chose should be ethically correct; that is, there should be no investments in arms industries or in alcohol or tobacco companies. Funds usually move in and out of a wide range of stocks, however, and few funds can guarantee that they will never own companies that some people find questionable, especially since criteria differ as to what is ethical. The most concerned individuals can turn to special ethical investment funds, especially those put together by particular brokerages, which can be very successful in their investment strategies.

In this large and varied group, many invested in funds rather than individual stocks. In the midst of careers and raising families, they did not feel they had the time to watch over a stock portfolio. Those who did chose individual stocks tended to keep them over long periods, which has been a wise strategy with the rising market of the past decade. Some people chose individual stocks based on their own field of work. Pernilla, who had a good job in a multinational technology company, decided to invest in a couple of smaller Swedish technology companies that she had dealings with through her work; likewise, she said that there were companies that she would never consider, because they had given her a bad impression when they did business with her. Mats, a dentist, was interested in the companies offering new dental technology.

Stock enthusiasm in the workplace sometimes also led people to participate in a stock investors' club, where members all save a certain amount each month and contribute to doing research on stocks in different sectors of the economy. The club then chooses some of these companies to invest in. Interestingly, such clubs sometimes led people to make individual investments. Irene, a university employee, explained that the first stock she bought on her own was one that she had done research on for her investment club, but that the group, to her disappointment, had decided not to buy.

A number of people I met had inherited stocks, and although not very interested in the stock market, they felt they had a responsibility to administer the wealth they had inherited. For them, their stocks had an intrinsic value as well as a monetary value. With the market volatility of the autumn of 1998, these shareholders had a difficult time, feeling they should do something, but at the same time not feeling sufficiently informed to be able to make decisions. Watching the market filled them with angst. Hans told me about his feelings for his grandfather, who had owned a business and had considerable stock investments that he left to his grandchildren:

Knowing that I have the stocks to fall back on in an emergency has always been a comfort. Although if I didn't have them, maybe I would have been

more ambitious in my career. For many years, I didn't pay much attention
to the stocks. I just sold a few now and then, for the down payment on my
apartment, and a couple of years ago, a summerhouse. But now the market's been doing so well for so long that the papers are always writing about
how it has to turn down, pretty soon. I feel I should know more, and be
ready to do something when the time comes. But if I sell something, I have
to buy something else, and then, there are the taxes. My grandfather knew
all about these things—it was his life—but I feel like I'm not doing a very
good job of administering what he left me.

Among those I interviewed were people who did not really have any
particular desire to participate in the stock market, but who had been
advised to buy funds as a way of saving to complement their retirement
pensions. A number of such investors were sympathetic to or active in
the political left and viewed the stock market as a legalized casino that
appropriated profits that rightfully belonged to the workers. Sylvia, a
teacher, stated:

I never in my life thought I would buy stocks, but I've had a lot of part-
time jobs, and I've spent time and money travelling. I know I'm not going
to qualify for a very big pension. My mother left me some money, and I
decided that the best thing to do was to invest it in funds. This is a capitalist
country, and even if I don't agree with it, I live here and have to watch out
for my future. A lot of people are doing the same; I have friends who have
bought funds that I never thought would do something like that. It's not
right—one day you read in the paper that a big company like Electrolux is
going to lay off 5,000 employees. And the next day, in the papers you read,
"Electrolux stocks take a leap." People are losing their jobs, the stockholders are getting rich, and now I'm a part of it.

The ambivalence that Sylvia feels is based on the complex relationships
between stock prices, company profits, and production. Ideas about job
security, social benefits, and full employment are prominent in discourses
on Swedish politics, especially since the beginning of the 1990s, when
unemployment statistics in the country rose and long remained at politically unacceptable levels. As noted earlier, Swedish companies move
abroad, merge with others, and have faced competition repeatedly from
emerging markets; the textile industry, shipbuilding, steel, and paper have

all had to compete in a global arena. When companies now restructure to meet competition and slash jobs, share prices tend to rise, making many feel that the market profits from others' misery. Often restructuring means ceasing production at some site, and when a town loses its main employer, problems quickly multiply. With many facing long-term unemployment, property prices dive, and families lose much more than their jobs: Homes, expectations and, because of dependence on unemployment and welfare, personal dignity can be jeopardized. Such processes have been very much in the public eye throughout the 1980s and 1990s and make the elimination of jobs a sensitive issue.

These ambiguities are troubling for many Swedish investors, even if they do not keep them out of the market. Frequently, people feel that their good fortune is someone else's misfortune, and other issues, such as the destruction of the environment and child labor, also have resonance when people speak about the global marketplace. One investor commented that she only had started to save in a fund because her local bank suggested it, and that she now wondered what mischief her money was up to, circulating around the globe. Such worries are probably fleeting for most, but their existence speaks to a different view of the market than those of the young investors, who voiced no such worries, and were, on the contrary, more concerned about the international competitiveness of Swedish companies. The mainstream Swedish investor seems to seek a compromise between competition and social responsibility. Susanna expressed this in an interesting way:

> Small investors—I believe in them. If many, many invest in stocks, we can influence companies. If they destroy the environment, or have unfair labor practices, small investors can sell their stocks, or exert pressure at the annual meetings. It can come to be a different way of having power over what goes on in companies.[15]

RETIRED GROUP

Retired people who are actively investing make up another group of investors with particular characteristics. Many are long-term investors, yet they resemble the young investors in some ways. They are less likely to use the Internet, but they are equally interested in ways of getting an edge and reducing risks, for example, by using technical analysis. They are also optimistic about the opportunities in the stock market, but more guardedly so; time is not on their side when it comes to the ability to take risks as it is for the younger group.

These people are usually long-time investors who have built a portfolio of stocks through a lifetime of saving. Part of their plans for retirement includes dedicating more time to their investments, more out of interest than need. Being retired, they want to conserve their holdings, but active trading can, of course, produce the reverse effect. Thus, ambivalent feelings arise. This group seems to have more faith in brokers and other experts, unlike the young investors, who believe they can beat the fund managers' records. The retirees are also the ones who can best afford expert advice. "This business of technical analysis is very interesting," said Per. "But it's not so easy to interpret the charts. Those curves could go in a lot of different directions. And we, who are amateurs—I think we'd have a pretty hard time beating the boys at the brokerage."

For the retired, investing is a hobby and for some of them it is also of social importance, for grey heads are often very visible in the audience at Aktiespararna's meetings with the directors of Swedish companies. In general, the older generation of investors is more concerned about the fundamentals of a company than their younger counterparts, and they are more serious about the idea that as investors, they become co-owners of a company. Some speak of investing as a contribution to the progress of the nation, a way of fomenting Swedish industry and welfare. They focus on Swedish stocks, and the success of particular Swedish companies is important to them in a way that it was not for younger investors, who cared less what shares they bought, as long as they were on the way up, and were quick to sell when they sensed a fall in price.

CONCLUSION

The radical changes under way in the global economy and their reflection in the financial marketplace have been discussed as a part of a transition from modernity to postmodernity (Harvey 1990; Jameson 1991). In an interesting article on the discourse and practices of the Swedish economic sector, Lindqvist (1999) focuses on the financial services offered at an annual exposition and questions whether one can see them as indicative of a shift to a new kind of economy, with different basic values.

Savings are no longer carefully accumulated for future needs, Lindqvist indicates, but are invested for growth, for a miraculous expansion of value. The issue of the risk inherent in these financial instruments is minimized; they come to provide the basis for a new understanding of how economic values are created. The productive work once necessary to accumulate capital is now of secondary importance; it is participation in the financial marketplace that is considered fundamental to wealth creation. While in earlier decades economic progress was a collective project grounded in the national production of export goods, today it has become an individual endeavor.

A broad sector of the population owns stocks through participation in funds, but has little knowledge about what they own, and interest is almost exclusively focused on the rise in value of their holdings, a point of view legitimized by the activities of fund managers. Lindqvist emphasizes the vital role that modern information technology and the media play in underpinning and legitimizing an illusion that economic values are represented by statistics, computer-generated charts, and market prognoses from different sources. He concludes that although speculation and an exaggerated focus on profit maximization are not new to financial markets, they are now so widespread and legitimate that one can reasonably speak of a fundamental sociocultural change: from a production-centered economy to one that considers financial operations to be the basis for both general and private growth in wealth.

I agree with Lindqvist that great changes are underway. Bernstein (1992) documented that the growth of investment choices in the United States have their counterparts in Sweden, and an unusually high proportion of the population invests. The financial world and the media have been quick to recognize new potentials; several popular Swedish magazines dedicated to personal investment information have started up in recent years, and even the evening papers have come to include weekly inserts discussing stocks' potential and new companies in terms that nonexperts can understand. From the financial world come specialized reports to which one can subscribe, software for analysis, and stock-picking models. The Swedish state has contributed by reorganizing the national pension system to include individual choice in the placement of a portion of ones' accumulated funds. All this attention serves to amplify the space that finance occupies in peoples' minds, and to legitimize investment as an activity. The fact that the industrial West has experienced a nearly unbroken two-decade-long period of rising stock prices is an overwhelmingly important aspect of any analysis of possible epochal change; how will things look a year or two after a turndown?

Based on my findings in interviews with shareholders, I would hesitate to say that people have come to accept speculation and heedless profit maximization as legitimate in a new economy based more on financial operations than on productive work. The issue seems more complex. The surge in online investment accounts—recently estimated to be increasing in Sweden by one thousand accounts a day—indicates that people are increasingly taking responsibility for their own investments.[16] When they do so, they inevitably face the need to contemplate risk, for the mass of new investors are salaried workers, and not in a position to ignore it. Risk assessment of any kind calls for information about placement strategies and about companies suitable for investment and their histories. The pervasiveness of risk in financial markets strongly links productive and innovative work—carried out by investors to gain capital and to invest it and by companies as they maneuver within the marketplace to prospective gains or losses.

Contrary to Lindqvist's assumptions, my interviews indicate that for most stock market investors, quite traditional ideas about productive work and competition permeate considerations of financial strategies. Investment growth is linked to innovative, productive, and often socially responsible work in particular companies. Interestingly, it is fund investors, those removed from direct investment by a layer of professional managers, who tend to be the most wary and ambivalent about their own participation in the financial arena. Here, however, the increase and success of ethical funds speak to investors' concerns with fundamental values and their desire for coherence between their convictions and investment earnings.

The relationship between investment and savings also needs more elaboration. In this chapter, I simply define savings as capital accumulated for future needs, and investment as ways of making it grow, specifically stock in companies. Lindqvist appears to object to calling money used for "speculation in the stock market" savings; to do so would be to imbue it with social values that existed when individuals' savings contributed to financing industries but that disappear when used for gain that is speculative and purely individual. But to what extent can one maintain that stock market investment only benefits individuals—that it provides nothing of social value?

The importance of financial markets for society is a huge question that can not be elaborated on here. What is evident, in any case, is that most market investors look on their placements as savings, be it capital to trade with as avid young investors or, more commonly, for retirement income. Some people also see their investments as providing a future nest egg for their offspring or grandchildren; investments are conceptualized as making possible improved homes, vacation retreats, or wider educational opportunities. These stocks and funds are kept through the years with the intention that they will provide. It is important to remember that all capital symbolizes delayed consumption, the conscious decision to forego certain things one would also like to do or to acquire.

Thus, when removed from the hype of financial professionals and media headlines, the act of investment comes down to the more mundane and vulnerable individual and his or her possibilities and belief in the future. Risk pursues investors and keeps them anchored to worldly realities. "Investing seems easy enough," I once commented cheerily during an interview. "Not at all," the interviewee replied, fixing me with a grim look. "It's just terrible," he said, "it's my money that's at stake."

NOTES

I thank the Tercentenary Foundation of the Bank of Sweden and Tore Browaldhs Stiftelse at Handelsbanken for the financial support for this research. Thanks go also to Jeffrey Cohen, Norbert Dannhaeuser, Richard Swedberg, and José Antonio Torres for their suggestions on a previous version of this chapter.

1. Abolafia's (1996) study on Wall Street traders, Hertz's (1998) examination of the Shanghai stock exchange, and Lindqvist's (1999) discussion of the financial service industry are exceptions.

2. This is an interesting term that transforms the intangible—assets, debts, confidence, doubt, and so on—into tangible products marketed to fill defined financial needs.

3. In his foreword to Cook and Diskin's edited volume, Mintz uses the word "speculum," a mirror made of polished metal.

4. The field of behavioral economics is a fairly new and very interesting area of economics that focuses on peoples' economic behavior, investigating how people

reason about money and risk but deals with people as individuals, rather than viewing them as networks or social groups.

5. In an article about *The Lonely Crowd*, McClay (1993:437) suggests that cultural contradictions are part of our condition as historical beings. He cites both Spanish philosopher José Ortega y Gasset, who noted that European man "has been 'democratic,' 'liberal,' 'absolutist,' 'feudal,' " and does "in some way continue being all these things: he does so in the 'form of having been them' "; and historian John Lukacs, who has pointed out that "nothing in history passes away completely" (1984:7).

6. Since September 1998 I, together with Miguel Montoya, have been collecting field data for anthropological studies of individual investors in stock markets. I am working in Sweden and Miguel is doing fieldwork with investors in Latin America (in Venezuela; see Montoya, this volume). Our studies are part of a larger research program in the Department of Anthropology at Stockholm University that began in 1998. It is entitled "Cultural Models of the Market: Trust, Risk and Social Change," and is funded primarily by the Tercentenary Foundation of the Bank of Sweden.

7. *Svenska Dagbladet* 1997b.

8. *Dagens industri* 1998b.

9. *Dagens industri* 1998a.

10. *Dagens industri* 1998c.

11. *Metro* 1997.

12. *Svenska Dagbladet* 1997a.

13. Fundamental analysis and technical analysis are two different prediction strategies used by investors to chose stocks and are, to an extent, different schools of thought. Fundamental analysis scrutinizes stocks on the basis of the company's intrinsic value, as determined from their balance sheet, cash flow, operating performance, leadership, and future prospects; technical analysis departs from past market and stock price patterns, with the assumption that they are useful in predicting future stock movement.

14. The automobile division of Volvo was acquired by Ford in 1999 through a deal that Aktiespararna did not oppose because it considered it fair to small investors.

15. Implicitly, Susanna is referring to the past strength of unions in Swedish com-

panies. Unions no longer have as much power as they used to, largely because of the exigencies of the global marketplace.

16. *Svenska Dagbladet* 1999.

REFERENCES

Abolafia, Mitchell
    1996 Making Markets: Opportunism and Restraint on Wall Street. Cambridge, MA: Harvard University Press.

Baudrillard, Jean
    1981 For a Critique of the Political Economy of the Sign. St. Louis, MO: Telos Press.

Beck, Ulrich
    1992 Risk Society. Towards a New Modernity. London: Sage.

Bernstein, Peter
    1992 Capital Ideas: The Probable Origins of Modern Wall Street. New York: The Free Press.

Bourdieu, Pierre
    1986 The Forms of Capital. *In* Handbook of Theory and Research for the Sociology of Education. J. B. Richardson, ed. Pp. 241–258. New York: Greenwood Press.
    1990 The Logic of Practice. Stanford, CA: Stanford University Press.

Carrier, James, ed.
    1997 Meanings of the Market: The Free Market in Western Culture. Oxford: Berg.

Cook, Scott, and Martin Diskin
    1976 The Peasant Market Economy of the Valley of Oaxaca in Analysis and History. *In* Markets in Oaxaca. Scott Cook and Martin Diskin, eds. Pp. 5–25. Austin: University of Texas Press.

Dagens industri
    1998a Utländska fondbolag intar Sverige ["Foreign fund companies advance on Sweden."]. Stockholm, Sweden. 2 March.
    1998b Småsparare sover ["Individual investors asleep."]. Stockholm, Sweden. 9 March.
    1998c Nya pensionssystemet ger 185 mdr till börsen ["New pension system will bring 185 billion to the stock exchange."]. Stockholm, Sweden. 25 March.

Dannhaeuser, Norbert
1989 Marketing in Developing Urban Areas. *In* Economic Anthropology. Stuart Plattner, ed. Pp. 222–252. Stanford, CA: Stanford University Press.
1996 Two Towns in Germany: Commerce and the Urban Transformation. Westport, CT: Bergin & Garvey.

Dilley, Roy, ed.
1992 Contesting Markets: Analyses of Ideology, Discourse and Practice. Edinburgh: Edinburgh University Press.

Eder, Herbert M.
1976 Markets as Mirrors: Reflectors of the Economic Activity and the Regional Culture of Coastal Oaxaca. *In* Markets in Oaxaca. Scott Cook and Martin Diskin, eds. Pp. 67–80. Austin: University of Texas Press.

Friedland, Roger, and A. F. Robertson, eds.
1990 Beyond the Marketplace: Rethinking Economy and Society. New York: Aldine de Gruyter.

Giddens, Anthony
1991 The Consequences of Modernity. Cambridge: Polity Press.

Granovetter, Mark
1985 Economic Action and Social Structure. The Problem of Embeddedness. American Journal of Sociology 91(3):481–510.

Gudeman, Stephen
1986 Economics as Culture: Models and Metaphors of Livelihood. London: Routledge and Kegan Paul.

Gyllenram, Carl-Gustav
1998 Aktiemarknadens psykologi, eller Vad styr upp- och nedgångarna på börsen? ["Stockmarket psychology, or what steers the ups and downs of the market?"]. Stockholm: Rabén Prisma.

Hannerz, Ulf
1992 Cultural Complexity: Studies in the Social Organization of Meaning. New York: Columbia University Press.
1996 Transnational Connections: Culture, People, Places. London: Routledge.

Harvey, David
1990 The Condition of Postmodernity. An Inquiry into the Origins of Cultural Change. Oxford: Blackwell.

Hertz, Ellen
1998 The Trading Crowd: An Ethnography of the Shanghai Stock Market. Cambridge: Cambridge University Press.

Jameson, Frederic
1991 Postmodernism or the Cultural Logic of Late Capitalism. London: Verso.

Lash, Scott, and John Urry
1994 Economies of Signs and Space. London: Sage.

Lindh de Montoya, Monica
1996 Progress, Hunger and Envy: Commercial Agriculture, Marketing and Social Transformation in the Venezuelan Andes. Stockholm Studies in Social Anthropology, vol. 36. Stockholm: Almqvist & Wiksell.

Lindqvist, Mats
1999 Igår var vi slösare. Idag är vi sparare. Etnologiska reflektioner kring en privatekonomisk mässa ["Yesterday squanderer, today saver."]. Kulturella Perspektiv (1):25–38.

Lukacs, John
1984 Outgrowing Democracy: A History of the United States in the Twentieth Century. Garden City, NY: Doubleday.

Marcus, George, and Michael J. Fischer, eds.
1986 Anthropology as Cultural Critique. Chicago: The University of Chicago Press.

McClay, Wilfred M.
1993 The Strange Career of The Lonely Crowd: or, The Antinomies of Autonomy. In The Culture of the Market: Historical Essays. T. L. Haskell and R. F. Teichgraeber, III, eds. Pp. 397–440. Cambridge: Cambridge University Press.

Metro
1997 Allt fler sparar—men utan att tänka på räntan ["More people are saving—but without thinking about interest."]. Stockholm, Sweden. 24 March.

Mintz, Sidney
1976 Forward. In Markets in Oaxaca. Scott Cook and Martin Diskin, eds. Pp. xi–xv. Austin: University of Texas Press.

Parry, Jonathan, and Maurice Bloch, eds.
1989 Money and the Morality of Exchange. Cambridge: Cambridge University Press.

Robertson, Roland
1992 Globalization: Social Theory and Global Culture. London: Sage.

Sassen, Saskia
1996 Losing Control? Sovereignty in an Age of Globalization. New York: Colombia University Press.
1998a Globalization and Its Discontents: Essays on the New Mobility of People and Money. New York: The New Press.
1998b Governance and Normativity in the Global Economy. Paper delivered at Globalizations, a conference organized by the Swedish Council for Planning and Coordination of Research (FRN) and its Committee on Global Processes in a European Perspective in cooperation with the Ministry for Foreign Affairs (UD) and the Swedish Collegium for Advanced Study in the Social Sciences (SCASSS), Stockholm, Sweden, October.

Svenska Dagbladet
1997a Hushållens börsägande borde öka ["Households shareholding should increase."]. Stockholm, Sweden. 7 April.
1997b Varannan svensk är aktieägare ["Every other Swede a shareholder."]. Stockholm, Sweden. 8 April.
1999 Aktiehandel via nätet ökar explosionartat ["Stocktrading via the net increasing explosively."]. Stockholm, Sweden. 10 October.

Swedberg, Richard
1994 Markets as Social Structures. In The Handbook of Economic Sociology. Neil J. Smelser and Richard Swedberg, eds. Pp. 255–282. Princeton, NJ: Princeton University Press.

Swidler, Ann
1986 Culture in Action. Symbols and Strategies. American Sociological Review 51:273–286.

Taussig, Michael
1980 The Devil and Commodity Fetishism in South America. Chapel Hill: University of North Carolina Press.

13

Emerging Markets, Globalization, and the Small Investor: The Case of Venezuela

Miguel Montoya

During the last few years, news about emerging markets have become daily fare in financial publications and in the media in general. In the late 1980s and 1990s, these markets were promoted as offering some of the best investment opportunities for those seeking rapid capital growth. The optimistic reports of the booming economies in the countries in the Far East and in parts of Latin America in the early 1990s have, however, been replaced with a series of crisis scenarios since the devaluation of the Mexican peso in 1994 and the fall of the Thai currency in 1997. Instead, the media has depicted scenes of despair, played out in far-flung continents and cultures: Mexico, Thailand, Korea, Indonesia, Malaysia, Russia, and Brazil.

Without a doubt, the rapidly accelerating rise of a global economy that ties people together through their invested savings—the essence of their labor, ingenuity, and sacrifice—will affect the way people think of the world and their place in it. As we read about the changes under way in the financial arena—new technologies, financial instruments, and fast, reliable, inexpensive communications—it appears that the world may be on the brink of a financial transformation where stock markets become a great common denominator, incorporating more and more nations and peoples into financial markets through mechanisms such as privatization, pension funds, and on-line brokerages. What are these developments likely to mean for investors in the industrialized countries and in the emerging markets themselves?

If there is little work and not much of it academic[1] on the behavior of small investors in industrialized countries,[2] even less is known about individual investors in the emerging markets. Yet these seem to be those likely to be most affected by the changes in store, and they may also come to have considerable impact on the more mature markets. As Hertz (1998) noted in the case of Shanghai, stock markets can, in particular circumstances, really seize the public imagination.

In this chapter, I examine the concept of the emerging market, looking at the circumstances that have given rise to the concept and examining a particular Latin American market—Venezuela. I explain some of the recent history of both the market and the state, before discussing some preliminary data from my fieldwork among Venezuelan individual investors. As will become clear, it is difficult to gain an understanding of financial markets and the actors within them without examining the context in which they exist, and that context is, in the first instance, made up of the state—the institutions and laws—in which they are embedded.

Theoretically, my research on Venezuela as an emerging market shares the framework of Lindh de Montoya's (this volume) study of Swedish stock market investors, departing from the point of view that even as the market becomes a global phenomenon, ways of conceptualizing it and acting within it must be culture bound and differ between regions and nations. Social relations, so varied around the globe, are central features of all market processes in modern societies. Gudeman's (1986) cultural economics and ideas about how societies model their participation in economic life in different ways can be a starting point for an anthropological examination of stock markets, providing a means by which social and political decisions about markets can be understood.

Economic modeling builds on earlier experience and values that give them a certain form, but models are constantly changing and constituted in use, arising out of new circumstances, information, and tools available to the individual. Consequently, models are likely to be contradictory, tense, and filled with gaps and ambiguities as societies become involved with new kinds of economic activities, but they can serve as readings of changing ways of perceiving a world in metamorphosis. In Venezuela, as in Sweden, people model the world in an attempt to explain it, searching for metaphors from daily life to use as tools for understanding (Gudeman 1986). In both countries, there is a preoccupation with, and public discourse on ideas of morality, the relationship between the individual and the community. In Venezuela, there has long been a desire for honesty in economic and political life, something taken more for granted in Sweden. Naturally, times that are perceived as economically difficult make such issues more resonant and relevant to the general public.

This chapter deals, then, with Venezuela, a so-called "emerging market."[3] Stock markets in developing countries can be analyzed from several different points of view. They are local financial arenas, in which citizens invest to secure personal economic goals; international fields in which investment can be made for profit; and spheres in which development aid agencies seek to enhance actors' competence in the hopes that stimulating activity will promote economic development. Worldwide, the nature and configurations of trade are changing,[4] and the rise of the emerging market as a concept is a consequence of new ways of looking at developing countries. The liberalization and globalization of trade as reflected in changing political and economic constellations, new trade agreements, and communication technology are beginning to focus the financial spotlight on the potential of the financial markets of particular countries that were previously more peripheral to the global economy.

HISTORY OF GLOBALIZATION AND THE CONCEPT OF THE EMERGING MARKET

Much has been written about the sociocultural aspects and consequences of processes of globalization (Appadurai 1996; Hannerz 1992, 1996; Robertson 1992; Sassen 1996, 1998). Perhaps Waters's (1995) definition of the phenomenon as "a reduction in the geographical contraints on social relations" (p. 164) is the most appropriate for my purposes in this chapter. From the point of view of markets, globalization is nothing new; indeed it was the search for new trade routes that gave us the knowledge that our world is a globe. In the Europe of the 1400s, Spain and Portugal competed for trade by striving for supremacy on the seas. Crone (1969) recounts that Spain controlled the Canary Islands, which were believed to be "the end of the West" at this time; but Portugal was in a good position in

regard to trade between northern and southern Europe, and toward
Africa.

During this period, the known world looked eastward; Cairo and Bag-
dad were the endpoints of the spice trade, and Jerusalem was the center of
the *mappa mundi*. Later, with the evidence provided by Magellan in the
early 1500s, European cartographers could design the Mercator chart,
divided by the Greenwich Meridian, with the New World and Asia placed
to west and east. Crone notes that these widening horizons initiated a revolution in international affairs by making statesmen and merchants think
globally: about the precise location, on the other side of the world, of the
Spice Islands; about the best route to them; about the best places for overseas colonization; and about the best markets for their own goods. The
story of peoples' search for new sources of wealth is the story of emerging
markets. Today, we have other economic centers (Sassen 1993)—New
York, London, Tokyo—but especially since the mid-1970s, with the deregulation of financial markets, privatization of state companies, and political
processes such as that which began in Poland and resulted in the fall of
the Berlin Wall, the centers of economic powers are again looking eastward—and to the south—trying to find ways of gaining a share of market
spaces. In doing so, they are dissolving the conceptual space between
national economies, reducing the role of the state, increasing trade, and
creating innovative ways for people to participate in each others' economic expectations.

What is an emerging market? The sailors and merchants of the 1400s
and 1500s were eager for information about trade routes, sources of trade
goods, and knowledge about the people they traded with. In part, emergence has to do with information, for information reduces risk and
enables trade. It is of great importance to potential investors; increased
and dependable information and communication processes are elements
that help create emerging markets. As their statistics become more reliable
and gain the attention of financial analysts, these countries' industries and
economies are discussed in the global financial media and they come out
of the darkness; they emerge, recognized as holding profitable investment
opportunities. One might compare the gradual accumulation of reliable
information about commercial enterprises in developing countries to the
mapping of new continents and trade routes in the age of exploration.
And clearly, it is particular people in the industrialized West who, for a

variety of reasons, "discover" these new financial markets, conceive of them as profitable, and direct attention toward them. But what has changed in these countries, other than our way of looking at them?

The concept of the emerging market is part of a shift in the conception of the economic potential of developing countries, but also of the role of the market in development. Much development aid worldwide has focused on the provision of the infrastructure understood to be necessary for economic growth: transportation, improved communications, and cheap and abundant energy (Montoya 1996). Investments have also been made in improving the technology of farming and local industry. Financial markets in developing countries were mainly overlooked, however, until 1986 when, as Mobius (1996) indicates, the International Finance Corporation (IFC) began to promote capital market development in less-developed countries.[5] A recent series of articles in the *New York Times*[6] reporting how the world financial landscape has changed with the vast amounts of money circulating the globe, notes that when the International Development Bank tried to awaken support for a Third World investment fund, a listener at a meeting protested that no one would want to put money into a Third World investment fund, and that a better name was needed. And therewith, the "emerging market funds" were born.

Investment in these markets has been promoted heavily by prominent financial analysts such as Mark Mobius, who worked for Templeton funds in the late 1980s and early 1990s. As money flowed into mutual funds, pension funds, and other institutional investors, investment capital increased greatly; by 1995, such funds controlled 20 trillion dollars, ten times that in 1986. The amount of pension fund assets moving into emerging markets has risen simultaneously; less than 1 percent of such assets were invested abroad in 1980, but in 1997, the figure was 17 percent; and in 1997, investors in industrialized countries spent 197 times more on overseas stocks than in 1970.[7] In this way, the capital markets of individual nations begin to merge into a global financial market.

It is important to keep a few developments in mind when thinking about individual investors, since several processes are currently transforming the small investors' situation within financial markets. Technology is one of them.

Digital systems have changed stock markets from the obvious "market-places" where traders meet and bid for shares, to the rows of young traders who sit watching computer monitors in banks and brokerages. The stock market has been silenced, and money markets have been moved from a place into cyberspace. But more important, these systems make investment easier and less expensive for the individual. Internet brokers charge minimal fees for executing trades.

Direct access to the market has been offered the public since 1997 in the United States (to Island at NASDAQ, via online brokerages), and there are similar systems in Europe. It is only a matter of time before they are worldwide; Venezuela's first such online brokerage advertised to the public in the end of 1998. The fall in price of computing power makes it possible for more people to acquire sophisticated computers, and the development of technical stock analysis software for amateurs allows stock enthusiasts to download trading information from data providers, create their own charts, and invest in stocks based on their own interpretations of trading patterns.

Day trading is also an outgrowth of these developments. Through the Internet, vast amounts of information about financial markets become available, such as international business newspapers, financial publications, and the home pages of companies and brokerages.

The emerging markets are also caught up in these processes of technological change; through them, their companies become more accessible and local investors also gain access to international markets.[8] The demand for increased transparency in and increasing institutional vigilance over financial markets is another process that improves small investors' situation, both by cutting down the abuses of powerful brokerages and traders and by making company information more accurate, both in mature and emerging markets.

One can characterize emerging markets as those in which processes of modernization, industrialization, and consumption move rapidly; consequently, investors can get a higher return on their money in these markets than in North America or Europe, where growth supposedly moves at a steadier pace. It has long been recognized that capital-creating savings are necessary for economic development. For example, the initial growth and success of the economies of East Asia have commonly been attributed to the high level of local savings in these countries, which provided capital that could be mobilized in productive ventures. The stock market is one important area in which savings may be invested, giving local companies the funds they need to modernize, expand production, find new markets, and research new products, processes that lead to increased economic activity and that can provide jobs and improve standards of living.

Theoretically, at least in the developed countries, small investors see their savings in stocks as long-term savings, while institutional investors are quick to move their capital at signs of trouble or decreased earnings. Thus, it is believed that small investors are important for the stability they can give to markets, as much in emerging markets as mature ones. But what factors lead to market confidence and long-term investment? Naturally, historical experience and the institutional environment are important.

THE BACKGROUND: OIL REVENUES, DEBT, CORRUPTION, REFORM

Known for its rich mineral resources—iron ore, bauxite, gold, and diamonds, in addition to the second largest oil deposits in the world, after the Gulf States—Venezuela was long one of the best-off countries in Latin America. The nation became a democracy in 1958, with the fall of dictator Pérez Jiménez, and two political parties, the Social Democrats and the Christian Democrats, alternated in power for forty years. Petroleum exports allowed the nation to modernize—investing profits in national industries, infrastructure, and public services—and kept the currency strong and stable for over two decades. The focus on the oil industry, to the neglect of agriculture, brought massive rural-urban migration. The state was organized to distribute petroleum income, partly through the construction of infrastructure, and through a large public sector.

More than being a capitalist country, in which a competitive productive sector exists, Venezuela can be considered a distributive society, where the state shoulders many of the costs that the productive sector normally must bear in capitalist societies (Rojas 1998:3–31). The party in power decides how to allocate oil revenues and favors its supporters. Consequently, accusations of corruption in public life have been a persistent theme in Venezuelan politics, but although wrongdoing is duly investigated, it is rare that anyone is punished for corrupt practices. With two powerful top-steered parties controlling political life and the inflow of oil income, there was no civil society to act as a counterbalance, and democracy gradually became bereft of meaning (Rojas 1998:39).

In 1983, years of economic mismanagement along with decreasing oil earnings led to a severe crisis in the economy and a sudden devaluation of the national currency, the bolívar, an event that shocked Venezuelans who had long been used to a stable currency and inexpensive imports. But the large foreign debt contracted during the 1970s, when oil prices peaked, had become too difficult to service when the economy began to deteriorate. In 1989, the debt was renegotiated, and International Monetary Fund (IMF) policies were implemented.[9] With the end of state subsidies for basic foods, milk, and energy, economic life became increasingly difficult both for the poor and for Venezuela's formerly relatively large middle class. Drawing on earlier public discourse about corruption in the country, new political parties (such as Causa R) sprang up and corruption in government institutions began to be discussed. Via the mass media, a lively and bitter debate began over morals in political life and the economic policies that should guide the distribution of the shrinking economic base brought in by oil exports.

The 1990s have been difficult years, marked by both economic and political instability. With the continuous devaluation of the bolívar, the state rescue of fourteen of the nation's banks that failed in rapid succession in 1994, and other fiscal crises in the 1990s, much of the national infrastructure and services cannot be maintained adequately, to the dismay of the population. With economic uncertainty—inflation and an overvalued currency—job opportunities also disappeared, and repeated strikes by public servants for pay increases contributed to the general economic malaise.

In December 1998, after years of declining popularity, the two traditional parties completely lost their power with the election of Hugo Chávez,[10] a former paratrooper who won the elections by a landslide on a populist platform that promised to clean up corruption and to write a new constitution. As my research began in Venezuela in early 1999, the country was in the midst of a deep economic and political crisis. The new administration has accomplished concrete political goals—the drafting and acceptance by popular referendum of a new constitution—but, as of this writing (January 2001), it has yet to produce any coherent market-oriented economic program.

STATE, MARKET, TAXES

There are important differences in the relationship between the state and the productive sector in Venezuela as compared with the United States or the European countries. Prior to the discovery of petroleum in the country, taxes on imports paid for the then-limited responsibilities and activities of the Venezuelan government. Petroleum has been the main source of income since about 1930 and has supported the modernization of the country, its large public sector, and, for many years, a wide variety of subsidies for food, housing, and transportation. Public taxation, that is a redistributive tax system, provides only a small part of the national budget.[11]

The state's ability to pay its way with oil income, instead of primarily through tax revenues collected from industries and citizens, creates fundamental differences in the relationship between the citizen and the state as compared to industrialized countries, one aspect of which is a lack of accountability and transparency; when the government is financed through taxes, the taxpayers demand to know where the money goes, and the state must publicly explain and justify its expenditures. In Venezuela, petroleum pays the bills; it is the national patrimony, a part of which, by right, supposedly belongs to every Venezuelan citizen. The debate about and accusations of corruption became vociferous when oil wealth decreased and peoples' quality of life declined. When the government had less to spend, peoples' expectations of the future were frustrated, and they began to demand more information and responsibility from politicians and government employees.

Another important difference is that redistributive taxation brings about a closer relationship between the state and the productive sector. In Sweden, for example, the last decade of economic difficulties has seen a dialogue between politicians, the public sector, industry, and citizens about how to best reduce costs, increase productivity, and create employment. In Venezuela, this dialogue is almost absent, since the state can stand autonomously from the needs and pressures of dominant social groups (Urbaneja 1992:38). The state takes the initiatives and has a monopoly on the country's most productive company, Petróleos de Venezuela, Sociedad Anónima (PDVSA), the national oil company, which was nationalized in 1976 and is dominated by state interests. Government spending is directed more by political than economic concerns, and its oil profits give the government in power relative independence vis-à-vis local industry.[12] As a result, there is little tradition of concerted cooperation between the state and the productive sector as a whole; rather, particular interest groups with political ties to the administration in power collaborate with the government to attain certain goals.

Since 1999, there has been intense debate in the Venezuelan media among scholars, politicians, and people in the financial sector about how to renew the failing economy by instituting long-term economic reforms.[13] But the administration seems to have turned a deaf ear to this discussion in favor of distributing rudimentary aid to the poor, primarily via the military establishment, members of which also make up a substantial portion of Chavez's cabinet and advisors. Venezuelans expect the administration to solve the economic crisis and look to the president to take measures, rather than looking toward the market for a solution.

According to Chávez and his supporters, the crisis in Venezuela is of a moral, rather than an economic, nature. The primary goal of his administration was to write a new constitution in order to be able to deal with corruption: The former constitution (from the 1960s), Chávez claimed, was not really democratic, because it focused power at the top of the political hierarchy. He says that the voice of el pueblo (the people) should be sovereign. Writing a new constitution embroiled Chávez in a power struggle with the congress and the Supreme Court over the process by which and by whom the new constitution should be written. Critics maintained that there was nothing wrong with the old constitution and that Chávez only wanted to write a new one to gain more power. What is certain is that in the process of creating a new constitution, many of the former gains made in the decentralization of power in the country were lost. Here, then, is a brief portrait of the environment in which this emerging market operates.

When reading about emerging markets in the economic press, one could get the erroneous impression that they are homogenous, but, in fact, they differ immensely, though they may experience similar problems in developing their economies. The valuation of companies in the various emerging markets may vary widely. Obviously, each country has different resources, but most have monostructural economies that focus on one or a few main products. Each has a particular economic history and a distinct political culture. Although it can be assumed that investors in all countries approach their stock markets in search of the highest possible gain on investment, they will have different perspectives on their investment activities, depending on the nature of the country's present and past economy.

THE CARACAS STOCK EXCHANGE

The Caracas stock market has a history dating back to 1805. Since its inception, it has undergone a variety of organizational forms, but the exchange in its current form was established in 1947, and began to gain prominence in 1989, when twelve of the forty-three seats were auctioned to financial institutions, incorporating this sector into the exchange. The same year, regulations for brokerages were established (Instituto Venezolano de Mercadeo de Capitales 1998). At present, about forty-three listed companies are traded regularly. Some listed companies are traded infrequently because the majority of their shares are held by a handful of people.

In general, Venezuelan companies have preferred to turn to the banking system for their financing, and their owners have often had social ties within the nation's banks that have made this a natural way for them to finance projects. Becoming listed on the stock exchange also involves a detailed and tedious procedure designed to make the company transparent to potential investors, and not all companies requiring financing believe that the end results will be worth this process. The need to reveal the intimate details of a company's history, sometimes a family history, can also be disturbing.

Thus, the stock market is relatively small, as is the body of investors. If half of the population invests in Sweden, in Venezuela not more than an estimated 5 percent of the population is active in the stock market. Little is known about investors' social composition, although it is assumed that investors are from the upper-middle and upper classes. Lindh de Montoya (this volume) suggests that in Sweden, the state's social welfare programs aid investment because people do not have to save for medical emergencies and for educational goals.

In Venezuela, the situation is quite the reverse. Middle-class Venezuelans send their children to private schools and universities; pay for medical services when uninsured, without coverage through their workplace, or when opting for a higher standard of care; and survive periods of unemployment without state assistance. They also have a myriad of social investments to face; baptisms, confirmations, coming-out parties (held for daughters when they turn fifteen), and weddings are rites of passage that are observed socially by holding a party for extended family and friends. Christmas holidays, Carnival, and Easter week are, when possible, celebrated with a trip to the beach or to visit relatives living out of town. Such social investments are important in this society, where family and friends still provide a vital socioeconomic and informational network than in more industrialized countries. The economic difficulties that people have experienced during the last fifteen years have changed consumption patterns, certainly, but have also increased the importance of social bonds and the necessity of accumulating savings for emergencies, and, when possible, to assist relatives in need. Nonetheless, investment in the stock exchange grows periodically.

Until the end of the 1980s, the Venezuelan stock market was small, with few transactions. But in 1990 and 1991, despite a generally gloomy economic horizon, the Caracas Stock Exchange expanded dynamically because of the favorable economic (if not social) impact of the IMF's economic policies of 1989, reforms in the market's legal structure, and rising oil prices. The middle class began to participate more actively in buying stocks. Stimulated by this increase in activity, the exchange modernized, acquiring a sophisticated electronic trading system imported from Vancouver to facilitate trading. In 1990, Venezuela was the best-performing stock market among the emerging markets, rising an amazing 584 percent, and ranked ahead of both Greece and Chile. By the last quarter of 1991, share prices had risen by a factor of eleven in less than two years.

Hugo Chávez's attempted military coup against the presidency in 1992 changed everything, and by the end of the year, the Venezuelan market was the second-worst performer among the so-called emerging markets. Since then, stock prices have fluctuated widely; oil prices, domestic political disturbances, rising inflation, negative domestic growth, and the collapse of the banking sector in 1994 brought an emergency economic plan involving foreign-currency controls (Keppler and Lechner 1997:335–337). In 1997, the nation seemed to be on the road to economic recovery with Caldera's *apertura* politics, which aimed at opening the oil industry to foreign investment, and the stock market surged again. Unfortunately, the plunge in oil prices during 1998 and the growing popularity of unpredictable Chávez quickly put a damper on enthusiasm, and shortly before the elections, the market was at its lowest point in many years.

Yet, despite the low volume of activity during the end of the 1990s, the administration of the Bolsa de Caracas invested in Infobolsa, a new information system imported from Madrid that they hoped would compete with Reuters within Latin America. They also installed yet another electronic trading system to handle higher volumes of trades, partly in expectation of pending legislation for a national pension system based on participation in funds and stocks that would bring capital and action to the exchange. Most members were optimistic about the future, and wanted to be ready for the next trading boom, but there was anxiety about what form the new government's economic policies would take. By 2001, the panorama had changed considerably. Because of the very low share prices due to economic recession, Electricidad de Caracas, the largest company listed, had been bought up by U.S.-based AES Corporation, and several more companies in a variety of branches (banking, telecommunications, the food industry) were candidates for acquisition by both national and foreign buyers. Consequently, stock prices rose dramatically in these companies (Armas H. 2001b; Prieto 2001).

I mention the foregoing to illustrate the nature of the Caracas stock market—its ability to go from the heights of euphoria to the depths of despair with few stops in between. It is also important to note the effect of oil prices; since oil gives the breath of life to the Venezuelan economy, rising prices revive the stock market. When oil prices are high, the government has money to distribute and has never refrained from spending. Foreign investors then enter this market where higher energy prices mean more consumption and better returns to industry, and are reflected in higher share prices, rather than the lower prices that are the case in most other markets.[14] Venezuela is part of a global economy, but dances to a different drummer, economically out of tune with most of the rest of the world.

PLAYING THE MARKET—INDIVIDUAL INVESTORS

How do individual investors reason in such a market? On the basis of twenty-five in-depth interviews I conducted with stock exchange officials, brokers, and small investors, certain tendencies can be noted. With regard to individual investors, the issues of trust, information, and investment alternatives merit discussion.

Because of the institutional situation surrounding the market, trust is difficult to establish. There is no active shareholders' association, few courses on stock market investing, little of the medial "how to" information that attracts small investors in more mature markets, and marketplace institutions are not always dependable. People invest through brokerages or through banks and say that when they started out, they went to a brokerage recommended by a relative or friend. A number of brokerages have gone bankrupt and closed in recent years,[15] as have banks, and this history is fresh in peoples' minds. "You have to watch the situation closely," said Antonio, a physician in his seventies. "You have to read the paper, listen to what people say, and figure out what might happen. If you hear rumors about your bank or your broker, it's better not to wait and see—get your money out. It's better to be safe than sorry." The first problem to be faced, then, is choosing a reliable bank or brokerage.

Because of the nature of the market, stock investments are nearly always short term—a few days, a couple of weeks, or a month or two. Long-term investments are those that are kept from several months up to a year. Few investors could imagine keeping their money in a stock for a whole year: "That would be really long term," said Marcelo, a finance student whose uncle ran a brokerage. "Here everything is short term, short term!" he insisted, referring as much to government planning and policies as his investment strategies. Indeed, the lack of long-term commitments to particular market-oriented economic goals and the ad hoc nature of economic policy is reflected in the ups and downs of the stock market. "I don't know what's going to be happening in a week, much less a month," Juan, an investor in his forties pointed out. "How can I invest long term?" Thus, a lack of faith in government policy affects the market and is reflected in the short-term nature of investment activity.

"If you read the newspapers you'll notice that some things printed don't have much to do with reality," one stock market official commented when explaining the exchanges' decision to adopt Madrid's Infobolsa system for their informational needs. "We have an almost genetic lack of information." This is certainly true for the average investor. Information about companies listed on the exchange is available, for example through the library at the stock exchange, but it is not readily available elsewhere. When I asked investors how they decided to invest in a particular company, I found that word-of-mouth was a common information resource.

"Someone who knows what's happening will give you a hint," said Antonio. "Maybe one of my patients, or a relative. 'This company has a good project,' they'll mention. Or 'take a look at such-and-such.' Then I'll read the papers, try to find out about it, and see what I think."

The people I talked to felt that there was adequate information in the newspapers to guide them in their investing, however. Then, they were talking about macroeconomic and political information, what is going on in the country and in the world. Those who work within the field of finance, such as two university teachers I interviewed, felt quite the opposite. One pointed out that it was when companies (five in Venezuela so far) first went through the rigorous procedure of having their stocks registered as ADRs[16] on the New York exchange that adequate information about the company became available. The information booklet that each was required to publish when being introduced in the United States was sought after by Venezuelans and considered by far the most complete source of data about a company. Certain foreign banks operating in Venezuela also provided good information, but it was not easy to obtain, and other specialized information services used by financial professionals in Venezuela and abroad were too expensive for average investors.

The investors I spoke with did not complain about the lack of financial data on companies, however. Generally, they did not appear to take fundamental analysis as seriously as I expected; rather they emphasized the gambling aspects of investing. "We call it *jugar dinero en la Bolsa*" (to play the stock exchange), Roberto, a former stock exchange official, pointed out. This was also noted by several of the people I spoke with. They did not save regularly in the market, accumulating stock in a company over time, but placed a lump sum in a stock, to see what it would do in the next few days or weeks. They tried to seek out winners, informing themselves with the resources at hand. "I use all three methods when I invest," confided Armando, in his mid-thirties, a regular in the Investors' Room at the exchange, where investors can watch the ticker, observe market depth on the trading system, and the information on Infobolsa. "I use fundamental analysis, technical analysis, and I use 'feeling.' I walk around the city, I talk to people, I try to take it all in. How are people feeling? Are they optimistic? Do they think life is going to be o.k.?"

Among Venezuelan investors, there was none of the ambivalence about the morality of the stock market found by Lindh de Montoya (this volume) among some fund investors in Sweden, nor the consciousness of owning part of an industry or being part of a global economy. People were aware that their shares signified ownership of part of the company, but did not indicate they felt a part of it in any way. Stocks were seen more as vehicles for possible profit, comparable, perhaps, to horses at the racetrack. And winnings, like racetrack or lottery winnings, held no negative stigma; there was no expression that one's winnings were another's losses. It would be interesting to see if one could link this perspective to the oil revenue economy, where bonanzas also arrive with no guilt attached. A mining economy does not seem to produce a society like the one described by Foster (1965) in his article on the image of the limited good.

For average Venezuelans with savings, there are not many alternatives for preserving their capital and making it grow. When I asked people what was the best investment today, all replied "real estate," and indeed, in rapidly growing Caracas, real estate values have risen consistently. But buying a piece of property, beside the family home, is not a realistic investment if one has a smaller sum to place since interest rates are high. Inflation quickly decimates money in savings accounts, so buying dollars has been a favorite strategy over the years. However, hoarding dollars is not safe and produces no interest. Thus, interest has grown in the stock market.

Other markets are available beside the Venezuelan one, however. Based on my thus far limited sample, it appears that a number of globalized Venezuelans invest abroad. Often, they have studied in the United States or in Europe, or have visited relatives living there; they speak English and acquire foreign stocks via North American Internet brokerages. It is easy and perfectly legal for Venezuelans to invest overseas, and the dynamic performance of the stock market in the United States has naturally been of interest to them.

Thus, a number of Venezuelan investors are leapfrogging over their own stock market into cyberspace. "Never again the Venezuelan market," one businessman nearing retirement intoned. He had invested, won, and lost on the Caracas exchange for several years but now had most of his savings invested in a U.S. portfolio of stocks and bonds via a Venezuelan brokerage. Investors from industrialized nations look to Venezuelan stocks hoping for rapid gains, while savvy Venezuelans turn to the U.S. market for its performance, transparency, and greater security.[17]

CONCLUSION

To judge from their economic investment in electronic trading and information systems (Infobolsa), the Caracas Stock Exchange is an institution in the process of modernization. Despite national economic difficulties and political uncertainties, it is going ahead with major projects with the goal of further incorporating the Caracas market into the global economy. Observing Venezuelan investors' conceptions of the stock market, however, one senses a deep divide between their way of thinking about their investments and those of small investors in the more developed financial markets, with a notable difference in their economic possibilities.

How can we explain this? Keppler and Lechner (1997:73) discuss the greater risk in stock markets of emerging markets, due to threats such as political instability, civil war, high levels of foreign indebtedness, trade restrictions, declining commodity prices, lopsided development, and the sudden withdrawal of capital by large short-term–oriented investors, such as occurred in Mexico during the peso crisis. Most of these risks (except civil war) are latent in Venezuela today, and for such reasons, foreign investment by large investors in the country's financial market is usually short term.

Everything considered, it is not unreasonable for Venezuelans to use short-term strategies in their local stock market, and to chose to invest more long term in the U.S.'s financial market. Many others do. Unfortunately, the current Venezuelan economic situation does not foster the development of more stable local financial instruments that might attract small investors' savings, nor the possibility of educating the public about the possible benefits of a viable local stock market for households' gradual accumulation of capital. In order to make the market more attractive, monetary stability, fiscal discipline, and banking supervision and transparency must be improved and trade liberalization agreements respected.

Venezuela lives primarily off the profit of petroleum exports that are subject to international price fluctuations. The instability of oil prices is directly reflected in the national economy and in the political decisions taken by the government, which operates in the short term. Consequently, people are accustomed to a fluctuating economy, and it is not surprising that their economic strategies should mimic those at the national level. The situation in Sweden is very different; a manufacturing country, Sweden depends on the taxation of industry and citizens (and some state monopolies) for income, and has a more stable economy. Politicians' economic planning is more long term. The reliability of financial institutions, variety of investment instruments, and wealth of good-quality information contribute to creating a situation in which the majority of investors invest over the long term.

If Venezuelans conceive of the stock market as a roller coaster that they have to be ready to jump off of at any moment, this can be linked to the rise and fall of international oil prices and their immediate effects on the national economy. It can be noted, too, that Venezuela's fortunes long have depended on commodity prices; prior to the petroleum-based economy that was consolidated in the end of the 1920s, the nation was a major coffee exporter. Thus, a view of economic life as uncertain and far beyond one's control is well grounded in historical experience.

There are two tendencies, or forces, within the Venezuelan economy today. One, apparent within the stock exchange, in the opinions of some academics and journalists, and within certain companies, is to reach out toward international exchange and competition and to participate as fully as possible in the global marketplace. The opposite tendency, most visible in the current administration, is to shy away from the demands of globalization, and to distrust the purported benefits of a completely open economy. Yet, as many commentators have noted, it is difficult for nations to escape this worldwide process.

But can the world marketplace be trusted to provide for the needs of a nation? Indeed, this is a question open to debate. Bello (1998) has reviewed the 1997 Asian financial crisis and indicated that the chief cause of the debacle was the massive influx of foreign capital to the region in the early 1990s, and its even speedier exit when the crisis developed in 1997. He also blames multilateral institutions such as the IMF, which pressed Asian governments to liberalize their capital accounts to encourage inflows of foreign capital, as well as the business press, investment analysts, and academics who hyped "the Asian economic miracle, too often without a careful analysis." The "crony capitalism" and lack of transparency in financial institutions that usually take the blame in accounts of the crisis are certainly also contributing factors, Bello indicates, but were part and parcel of the Asian investment environment from the beginning and not instrumental in the collapse.

The benefits and detriments of foreign investment in the financial sector of growing economies can certainly be debated. Some Venezuelan economists speak disparagingly of *capitales golondrinas* (swallow capital), which nests in the country over a sunny summer season only to fly off when autumn winds blow. Others feel that the benefits outweigh the drawbacks. Within the social sciences, anthropologists such as Carol Smith (1976) have noted that markets in peripheral regions are as much organized to draw off the wealth produced in hinterlands, as to supply them with imports; and sociologists Frank (1967, 1969) and Wallerstein (1974) have developed convincing models of how these processes of extraction function at a global level. Certainly, the institutional actors in capital markets have the potential to extract speculative profits from the markets of developing countries. They are liquid, diversified, and well informed.

My concern in this chapter, however, has been with the small investor in a developing country, the Venezuelan citizen, who looks toward the stock market as a way of increasing his or her personal savings. Shareholders in North American and European countries have made substantial economic gains in recent years by investing in the technological advances—in information, communications, medicines—that are transforming our lives. Very few Venezuelan investors—only those able to invest outside of the country—can say the same. The local stock market is too little diversified and too erratic to provide the relatively stable growth necessary to attract small investors' long-term savings portfolios.

However, with time, Venezuela's continuing integration into the global marketplace could increase the opportunities for local investors, as the country and its companies and institutions increasingly comply with international standards for information and transparency, and as Venezuelan companies learn to compete in the international marketplace. A strengthening of democratic principles and of the accountability of national institutions to the public are political reforms that also need to go hand in hand with economic globalization. The main challenge that Venezuela faces is to diversify its economy, putting an end to its dependence on the mining sector. To achieve this, a space for dialogue and understanding must be established between the political and economic sectors of the country. At the moment, this seems unlikely, but time will tell.

NOTES

I thank the Tercentenary Foundation of The Bank of Sweden for funding this research and am also grateful to the Caracas Stock Exchange for their cooperation and enthusiasm for the study; Alejandro Ravard of the Instituto Venezolano de Mercado de Capitales was particularly helpful. The exchange allowed me to interview freely within the institution, and provided me with much valuable material. I also thank the Instituto de Estudios Superiores de Administración for its academic support during the research period. I am indebted to Jeffrey Cohen, Norbert Dannhaueser, Richard Swedberg, and José Antonio Torres for their comments on an earlier draft.

1. The work being done in the branch of economics called behavioral economics is an exception. See, for example, the work of Kahneman et al. (1982) and Richard Thaler (1993, 1994). This work deals with individuals and not societies, however, and research has been undertaken primarily in the United States.

2. See *Barron's* [1998] on investor reactions to recommended stocks and the *New York Times* [1997] as well as the *Wall Street Journal* [1997a, 1997b] on how anxiety and "psychological traits" affect investors' buying and selling behavior.

3. Fieldwork began in January 1999. This article is based on the first twenty-five interviews, of a projected total of seventy-five. In these, I have concentrated on the structural aspects of the stock market, carrying out interviews primarily in the stock exchange, with Venezuelan scholars working on financial markets (at the Instituto de Estudios Superiores de Administración) and with a number of small investors.

4. In Europe, the efforts to establish an economic community have been of political and economic importance for a quite a number of years. Similar efforts focused on integration and trade are under way in the Americas, with the Andean Pact, Mercosur, and the North American Free Trade Agreement. The Asian countries have also united, into the Association of Southeast Asian Nations Free Trade Area and the Asia Pacific Economic Corporation. While on one hand the world appears to be dividing up into large trade blocks, on the other, the World Trade Organization attempts to encourage free trade globally.

5. The IFC is a subsidiary of the World Bank supported by over 160 member countries. Its task is to promote the productivity and profitability of private companies in emerging markets through targeted investment assistance programs. In recent years, the IFC has worked intensively to promote development of capital markets that could finance projects in the emerging markets, and thus its input to

the upswing in this rapidly growing sector has been substantial (Keppler and Lechner 1997:11).

6. The series ran 15–18 February 1999 and was entitled "Global Contagion, a Narrative: Networked Economies, Stunted Lives."

7. See Kristof and Wyatt 1999.

8. For some of the latest developments in the business of stock trading, see Caruso 1998 and Hansell 1999.

9. One response to IMF policies, specifically the raise in local gasoline prices, was the four-day "Caracazo" riots in Caracas in the end of February 1989. The uprising was brutally put down by the armed forces.

10. On 4 February 1992, Chávez, then a paratrooper, staged a coup attempt against President Carlos Andrés Pérez. He failed, and was tried and jailed for a thirty-year term. Pérez's successor, Rafael Caldera, pardoned Chávez after two years, however; and upon his release Chávez formed his own political party, the Movimiento V República and ran successfully for the presidency.

11. Rojas (1998:37) notes that after the 1995 tax reform, less than 10 percent of the gross national product consisted of public taxes, and that there was a 60 percent rate of tax evasion.

12. To take a Swedish example: When political decisions are made, journalists inevitably comment "and tomorrow, we'll see what the market has to say about this." Unfavorable reactions may eventually bring policy revisions. In Venezuela, focus is on political power, and there is less interest in what "the market will say." Although the market is not ignored, it has less impact on state economic decisions, and, in general, promarket reforms are taken only when there is no other alternative.

13. When Chávez took office, oil prices were the lowest in twenty-five years and Venezuela faced a huge deficit in its budget. Inflation was at about 35 percent, then the highest in Latin America, and interest rates were also high. The currency was overvalued by as much as 35–40 percent, according to some analysts. Seven hundred factories had closed during 1998 because they could not compete with cheap foreign imports, causing even greater unemployment than the normally high rate. But the new administration benefited greatly by OPEC's policies that raised oil prices starting in the spring of 1999 and it has no plans to undertake the devaluation that many economists feel is necessary to make the Venezuelan economy competitive.

Some analysts argue that PDVSA should be truly nationalized by removing it from state control, which in practice means that it should be privatized (Malavé Mata 2000:xvii). The oil economy is a cyclical one, which periodically increases or decreases fiscal income. As of 2001, repeated OPEC decisions to defend prices by cutting production have kept prices high, within the $22–28 per barrel target range (*Daily Journal* 2001).

14. Salomon, Smith & Barney estimates that the Venezuelan gross national product will rise by 5.2 percent in 2001 due to increasing oil income and government spending (see Hernández Lavado 2001), while growth is declining in the United States and Europe. This slump in mature markets, is, according to the *Financial Times* (see Ostrovsky 2001), encouraging investors to invest more in emerging markets, some of which are beginning to recuperate.

15. The government has recently passed laws tightening the capital requirements for starting a stock brokerage, and some members of the stock exchange are merging to be able to meet these stricter requirements.

16. American Depository Receipts, a mechanism through which registered foreign stocks can be traded in the United States.

17. It should be noted that even mature markets, such as that of the United States, which extols its transparency, still find it necessary to continuously tighten regulations to avoid abuses. Serious incidents that come to mind are the 1991 case against Solomon Brothers for rigging the treasury bond market, and the failure of the LTCM (Long Term Capital Management) hedge fund in 1998.

REFERENCES

Appadurai, Arjun
   1996 Modernity at Large: Cultural Dimensions of Globalization. Minneapolis: University of Minnesota Press.

Armas H., Mayela
   2001a La Bolsa ha crecido 20% durante este mes. El Universal, Caracas, Venezuela. 25 January, part 2, p. 1.
   2001b Polar eleva su presencia en alimentos gracias a Mavesa. El Universal, Caracas, Venezuela. 28 January, part 2, p. 6.

Barron's
   1998 Discordant Notes, Barron's Roundtable '98. 26 January, no. 2, p. 32.

Bello, Walden
   1998 Speculations, Spins and Sinking Fortunes. Development Dialogue 1998(1):42–53.

Caruso, Denise
   1998 The Online Day-Trader Phenomenon. New York Times. 14 December.
   Online copy.

Crone, G. R.
   1969 The Discovery of America. New York: Weybright and Talley.

Daily Journal
   2001 Oil Prices Surge on Cold US Forecasts. Caracas, Venezuela. 3 February,
   p. 14.

Foster, George
   1965 Peasant Society and the Image of Limited Good. American Anthropologist 67:293–314.

Frank, André
   1967 Capitalism and Underdevelopment in Latin America. New York:
   Monthly Review Press.
   1969 Latin America: Underdevelopment or Revolution? New York: Monthly
   Review Press.

Gudeman, Stephen
   1986 Economics as Culture. Models and Metaphors of Livelihood. London:
   Routledge and Kegan Paul.

Hannerz, Ulf
   1992 Cultural Complexity. Studies in the Social Organization of Meaning.
   New York: Columbia University Press.
   1996 Transnational Connections: Culture, People, Places. London: Routledge.

Hansell, Saul
   1999 New Breeds of Investors, All Beguiled by the Web. New York Times. 16
   May. Online copy.

Hernández Lavado, Vladimir
   2001 Salomon, Smith & Barney también prevé alto crecimiento para la eco-
   nomía local. El Nacional, Caracas, Venezuela. 23 January, part D, p. 6.

Hertz, Ellen
   1998 The Trading Crowd: An Ethnography of the Shanghai Stock Market.
   Cambridge: Cambridge University Press.

Instituto Venezolano de Mercadeo de Capitales
   1998 Información general de la Bolsa de Valores. Caracas: Instituto Venezolano de Mercadeo de Capitales.

Kahneman, Daniel, Amos Tversky, and Paul Slovic, eds.
1982 Judgment under Uncertainty: Heuristics Biases. Cambridge: Cambridge University Press.

Keppler, Michael, and Martin Lechner
1997 Emerging Markets. Research, Strategies and Benchmarks. London: Irwin.

Kristof, Nicholas D., with Edward Wyatt
1999 Who Sank, or Swam, in Choppy Currents of a World Cash Ocean. New York Times. 15 February. Online copy.

Malavé Mata, Héctor
2000 El petróleo, el bolívar, y el fisco. Caracas: Monte Ávila Editores Latin-oamericana.

Mobius, J. Mark
1996 Mobius on Emerging Markets. London: Pitman Publishing.

Montoya, Miguel
1996 Persistent Peasants: Smallholders, State Agencies and Involuntary Migration in Western Venezuela. Stockholm Studies in Social Anthropology 35. Stockholm: Almqvist and Wiksell.

New York Times
1997 Why These Students Smiled as Your Broker Fretted. 9 November. Online copy.
1999 Global Contagion, a Narrative: Networked Economies, Stunted Lives. 15–22 February.

Ostrovsky, Arkady
2001 Se recuperan mercados emergentes. Maryflor Súarez, trans. Financial Times. Appeared as an insert in El Universal, Caracas, Venezuela. 2 February, pp. 2–6.

Prieto, Hugo
2001 Este es el año bueno . . . el que viene es el malo. El Nacional, Caracas, Venezuela. 14 January, part F, p. 7.

Robertson, Roland
1992 Globalization: Social Theory and Global Culture. London: Sage.

Rojas, Andrés
1998 Venezuela: Estado, acumulación y estructura de poder ante la apertura internacional. Fermentum. Revista Venezolana de Sociología y Antropología. Universidad de los Andes: Mérida, 8(21):27–58.

Sassen, Saskia
1993 The Global City: New York, London, Tokyo. Princeton: Princeton University Press.
1996 Losing Control? Sovereignty in an Age of Globalization. New York: Colombia University Press.
1998 Globalization and Its Discontents: Essays on the New Mobility of People and Money. New York: New Press.

Smith, Carol
1976 Regional Analysis. Vol. 1: Economic Systems. New York: Academic Press.

Thaler, Richard H., ed.
1993 Advances in Behavioral Finance. New York: Russell Sage Foundation.

Thaler, Richard H.
1994 The Winner's Curse: Paradoxes and Anomalies of Economic Life. Princeton, NJ: Princeton University Press.

Urbaneja, Diego Bautista
1992 Pueblo y petróleo en la política venezolana en el siglo XX. Caracas: Monte Avila Editores Latinoamericana.

Wall Street Journal
1997a On the Couch: Your Personal Quirks May Be Keeping You from Making the Smartest Financial Decisions. 1 December, online edition.
1997b Put Human Frailties to Work for You when You Make Financial Decisions. 30 September, online edition.

Wallerstein, Immanuel
1974 The Modern World-System. New York: Academic Press.

Waters, Malcolm
1995 Globalization. London: Routledge.

Index

About the Contributors

Michael Chibnik is professor of anthropology at the University of Iowa. He has conducted research on household economies, work organization, agricultural systems, and craft production in Mexico, Peru, Belize, and the United States. He is the author of *Risky Rivers: The Economics and Politics of Floodplain Farming in Amazonia* (1994), and is writing a book about the production and marketing of painted wood carvings from Oaxaca, Mexico.

Gracia Clark is associate professor of anthropology at Indiana University in Bloomington. She has worked with market traders in Kumasi, Ghana, since 1978. After her Ph.D. research in social anthropology for Cambridge University, she consulted for the International Labor Organization and UNIFEM for several years before teaching. Her 1994 book, *Onions Are My Husband*, was followed by articles in *Africa* and *American Anthropologist*. She is currently editing life histories of Kumasi market women.

Jeffrey H. Cohen received his Ph.D. from Indiana University in 1994 and is assistant professor of anthropology at Pennsylvania State University. His current research is on transnational migration between Oaxaca, Mexico, and the United States and the social impacts of migration and remittances investment in rural communities as well as a multidisciplinary project on community, cultural identity, kinship, and descent in the San Juan Mission, Texas. Publications include *Cooperation and Community: Economy and Society in Oaxaca* (1999).

Lee Cronk is associate professor of anthropology at Rutgers University in New Brunswick, New Jersey. His specialty is human behavioral ecology, and he has conducted fieldwork among the Mukogodo of Kenya as well as in the Honduran Bay Islands. He is author *of That Complex Whole: Culture and the Evolution of Human Behavior* (1999) and coeditor with Napoleon Chagnon and William Irons of *Adaptation and Human Behavior: An Anthropological Perspective* (2000).

Norbert Dannhaeuser is professor of anthropology at Texas A&M University and received his Ph.D. from the University of California, Berkeley (1973). He has done fieldwork in market towns in the Philippines, India, and Germany. He is the author of *Contemporary Trade Strategies in the Philippines: A Study in Marketing Anthropology* (1983), *Two Towns in Germany: Commerce and the Urban Transformation* (1996), and he is the coeditor of *Research in Economic Anthropology* (with Cynthia Werner).

Nils Gilman holds a doctorate from the University of California, Berkeley, and is the author of *An Intellectual History of Modernization Theory* (forthcoming 2003), and the coeditor of *Staging Growth: Modernization Theory and the Global Cold War* (forthcoming 2002).

Rhoda H. Halperin is professor of anthropology at the University of Cincinnati. Her previous works include *The Teacup Ministry and Other Stories: Subtle Boundaries of Class* (2001), *Practicing Community: Class Culture and Power in an Urban Neighborhood* (1998), *Cultural Economies Past and Present* (1994), and *The Livelihood of Kin: Making Ends Meet "The Kentucky Way"* (1990). Current research and advocacy work involves documenting the development and early stages of a community-based public charter school in an urban neighborhood in Cincinnati. This work builds on her long-term ethnographic fieldwork in urban Cincinnati.

Nitish Jha is a postdoctoral fellow with the International Water Management Institute and is stationed in South Africa. He received his bachelor's degree from Delhi University, India, and his master's degree in economics from Jawaharlal Nehru University, India. His doctorate in anthropology from Brandeis University is based on research he conducted on the social organization of an irrigation community in Bali, Indonesia. His research interests include irrigation, agricultural, social and economic development, and issues of resource management in South and Southeast Asia.

His article, "Giving Way to the Elephant: The Dynamics of Participation in the Management of a Balinese Subak," is forthcoming in the *International Journal of Water*. Another piece "Gender and Decision Making in Balinese Agriculture," is due to appear in *American Ethnologist*.

Patricia L. Johnson is associate professor in the Department of Cultural Anthropology, Demography, and Women's Studies at Pennsylvania State University. Her research focuses on socioeconomic change, particularly as it affects women in traditional societies. She has worked in highland New Guinea since 1977 and in Bangladesh. Her interests include social organization, gender ideology, demography (especially fertility and household structure), women's labor, and especially the demographic outcomes of the interaction of biology and culture.

Elizabeth T. Kennedy is in the Conservation Enterprise Department at Conservation International, Washington, D.C.

Ty Matejowsky received his Ph.D. in anthropology from Texas A&M University. His work focuses on the effects of globalization in Southeast Asia, specifically the Philippines.

Miguel Montoya received his Ph.D. in Social Anthropology from Stockholm University in 1996. He is the author of *Persistent Peasants: Smallholders, State Agencies, and Involuntary Migration in Western Venezuela* (1996). His research interests include agricultural development, frontiers, and the anthropology of the environment; he is presently carrying out a study of the economic processes involved in the colonization of a forest reserve in Venezuela. His contribution to this volume is part of his current research with the project Emerging Markets: Models and Practices of Investment in the Venezuelan Stock Exchange being conducted at the Department of Social Anthropology at Stockholm University, Sweden.

Monica Lindh de Montoya was educated at Vassar College and The Johns Hopkins University and received her Ph.D. from the Department of Social Anthropology at Stockholm University in 1996. She has carried out research on rural development and is the author of *Progress, Hunger and Envy: Commercial Agriculture, Marketing and Social Transformation in the*

Venezuelan Andes (1996). She spent the 1997–98 academic year as a post-doctoral researcher at the Population Research Center at the University of Texas at Austin. Her research interests center on economic anthropology, and she is currently studying small investors in the Stockholm stock market as part of the project Modeling the Market: Views of the Stock Market Held by Small Investors in Sweden, being conducted at the Department of Social Anthropology at Stockholm University.

Shannon Steadman conducted fieldwork on Utila in the Honduran Bay Islands while an undergraduate in anthropology and psychology at Texas A&M University in College Station, Texas. She now lives and works in Houston, Texas. She will start in the MA program at Texas A&M University in fall 2002.

Cynthia Ann Werner is assistant professor of anthropology at Texas A&M University. She received her Ph.D. in anthropology from Indiana University in 1997. Her fieldwork in post-Soviet Kazakstan and Kyrgyzstan has examined a number of issues in economic anthropology, including gift exchange, household networking, market women, and tourism development.

Michael Woost is associate professor of anthropology at Hartwick College in New York. He has been conducting field research in Sri Lanka since 1983.